W. Drotts

I STAND BY THE DOOR

I STAND
BY THE DOOR

The Life of Sam Shoemaker

Helen Smith Shoemaker

HARPER & ROW, PUBLISHERS

NEW YORK, EVANSTON, AND LONDON

The author is grateful to all the persons who have given permission for their letters to be quoted in this book and to publishers and authors who have given permission for quotations from the following materials:

Kromer, Helen. *One Man Awake!*

Norton-Taylor, Duncan, "Businessmen on Their Knees," in *Fortune*, Oct. 1953.

Reynolds, Amelia S. *New Lives for Old* (Westwood, N.J.: Fleming H. Revell, 1929).

Wilson, William. *Alcoholics Anonymous Comes of Age* (New York: A.A. Publishing, Inc., 1957).

In addition, material has been quoted or adapted from the following books by Samuel Moor Shoemaker:

A Young Man's View of the Ministry (1923), published by Association Press; *The Church Can Save the World* (1938), *Freedom and Faith* (1949), both published by Fleming H. Revell; and *Revive Thy Church— Beginning with Me* (1948), *By the Power of God* (1954), *The Experiment of Faith* (1955), *With the Holy Spirit and With Fire* (1960), all published by Harper & Row.

FIRST EDITION

LIBRARY OF CONGRESS CATALOG CARD NUMBER: 66-20784

M-Q

To Eugene Exman
Whose belief in Sam's ministry encouraged the
writing of this book
and
To all our friends everywhere who through the
years have "stood by the door" with us

Contents

III THE PITTSBURGH MINISTRY

IV A CAMPUS MINISTRY OUT OF A LOCAL PARISH
College Work by Rev. Dr. Ernest Gordon

V THE LAITY IN ACTION

VI THE BATTLE WON

I Stand By the Door

AN APOLOGIA FOR MY LIFE
by Samuel Moor Shoemaker

I stand by the door.
I neither go too far in, nor stay too far out,
The door is the most important door in the world—
It is the door through which men walk when they find God. *near its where men find God. That an exciting place.*
There's no use my going way inside, and staying there,
When so many are still outside and they, as much as I,
Crave to know where the door is. *Here.. Here — it is*
And all that so many ever find
Is only the wall where a door ought to be.
They creep along the wall like blind men,
With outstretched, groping hands. *Search for God.*
Feeling for a door, knowing there must be a door,
Yet they never find it . . .
So I stand by the door.

The most tremendous thing in the world
Is for men to find that door—the door to God.
The most important thing any man can do *Soul winning*
Is to take hold of one of those blind, groping hands,
And put it on the latch—the latch that only clicks
And opens to the man's own touch.
Men die outside that door, as starving beggars die
On cold nights in cruel cities in the dead of winter—
Die for want of what is within their grasp. *(Oh people.. don't the*
They live, on the other side of it—live because they have not found it.
Nothing else matters compared to helping them find it,
And open it, and walk in, and find Him . . .
So I stand by the door.
Go in, great saints, go all the way in—
Go way down into the cavernous cellars,
And way up into the spacious attics—
It is a vast, roomy house, this house where God is.
Go into the deepest of hidden casements,
Of withdrawal, of silence, of sainthood.
Some must inhabit those inner rooms,
And know the depths and heights of God,

And call outside to the rest of us how wonderful it is.
Sometimes I take a deeper look in,
Sometimes venture in a little farther;
But my place seems closer to the opening . . .
So I stand by the door.

There is another reason why I stand there.
Some people get part way in and become afraid
Lest God and the zeal of His house devour them;
For God is so very great, and asks all of us.
And these people feel a cosmic claustrophobia,
And want to get out. "Let me out!" they cry.
And the people way inside only terrify them more.
Somebody must be by the door to tell them that they are spoiled
For the old life, they have seen too much:
Once taste God, and nothing but God will do any more.
Somebody must be watching for the frightened
Who seek to sneak out just where they came in,
To tell them how much better it is inside.

The people too far in do not see how near these are
To leaving—preoccupied with the wonder of it all.
Somebody must watch for those who have entered the door,
But would like to run away. So for them, too,
I stand by the door.
I admire the people who go way in.
But I wish they would not forget how it was
Before they got in. Then they would be able to help
The people who have not yet even found the door,
Or the people who want to run away again from God.
You can go in too deeply, and stay in too long,
And forget the people outside the door.
As for me, I shall take my old accustomed place,
Near enough to God to hear Him, and know He is there,
But not so far from men as not to hear them,
And remember they are there, too.
Where? Outside the door—
Thousands of them, millions of them.
But—more important for me—
One of them, two of them, ten of them,
Whose hands I am intended to put on the latch.
So I shall stand by the door and wait
For those who seek it.
"I had rather be a door-keeper . . ."
So I stand by the door.

Credo

by SAMUEL MOOR SHOEMAKER
(written two months before his death)

As I sit in the study on a beautiful, cool August afternoon, I look back with many thanks. It has been a great run. I wouldn't have missed it for anything. Much could and should have been better, and I have, by no means, done what I should have done with all that I have been given. But the over-all experience of being alive has been a thrilling experience. I believe that death is a doorway to more of it; clearer, cleaner, better, with more of the secret opened than locked. I do not feel much confidence in myself as regards all this, for very few have ever "deserved" eternal life. But with Christ's atonement and Him gone on before, I have neither doubt nor fear whether I am left here a brief time or a long one. I believe that I shall see Him and know Him, and that eternity will be an endless opportunity to consort with the great souls and the lesser ones who have entered into the freedom of the heavenly city. It is His forgiveness and grace that give confidence and not merits of our own. But again I say, it's been a great run. I'm thankful for it and for all the people who have helped to make it so, and especially those closest and dearest to me.

Foreword

by BARDWELL SMITH

Samuel Moor Shoemaker was not a saint but a prophet, not a be-stower of peace but a disturber of it, at least of false peace. While sanctity may be the standard by which men are judged by God, Christian sainthood is often so narrowly defined that only those con-forming to traditional images are thought to qualify.

On the other hand, if by sainthood one means a vocation to Christ-centeredness, to a constant process of transformation, then Sam Shoemaker would have accepted this as his vocation. While saint neither by temperament nor yet by achievement, he was still called to this destiny.

To evaluate him by what he was not is to miss the extraordinariness of what he was; to see him in the light of what he struggled against may be closer to the point. With clear objectives in mind, Sam Shoe-maker's was a life filled with struggle—with himself, with various "roadblocks to faith," with self-righteousness in any form, with the Church's constant tendency to honor the vessels while ignoring the treasure.

I first met him in the early postwar years. Like so many former G.I.s, I had come back to civilian life shocked by the violence of warfare and disturbed about the emerging dilemmas of an atomic era. Even more than combat during the war, the experience of being a member of an occupying army had shattered my former preoccupa-tion with self, jarring me first out of apathy toward others and then into anger against injustice. I had begun to seek for an interpretation of existence radically different from the one I had known before, the one I had inherited. Of several influences upon my life in those years from 1946 to 1950 that of Sam Shoemaker still appears as formative and crucial.

The remarkable thing about Sam's influence was his uncanny way of shaming another into honesty about self without ever dismissing the injustice or hypocrisy against which one fumed. Becoming a radical without personal honesty, after all, is a contradiction in terms. A true radical is not, as has been said, "way out, but way down," that is, one who knows that the deepest changes in circumstances always include changes within persons. "Revive thy Church—beginning with me" was not only a title for one of his books but also a characteristic way in which he faced most situations. Personal change, like social, is a constant process, but it begins perhaps by honest looks into the mirror. Sam's first gift to persons was to raise this mirror to himself, a form of honesty that then enabled another to level with himself in the bargain.

Because of this honesty about himself (because he never forgot the image of the natural man) and because of his having gone through a similar experience of disillusionment following World War I, Sam Shoemaker was able to understand and speak to the condition of countless college students over the years. In the present hour there is considerable talk about the "new morality," about the Church's need to rediscover her mission in a world which sees the Christian word as irrelevant and its institutions as archaic. While it is not always simple knowing what this new morality is, since its spokesmen are so varied, there is a sense in which Sam Shoemaker's ministry reflected a genuine appreciation of those who struck out against "the establishment," whether from within or from the outside.

There was throughout Sam Shoemaker's ministry a deep sensitivity to this unrest both within and outside the Church. This reflected itself not only in his being able to speak honestly with young persons especially, but in his own continuing struggle with and love for the Church. The catholic nature of his theology always possessed a sharply "protestant" cutting edge. It would perhaps have been easier for him in this respect had his ministry been one generation later, since it has become increasingly common in recent years for this attack to take place openly. In fact, there is little else but "open season" on the Church in our time. Few creative leaders within it would have this otherwise. But this was not always so. One generation back the attack came principally from the outside. It was therefore all the harder for the prophets within to call the Body of Christ to task for failing to be the *Body of Christ*. A person of Sam's outspokenness could not fail to cause rancor among those less willing to be self-critical. His own ministry was clearly not without its scars in the battle against ecclesiastical rigidity and religious pretentiousness. In any ministry which is truly prophetic, the scars can seldom be avoided. Part of Sam's weakness, it is true, may have lain in his relative inability to be healed of these in the deepest sense.

Sam Shoemaker was not essentially, however, a bitter man. While not free of bitterness, especially in his later years, he combined a ministry free of cant with responsibly powerful preaching, profound pastoral effectiveness, and an infectious personal gaiety. The power of his preaching lay in its being truly existential and at the same time faithful to the full biblical context. Without question, he stressed certain themes to the partial neglect of others. Sam was not what one would call a "balanced thinker"; he was hardly a scholar. But what he dealt with in his sermons was the heart and core of the Christian message: the centrality of a God who in creation, governance, and redemption calls men into obedience, into loving service to the world. His preaching was Christocentric clearly, although emphasis upon the Holy Spirit tended to characterize the way God was presented. For this, certainly, he was on the soundest of biblical grounds.

Sam's convictions about the priority of personal conversion were inevitably both a challenge and a threat to those who heard him speak. During the postwar period, in the late 1940s particularly, I know of few men making the rounds in eastern United States college pulpits who matched his impact upon undergraduates. He had an aliveness of mind and a clarity of presentation which were extraordinary. To those to whom the Christian position was either foreign or dulled by inept nurture, he spoke with a vividness and authority which compelled attention. In a profession in which the parish is too often one's world, it was true of him (as with John Wesley) that the world was his parish. The contagion one caught through his preaching carried over into his work with small groups and into his counseling with individuals as well.

Not infrequently, he was criticized for "railroading" young men into the ministry. Doubtless, there were cases in which he prematurely or unwisely pressed this vocation upon certain persons. There are scores of others, however, who might never have considered such a step without "pressure," many whose lives still give evidence of his insight. Here, as in general about Sam, one should say that he was willing to take risks. While there was little doubt about his pressing the ministry upon "likely candidates," one could rarely accuse him of violating another's free choice.

Another area of his appeal in those days was his ability to stimulate thinking about the relevance of the Christian gospel to contemporary life. Though I personally came to be influenced more deeply by the social ethic of Reinhold Niebuhr, for instance, my first thoughts in these matters were prompted by Sam Shoemaker's concern for the whole nexus of social relations. He has sometimes been criticized for not having a social ethic at all, for being concerned for individuals alone. This is not accurate, however much one might challenge his conviction that creative social change occurs primarily through the changing of individuals. Disagreement with him at this point is not to suggest the two should be separated. It is merely to contend that social change frequently proceeds without or before the response of individual consciences. Otherwise, social reconstruction is put upon a perilous base. Yet it remains valid to insist, as he did, that authentic social reconstruction and reconciliation must include personal transformation.

As one whose life was profoundly influenced by Samuel Moor Shoemaker, I cannot but express my gratitude for the immense self-giving which characterized his ministry. As a human being, he was a thoroughly attractive person. Filled with wit and spontaneity, he was a joy to be with. While these personal traits are what gave his prophetic powers and his pastoral abilities much of their appeal, beneath them lay a depth of commitment that made him what he was. Undeniably, there were weaknesses to the man. But the overriding impression with which one is left is of a person deeply in touch with the living God. Because of this, literally hundreds of lives came alive to the same experience. Such, at least, is part of what constitutes the vocation of sainthood. And it is without question the road by which prophecy is marked, the road along which one dare not forget what the natural face was like.

Department of Religion
Carleton College
March, 1966

Author's Preface

As I have thought and prayed about this biography, I have been astonished to discover that Sam was even more versatile than I had known. He combined many ministries in one; he was truly "a many-sided man": a parish priest, a prophetic preacher, a prolific writer, one of the most popular religious radio personalities in America, an outstanding counselor and life changer (especially on college campuses), and an initiator of several living movements of the laity, such as Faith at Work, the Pittsburgh Experiment, and Alcoholics Anonymous.

Sam decided when he made his Christian commitment as a young man—and he never drew back from it—that he would throw his life into the breach for others. He often quoted to me the great insight of St. Paul, "Without shedding of blood there is no remission." He knew that if he stood by the door and remained willing to reach out to men and women involved in even the most sordid kind of sin, inevitably he would be given supernatural grace and power with which to help them. At the same time, he might risk the slander of a stung conscience, but he was not willing to neglect the sinner for fear of his backlash, as clergy and laity sometimes do.

Sam took this calculated risk throughout his life. And because he was human he sometimes failed. Yet he continued to reach out to human souls until he was called to lay his burden down.

A few have hated him, but countless thousands of others, of all sorts and conditions, have risen up to call him blessed. It is for these people that I undertook to write this book.

Both of our daughters have committed themselves to our Lord for His service. One of them is serving with her husband in the mission field in Korea and the other with her husband in Africa with the State Department of the United States government. Sam's thousands of "spiritual children" are serving in countless ways all over America and the world.

In the long haul, as our Lord said, "By their fruits ye shall know them."

HELEN SMITH SHOEMAKER

Burnside
Stevenson, Maryland
August, 1966

I
THE EARLY YEARS

Burnside ▓ 1

THE YEARS BETWEEN 1890 AND 1900 HAVE been called the happiest decade in human history. We remember them as the Gay Nineties. It was a time of impossible houses with gingerbread fretwork around corners and turrets, stained glass, and dark heavy woodwork. There were brass bedsteads and built-in tin bathtubs; iceboxes with drip pans; coal ranges and water coolers and cast-iron flues all through a house. Oil lamps, gas chandeliers, and candles supplied the light. Every night the silver was put in flannel bags and carried upstairs in a basket. Axminster carpets covered the floors. The heavy-framed pictures were sheeted in summer and striped linens covered the overstuffed furniture. The "parlor" was dark except on special occasions. Usually there was a gas lamp, held aloft by a bronze Nubian, on the newel-post at the foot of the stairs.

In those days gentlemen wore mustaches, bowlers or flat-topped straw hats, and shirts with stiff wing collars and starched cuffs. Ladies squeezed themselves into tightly laced corsets and gave their arms plenty of air in blousy, bulging sleeves. It was a time when the well-to-do enjoyed the luxury of horse-drawn carriages upholstered in broadcloth—the "surrey with a fringe on the top." The delicious plop-plop of the horses' hooves, and the hard-rubber tires of the carriage wheels cutting into the pebbles have a kind of echo in the sound of car tires on modern gravel. A family that owned an upright piano had a conversation piece. It was a happy, tasteless, hard-working, lovable time. The very tombstones and mausoleums were built to stand until doomsday. Sam used to say how glad he was to have been born in time to see at least the edge of this era.

In the winter of 1893-1894 the Shoemaker family rented a house in Baltimore. And there, in a second-story front room on Read Street, Sam was born on December 27, 1893.

When Sam was two years old the family moved to their country place, Burnside, about ten miles north of Baltimore. To Sam, throughout his life, this was home. Burnside is a lovely piece of land nestling between two lines of gently rolling hills in the Green Spring

Valley. Between the years 1860 and 1863 Sam's grandfather had bought thirteen tracts of land which added up to about 467 acres. The heart of Burnside was, and is, the "Big House," which was built about 1862. Sam remembered hearing his grandmother, "Nana," tell how they had sat on the porch of the Big House and listened to the guns roaring at Gettysburg.

Originally the Big House was a huge three-story Victorian mansion of twenty-eight rooms—not counting the laundry and servants' quarters. The house was of clapboard, had a mansard roof. A circular, cast-iron staircase led to a square cupola at the top. Here were kept the enormous chests that held all the fancy-dress costumes used in charades and dramatics. In 1911, four years after Nana's death, Sam's parents had the mansard roof removed, turned the third story into an attic, and crowned the house with gables.

For a time Sam's grandparents spent only part of the year at Burnside, although they sometimes came out for winter weekends. In those days the house had no furnace, so more than twenty fires were always kept burning. In the summers, however, the Big House was usually overflowing with relatives and friends of all ages, and many were the romances that began there. When the six daughters and three sons of the house were growing up, each girl had her own maid and her own horse and carriage. There were two Negro butlers, two cooks (a third one came in the summer to help with the canning), two chambermaids, and two laundresses. Breakfast was served from eight o'clock on, and there were usually three kinds of meat and three kinds of hot bread. Sam's grandmother thought nothing of having twenty to thirty guests for Sunday dinner after church.

Extending from the Big House were fields that reached to the Valley Road, about half a mile away. Three men with horse-drawn mowers worked all summer to keep the fields in short grass. The horses were leather-shod so they would not cut the turf. Later, when more land was needed to feed the increasing number of animals, much of this soil was turned under and sown with alternating crops of corn and alfalfa. The corn, planted in thick, straight rows, sometimes reached a height of fourteen feet. Some of it was cut green for silage for the cows; some left to ripen for the horses and mules. North of the Big House is a smaller house in which Ma'am Dorsey lived, a Pennsylvania Dutch woman who was in charge of the milk and butter and cheese. And close by is a still smaller house, in the basement of which were kept tanks of acetylene gas while upstairs were stored the family's dozens of Saratoga trunks. This is still called the Trunk House. Beyond these houses were the vegetable gardens and grape arbors, and not far away is a small building shaped like a frying pan that was called Ten Pin Alley. Sam's Uncle Ned had it built to contain a bowling alley and, Sam always suspected, to stash liquor. Nana sternly forbade liquor in any form at the Big House except "on the horizontal" in brandied peaches and wine jellies.

East of the Big House was a large fountain, and beyond it were seven greenhouses and the florist's house. In the farmyard there were barns, sheds for wagons and carriages, and the stables. A separate, tiny stable held the goats and later on the donkeys, and to the south were the cowsheds.

Grandfather Shoemaker had owned one of the most valuable herds of Jerseys in the country, but Sam's father preferred Guernseys. In 1898 he went into the milk business and Burnside became a dairy farm. The herd was stepped up and new barns were erected. In 1906 an elaborate stone dairy was built, connected with the barns by an overhead monorail track on which ran cars attached by hooks.

The cows had begun to outnumber the horses, but the family still had Sirrah, the magnificent Hackney stallion that won a prize in Madison Square Garden in 1893, and Victoria, a beautiful Hackney mare. In Sam's childhood the Green Spring Valley was a great fox-hunting country, and hunters came and went freely over Burnside's fences and through the gates and across the meadows. Both the Maryland Hunt Cup and the Grand National were run over various parts of the Valley.

It became out of the question to operate the farm on a full-scale basis after the death of Sam's father in 1933. World War II marked the end of the greenhouses. Sam and his mother and sister began selling off some of the outlying portions of Burnside, and doing over many of the tenant houses for rental. Sam's sister kept "the Cottage" and about fifty acres and, after his mother's death in 1954, Sam succeeded to the Big House and some fifty surrounding acres. On this smaller scale the place is still manageable.

The sense of "family" was deeply ingrained in Sam, and so was old Burnside itself, for here took place many events that had much to do with molding his character.

One of Sam's fondest recollections of his early childhood was the discovery that the children of one of the men on the place owned a goat. He also discovered a small sulky. Soon Sam was given a goat of his own, and how he loved to drive it, with a few butts of disapproval whenever the goat would catch him standing in front of him! Once a friend gave Sam a donkey, which he named Lavinia. For years these two were Sam's inseparable companions, and he would often drive them in tandem. One winter his father gave him a large Flexible Flyer sled, and had a pole made for it in the carpenter shop. Sam would harness up his pets and, followed by a string of boys on other sleds tied on behind, go flying across the snowy countryside. Some time later came the ponies: Meekness, Freckles, Taffy, Sirrah II, and with them the beginning of serious riding.

"One day when I was about eleven," Sam recalled, "a man stopped by with a wagonload of sheep and offered to sell them to me. I had made some money on my chickens and I wanted those sheep 'til I could taste their mutton! So I approached Father, but he reminded me the place belonged to Nana. I thereupon marched myself down to the Big House and laid the scheme before her, and returned with her glad permission: apparently Nana had always wanted some sheep on Burnside! How I enjoyed those sheep—feeding them, shearing them, and, of course, tantalizing them!

"When I was still very small I used to slip into the office and try my hand at the typewriter. Father noticed this and it was not long before he gave me an Underwood—not a toy typewriter, but a good, substantial machine which I kept and used for years."

One of Sam's closest pals at Burnside was Hen Bodley, the son of the Negro driver of the milk truck. The Bodleys lived on Caves Road, and before Hen and Sam could have time off for play, Hen had to cut wood and milk the cow. Sam would ride Taffy back through the woods, chop some logs while Henny did the milking, and thus cut the "chore time" in half. Hen would then hop up on Taffy behind Sam and off the boys would head for another adventure!

Years later Sam wrote in his diary,* of this period:

"There was always something to do at Burnside and always somebody to keep me company. The most important somebody, and the somebody with whom I spend most of my time, was James. James's real name was Richard Hugh Gwathney, and he had been born near Fredericksburg, Virginia. He came to Burnside in 1898 and was with us until his death sixty years later.

"I remember going out to James's room off the kitchen and climb-

---

* Sam kept a sporadic account of his life, his work, and his impressions from his boyhood until close to the end of his ministry in Pittsburgh.

ing up on his lap and getting him to tell me how he used to catch rabbits and fish in Virginia. He had a faculty for simple narrative and an engaging way of bringing me into the stories as if I had been there. So I got into the habit of suggesting, 'Let's talk some more *ш* about when me and you was boys.'

"When James got through serving lunch I would dragoon him at once into playing with me; it never occurred to me that he might want some time to himself. He was indispensable when I wanted to ride the donkeys, or have any other kind of fun on the place. He was able to fix anything, he knew how to do everything, and he was tireless. I loved him as a brother. He used to say, 'When the Boss dies you'll see how he lists us—my son Sam and my son James— share an' share alike.'

"On James's twenty-fifth anniversary at Burnside, he came downstairs and stood as usual behind Father's chair in the dining room. Father was never very communicative in the early morning. After a moment of silence, James cleared his throat. 'Mr. Shoemaker,' he said, 'do you know I've been with you twenty-five years today?' Father turned and looked up at him with a mock frown and demanded, 'Do you mean to say that I've been putting up with you for twenty-five years?' 'Yes, sir,' replied James, 'and I've been putting up with you, too!'

"A quarter of a century later, to mark his fifty years at Burnside, we gave James a surprise party and presented him with a gold watch. Friends came from all over; it was a completely mixed gathering. James's comment to me the next morning was: 'Mr. Sam, we had all the colored elite and all the white elite in the Valley!' And so we did.

"Once in a while I listen to my own radio programs and am struck by the southern tones in my accent. This does not come from my } x family, but from James, my constant childhood companion.

"Another person at Burnside who meant a great deal to us all was Seymour Diggs, who for some fifty years was Mother's coachman and chauffeur. Seymour taught me the elements of horseback riding before Mr. Redmond Stewart took me on. Seymour was an exceedingly good driver, and a man of the finest, most trustworthy character.

"To be constantly associated with such men, and never to hear from them a questionable word or story, but often to hear from them quite as good sermons in living as were ever heard in church, was

colored people — but also human

one of the great privileges granted to youngsters whose families enjoyed old family servants.

"I wonder whether children are naturally kindhearted or naturally cruel? I don't think I had much mercy for my donkeys when they were ornery, yet animal suffering bothered me. But I'll never forget little Nathan Allen, the son of the florist at Burnside. Nathan suffered from edema, or what was then called dropsy. I can still see him, pale and lame, coming out to play with us beside the greenhouse and then, tiring so quickly, toddling back into the house to lie down. It bothered me, for there I was, a healthy, domineering, privileged kid with everything to live for, and there was Nathan without half a chance even to survive. It was experiences like this that made me realize there was evil in the world to be fought and that I ought to find out if there was anything I could do about some of it.

"One might suppose that such seemingly ideal circumstances as those in which I spent my early life would produce only happiness. But this is never so. Apart from the general stresses of childhood, and especially of adolescence, there were the usual family tensions and personal frustrations to which every individual is subject. These are not resolved by material blessings. I always had good friends— companions among the children of our neighbors in the Valley, and especially among the boys who belonged to the families that lived at Burnside. But until I was several years more than grown, I had not found anyone with whom I could really *talk* in the intimate way we all need to talk with someone. Being eight years younger than my sister, it was as if I were an only child. I did not care much for organized sports, but enjoyed riding and gardening and the kind of spontaneous play that country boys find natural. This made me something of an individualist, but at times very lonely. In a way I have grown younger as I have grown older; certainly this is true with regard to social contacts. As a youth, I was more interested in things that interested older people, but I had difficulty in communicating with people in general. I knew words that might have conveyed my thoughts, but the words were too long or too pretentious for a youngster to use, at least around home.

"Often I would ride or walk in the woods alone. The huge white oaks would speak to me, and I would talk aloud, framing ideas for essays or talks or poems. I had a consuming desire to express myself. This is hard for a youngster, who seldom has something truly of his own to express but rather the half-digested ideas he has picked up from other people.

"Walking alone in the deep woods, however, did something for me. I loved to be where there was utter stillness save for a squirrel darting here and there or the sound of a bird in song. Many years later a friend of mine, who returned from a solitary walk in these same woods, said to my sister, 'Now I know why Sam went into the ministry.'   *In cottage lou*

"Burnside played such a special part in my life. My attachment to it was so deep that it became one of the things which, when I tried to face real commitment to Christ, I had to surrender.

"There is the beauty of something which in itself is aesthetically good and satisfying, and would be so by any standards, and there is the less striking beauty of what is merely familiar and beloved. I believe that in the long run it is this daily and pedestrian beauty that satisfies us most.

"There are memories of Burnside that will be forever with me. I can still see icicles hanging from the roof of the old porch and melting onto the terrace with a clear, watery smell. Every summer brings back the sight of robins on the lawn and the delicious rain that bounced and dripped off the slates during a sudden shower; I can still hear the tinkle of a pitcher of iced tea, and see the sun going down and long golden evenings before night. Nowhere else have I ever scented such pure air as that under the big spruces just at the back of the house. There was a special sadness to the moan of the doves thereabouts, and a particular quality to the 'bob-white' cries of the quail. And suddenly there comes to my ears the sound of sleigh bells—not the usual kind that are attached to a belt around the horse's middle, but a little epergne of bells fastened to the harness just behind the horse's shoulders.

"Probably it all glows and grows in retrospect, but it was pretty wonderful in the happening."

A Goodly Heritage   2

BENJAMIN FRANKLIN WROTE TO HIS SON, "I have ever had pleasure in obtaining any little anecdote of my ancestors." There is usually someone in every family who takes a particular interest in its past; Sam first felt such an interest when he was about fourteen.

The Shoemakers, formerly Schumacher, "originated entirely, so far as is known, in the German states and in Holland and Switzerland. The early German martyr books contain accounts of the exploits and sufferings of many of this name. They were, in the main, dissenters from the Catholic faith. One terse phrase sums up the frequent end of their idealistically uncompromising careers . . . 'tied to the stake and *verbrannt zu aschen.*'"

Some of the early members of the family were Mennonites. The Schumachers had been prosperous farmers, but in 1655 the German branch were forced to sell their possessions and vacate their land. A genealogical record of the family, in its possession, states, "From Mainz the family moved to Kriegsheim, near Worms, and it is well known that Peter and George Schumacher were converted at Kriegsheim about 1659 from the Mennonite to the Quaker faith by William Ames and George Rolfe, missionaries of William Penn."*

In *The History of Quakerism,* Elbert Russell writes: "Penn . . . made visits to Holland and the Rhineland partly in order to interest prospective colonists. . . . A colony of former Dutch Mennonites from Krefeld and Krisheim [Kriegsheim], whose conversion to Quakerism was begun by William Ames in 1659, emigrated in a body and settled Germantown, now a suburb of Philadelphia. Their leader was Francis Daniel Pastorius, a German scholar, who became a Friend under Penn's influence."

Sarah, the widow of George Schumacher, emigrated to America in 1686 with her twelve children and settled on a farm in Germantown.

* B. H. and R. K. Shoemaker, *Shoemaker Pioneers* (Philadelphia: Privately printed, 1955).

In 1935, nearly two and a half centuries after these courageous people set out upon their dangerous journey across the sea, Sam visited the little town of Kriegsheim. He went to the church, and stood for a moment in its pulpit at the behest of the local minister, who knew all about the family's emigration. The minister showed Sam the old underground tunnel that ran from his house to the church, a vivid reminder of the peril in which the dissenters once lived. Sam saw also the old brownstone gateway through which the dissenters passed as they made their way down to the ship waiting for them on the Rhine.

Among Sam's forebears, Gerhard Hendricks holds a distinguished place. On February 18, 1688, in the house of Richard Worrell in Germantown, the first petition against slavery in this country was adopted. "There are reasons," the petition began, "why we are against the traffick in men-body as followeth." Gerhard Hendricks was the first person to affix his signature to the protest. This was always a source of pride to Sam, and perhaps had something to do with his strong affinity for the Quakers. He was a long-time member of the Wider Quaker Fellowship and maintained a close friendship with Dr. Rufus M. Jones, the Quaker leader.

One of Sam's most colorful ancestors was Samuel, the grandson of Isaac and Sarah Hendricks Shoemaker. Born in 1725, this early Samuel served two terms as mayor of Philadelphia and is still referred to by this title. "The Mayor" opposed the Revolution, not only from pacifist principles but from loyalty to King George. In 1778 he was found guilty of treason and was forced to flee to England, where he spent the rest of his life seeking the restoration of his confiscated estates.

Samuel Moor Shoemaker, Sam's grandfather, was born at Bayou La Fourche, Louisiana, on June 28, 1821. At sixteen, Samuel Moor began working in his stepfather's wholesale grocery business in Baltimore. Four years later he realized that his vocation was not in marketing but in transportation. In 1843 he joined E. S. Sanford, then agent for the Alvin Adams Express Company in Philadephia, and helped to organize an express transportation line between that city and Baltimore. Later the line was extended to Richmond and Charleston. Still later, he and his partners organized the Great Western Express between Baltimore and St. Louis. They expanded the service by rail to Cumberland and thence by stage and river to Wheeling, Pittsburgh, Cincinnati, Louisville, and St. Louis. A year before his death in 1884, Samuel Moor became vice president of the company.

His widow, the former Augusta Chambers Eccleston, of Chestertown, Maryland, was always referred to as "Dear Nana." Grandfather Samuel Moor died years before Sam's birth, but Nana lived until he was thirteen. She was the daughter of Judge John Bowers Eccleston, chief justice of the Maryland Court of Appeals. Nana was short and not really pretty, but she was vivacious and charming. From Chestertown she had come as a bride to the house at 901 St. Paul Street, in Baltimore. With her there came a colored maid, Aunt Gracie, who had convinced Nana's mother that it was not respectable for a young woman to leave her parents' home "without some servants of her own." Sam's father was fond of quoting Aunt Gracie's most famous saying, "If you ain't got no religion at home, you ain't got no religion nowhere."

Sam remembered his grandmother as an old lady who stayed up till all hours. She read her Bible and the newspapers in bed and was never seen until lunch. Nana's clothes were extraordinary; Sam recalled seeing the outer layers of them being put on when he came to her room to eat creamed sweetbreads for breakfast. Nana believed that nothing should ever bind the body, so she wore a loose armor of stays and straps. Her black polonaise dresses were identical in pattern, differing only in materials which ranged from the heaviest of wools to the lightest of silks. The dresses were so much alike they had to be numbered, and Nana would call to her maid, "Mason, bring me number two," or seven, or eleven, as the case might be. She wore lawn caps made by the two elderly sewing women who lived in the house. The final touch to her *toilette* was a crepe collar that went on separately and was pinned into place with a cameo brooch.*

Someone once said that Nana's stories were like Chinese boxes—there was always one inside the one she drew out. Sam remembered Nana as one of the most absolute Victorians he ever knew, holding to many of the views of the queen she so extravagantly admired. And how she loved people! So many people came to Burnside! Where else were there so many horses to ride and drive, so many things to do and friends with which to do them?

Nana's musical accomplishments were a source of great joy to everyone. Her tastes were not precisely classical, but when she sat

* This material is based on a piece called "Burnside Plus" by Sam's sister, Mrs. Bartlett F. Johnston.

down at the old rosewood piano or picked up her guitar and began
to play the old-fashioned southern melodies, she was captivating.
(Her delicate and beautiful little guitar is still at Burnside.)

The Shoemaker family have been Episcopalians since the early
1800s. Going to church was *de rigueur* for Nana, although she never
managed to arrive until after the General Confession. Easter was
Nana's great moment. All year long the Victorian greenhouses at
Burnside grew the plants and flowers that were to decorate Emmanuel Episcopal Church, in Baltimore, where her brother, Dr. J.
H. E. Eccleston, was the rector. One of the delicious memories of
Sam's childhood was early Saturday morning before Easter when
two big horse vans drew up to the greenhouse door and were filled
with Easter lilies, geraniums, hyacinths, azalea, junista, lilies-of-the-
valley, jonquils, and narcissus. Sam was allowed to climb up beside
the driver for the hour-long drive into Baltimore. At the church they
would be met by his aunts and other members of the family who
came to help decorate. He recalls his excitement when the
seventeen-foot cross of lilies with crimson azaleas at its heart was
raised into position above the chancel and the wide frame of lilies-
of-the-valley was placed around the window in memory of his Uncle
Eccleston who had died in childhood. Sam always said that this
lavish gift was Nana's alabaster box.

When at Burnside, Nana always held Sunday school for all the
children on the place. She would play hymns—often Moody and
Sankey ones—give a rambling lesson on whatever subject struck her
fancy, or read a story. One day Nana said to her cousin, Sophie
Clark, "You know, I've always prayed that I wouldn't be just like
everybody else." And Cousin Sophie replied, "My dear, you should
have the satisfaction of knowing that your prayer has been abun-
dantly answered."

In 1861 Sam's father was born, the second Samuel Moor Shoemaker. He loved all the workings of a farm, and was well suited to
run Burnside after his father's death. He also became a member of
the Baltimore County School Board and subsequently its president.

Before 1903 the roads in Maryland were so bad that automobiles,
then coming more and more into use, were often stuck in the mud.
Sam's father decided that something had to be done about this situation and, with the cooperation of others, he wrote the Shoemaker
Road Law, which is still in effect. The first experimental road in the
state was built on land given by the Shoemaker family.

For many years a small agricultural college, built on Land Grant property, had operated at College Park. The outstanding contribution of Sam's father to the state was the part he played in developing that institution into the present University of Maryland. When the university's Board of Regents was organized, he was appointed chairman, a position he held until his death.

Sam's father had many brilliant and lovable qualities, including a gift for telling funny stories with a perfectly straight face. He was handicapped, however, by a terrific shyness that cut him off from many persons, including Sam.

Sam's mother's family, the Whitridges, came from England in 1635 and settled in Rochester, Massachusetts. Thomas, the youngest son of William and Mary Whitridge, went to Baltimore in 1826 when he was twenty-four years old. Starting out with a loan of four hundred dollars, he proceeded to make a considerable fortune from a fleet of clipper ships. The most famous of these clippers, the *Mary Whitridge*, made a record run in 1855, sailing from the mouth of the Chesapeake to the English Channel in thirteen days and seven hours. Some of Uncle Tom's clippers sailed to the Orient and brought back as ballast quantities of Oriental Export China and Rose Medallion called in Baltimore in the old days "India China").

John Augustus Whitridge, Sam's maternal grandfather, died when Sam was thirteen. He was a small man with a very large mustache. He could not stand dust, and anywhere he saw a spot of it he would rub it off with his handkerchief. As a small boy, Sam loved to watch his grandfather manage that huge, white, overhanging mustache when eating black bean soup.

Sam's mother was the eldest child. Sam's father first saw "Nellie" Whitridge at Emmanuel Church. One day he put his sister up to inviting the good-looking girl to go on a sleigh ride. Nellie's father opposed her accepting the invitation, saying he knew nobody named Shoemaker. "Oh yes, you do, John," stated his wife, "they sit right behind us at Emmanuel Church, and Mrs. Shoemaker is Dr. Eccleston's the Rector's sister!" When the sleigh arrived at the Whitridge door, Sam's father was on the box and he asked Nellie to come up and sit beside him, and so the romance began.

Nellie Shoemaker understood her husband's shyness and was devoted to his family, especially to Nana. A dedicated churchwoman, she was head of the St. Cecilia Guild at Emmanuel Church and, later, president of the Woman's Auxiliary of the Diocese of Maryland. Soon after her marriage she began to sing in the choir of St. Thomas' Episcopal Church, Garrison Forest, the Burnside parish church, and led it for forty years.

Sam and his mother were always congenial. She was in on all that he was doing, but was never inquisitive or inclined to make his decisions for him, although she never understood the evangelical side of Sam's temperament. She was the epitome of the old-fashioned organizational Episcopalian churchwoman and was content with the church as she knew it. But when various people were critical of Sam's work she would say, "They're all saying that evangelism is important. If what Sam is doing isn't evangelism, I'll be switched if I know what it is." Her belief in her son was a very important factor in his life.

New Horizons   ▓ 3

WHEN SAM WAS FOURTEEN THE FAMILY wisely decided that he should get away from home and go to boardingschool in a different part of the country. He needed an environment where his every wish was not immediately granted, and where he would have to make it on his own and among his peers. So in the fall of 1908 Sam was enrolled at St. George's, an Episcopal school for boys in Newport, Rhode Island.

At first Sam was homesick. He didn't feel comfortable among these "Yankees" and, of course, did not realize until he was older how provincially southern his viewpoint was. His adaptation to this new environment was not helped by the headmaster's inadvertent query as to whether they celebrated Thanksgiving in Maryland. After a time, however, Sam learned that northerners were just as warm-hearted as southerners, only perhaps not as demonstrative.

The headmaster of St. George's, the Rev. John B. Diman, had gathered about him a group of fine-spirited men. "Mr. John," as he was called by the boys, had a strong influence on Sam's early life. Sam remembered him as a tall, craggy-browed man with piercing blue eyes and a friendly, although rather aloof, manner. None of the boys apparently felt close to him, but they all revered him without fear. At the time that Sam was a student of his, Mr. John was torn by an inward conflict that finally carried him into the Roman Catholic faith and, a few years later, to the founding of the Portsmouth Priory, not far from St. George's.

Sam's best friend at St. George's was Edward Barry Wall, later his roommate at Princeton. Barry had lost his parents when he was very young, and had been brought up in Columbus, Ohio, by his mother's family. Sam always described Barry as an outstanding example of the *anima naturaliter Christiana*. During their senior year at St. George's, Barry was head prefect. One night a young foreign student climbed out of his window, shinnied down the rainpipe, and went off into Newport. His case came up before the prefects, of which Sam was one. What a chance for the inherent cruelty of youth to assert itself!

The boys shook their heads in disapproval and discussed the penalty that should be imposed. Should the offender be dismissed, or merely suspended? Barry listened while the recommendations were being made. Then, quietly, he announced that if the boy were dismissed, or even suspended, he would resign as head prefect. He had recognized the misdemeanor as a prank not a sin. How quickly the other boys changed their moralistic minds!

Barry was a flier in World War I, and after the Armistice he began teaching flying in California. He was subject to fainting spells and, whether or not this was the cause Sam never knew, one day he went up for a spin, the plane crashed, and he was killed instantly.

Sam readily admitted that he was not an especially good student at St. George's. He hated math and science and gravitated toward English. In his diary, the spring before graduation, he wrote: "Stayed in the house all day and worked on that infernal square root. Mathematics is the abomination of my existence!" But in the nonacademic areas of school life Sam was about as active as it was possible to be. In his senior year he not only served as one of the six prefects but was editor-in-chief of *The Lance* (the biennial school yearbook), business manager of *The Dragon* (the monthly magazine), secretary of the dramatic club, president and manager of the musical club, president of the Missionary Society, and vice president of the St. George's Society. An active schedule for any young man, even if there were only fifteen boys in the graduating class of 1912!

Like every other freshman class of the time, Sam and the other boys who entered Princeton in the fall of 1912 turned up in nondescript black jerseys, black skullcaps, and corduroy trousers. The newly inducted president, John Grier Hibben, opened the college year with a service in old Marquand Chapel. Dr. Hibben was a gracious gentleman—"the whitest man in all the fac," as a senior song described him—and Sam came to know him well.

In 1912, however, and for many years afterward, no student could attend Princeton without being cognizant of the controversy over Woodrow Wilson. Sam became closely acquainted with Charles W. McAlpin, the secretary of the university under both Dr. Wilson and Dr. Hibben. McAlpin, although loyal to both men, once showed Sam a letter from Woodrow Wilson to Moses Taylor Pyne (long before it had been made public in the historical records) that convinced Sam that Wilson was right in two major issues: (1) the solution to the "club" problem would be to create separate colleges in the university, like those at Oxford and Cambridge, and (2) the graduate school should be located on the site of the president's house, Prospect, near the library rather than on a hilltop a mile away.

Wilson had all but persuaded the trustees on these two issues when Isaac Wyman, the philanthropist who had promised several million dollars toward the building of the graduate school, died. Wyman left the decision of how and where the money should be spent to Dean Andrew Fleming West, Wilson's implacable foe in this controversy. A number of years later, Eleanor McAdoo, Wilson's daughter, described to us how her father had handed her mother the telegram notifying him of Wyman's demise and, with a rather cynical smile, had said, "My dear, you can't beat death!"

It didn't take long, after the college year began, for personalities to emerge among the freshmen. In addition to Barry Wall, his classmate at St. George's and now his roommate, Sam soon made other friends. He got to know Bill Osborn, whose father, William Church Osborn, had been a classmate of Sam's father in 1883. Thayer Field also was the son of a member of the class of '83; he, too, became a good friend of Sam's, and later Sam was best man at his wedding. Hamilton Fish Armstrong, the distinguished editor of *Foreign Affairs*, was another close friend. Then there was Moore Gates, with whose family Sam vacationed on the shores of the Bosphorus some ten years later.

Edmund "Bunny" Wilson, the critic, was another classmate, and although he moved in an intellectual atmosphere too rarefied for Sam, Sam always enjoyed his brilliant wit. We once got a postcard from Bunny from the St. Francis Hotel in San Francisco. On it he had written that he was "eating in a hostelry named for a saint who only with difficulty could be prevailed upon to eat at all."

Sam noted in his diary, "Scott Fitzgerald was a year behind me and I seldom saw him. On one occasion, however, a dozen or so of us were gathered in a room at Holder. No one was drinking except Scott. He had brought a bottle of red wine and he quietly, steadily consumed it until he passed out. I can understand getting tight in certain circumstances, but Scott's performance really stumped me for its psychological basis. It still does."

Dr. Arthur Lincoln Frothingham, one of the Boston Frothinghams, was connected with the art department. He was an extremely handsome man with a great shaggy, leonine head. A friend of his, commenting on his good looks, remarked that he could have sat for

Michelangelo's *Moses.* "Moses!" rejoined Dr. Frothingham, "I've been painted twice for God Almighty!"

George Dobbin Brown, who first taught at Marston's, the school in Baltimore which Sam attended as a small boy, was also an influence at Princeton. "I remember long walks and talks with Dr. Brown at Princeton." Sam further recalled, "He attempted to make me face some of the intellectual issues about faith and the Bible. Thanks to Dr. Brown I was awakened to the importance of what he called 'the life of the mind.' "

At the end of his sophomore year Sam went to Europe. On his return in the fall he wrote in his diary: "I came back to Princeton from the summer abroad eager to know more about the history of the things we had seen."

Before the end of his sophomore year Sam had begun to feel what he called "a kind of mental emancipation," and had certainly begun to develop self-confidence. That year he wrote: "I'm going through a change. I can't find the secret of it. It's a certain falling away from strictness and severity with myself. I never was squeamish about theaters, cabarets, et cetera—it's not an external thing, but a broader, freer, more tolerant view of the world about me. I am freer, happier, easier to get along with. I have grown mentally on the creative side."

In an editorial in the *Daily Princetonian* of March 1, 1916, Sam and four other seniors openly protested military drill and war propaganda at the university. They did not oppose "preparedness" (the much-used word of General Leonard Wood and Dr. Hibben) but maintained that if the current army and navy forces were inadequate, the government should take steps to improve them. "Colleges are not the place for drilling or for instruction in military matters," the editorial stated; "patriotism which shoulders a rifle is not the only kind of patriotism." The *New York Times* subsequently noted that the editorial had "aroused a storm of discussion in which both students and faculty have taken sides."

Sam noted: "I cannot speak for the others, but for myself this stand represented a growing conviction that a Christian could not have a direct part in war. In about a year America would be in it with the Allies, and I think that when we signed that editorial none of us had any idea of what forces were being loosed into the world, nor of the tremendous reality of *evil* which America's relative isolation and seeming safety still further obscured for us. I wrote that 'it is madness to accept Germany's challenge because they are out of their minds. It seems to me we should be coming to their level if we meet them on their own ground.' I said I could not see Jesus Christ in a Sam Brown belt.

"What I did not face then or for some while afterwards, though of course it troubled me, was what was the alternative? You cannot simply take a personally idealistic stand in accord with your own conscience; what if this means refusal to defend a weaker person, or group, or nation? If one were a totally isolated individual he might be able to do it, but none of us is. I saw this slowly and reluctantly. At the time I was going through the deepest kind of questioning and heart-searching. Few will believe this in the light of my later deep convictions about the relation between our inherited faith and our Western freedom, including free enterprise, and my passionate belief that freedom must again and again be defended if it is not to be lost. People say it is a good thing for young persons to go through a 'radical' period, but this is only true when there are other forces to set their thinking straight about faith and especially in its relation to freedom."

In spite of the war, however, Sam's senior year was happy. He had felt increasingly during his last two years at St. George's and his time at Princeton that he would go into the ministry. His extra-curricular activities at college included participation in the campus Christian organization the Philadelphian Society (of which he was student president during his senior year), and its outreach activities in the community, as well as being manager of the musical club and a member of the Senior Council. He also wrote two songs for the Triangle Club, and some of his poems were included in two editions of *The Book of Princeton Verse*. At graduation he received the Manners Prize for excellence in English, and he had written the words and music for the Class Ode.

Sam had a cousin named Sam Harper, who was a great crony. In Sam's own words: "Sam Harper was a family institution. He looked like a small edition of G. K. Chesterton. Sam's mother, Aunt Minnie, took him to Europe when he was very young. There he learned to speak French and to read the entire *Nibelungen* in German by the time he was fourteen. Sam never earned a living, but he did some translations that netted him a little and he wrote one novel. We saw him on occasional visits to this country and I adored him. I remember taking walks with him back in 1909 while he began urging me to get beyond the horse-and-dog interests of the countryside and waken to the beauties of European culture.

"In 1914, when I was midway through college, Sam Harper and his mother returned to the States and settled in Princeton. Like myself, Sam was an ardent Woodrow Wilson fan. Sam had visited Princeton the year before, and was there on March 1, 1913, when the Woodrow Wilson 'finale' at the university took place three days before his inauguration in Washington. Sam, Nat Griffin, and I had dinner together and then joined the some five thousand people making their way toward Wilson's house in Cleveland Lane."

Aside from the friends and teachers at Princeton, Sam remembered famous visitors who came to lecture at the university: "Offhand I recall Lowes Dickinson, Walter de la Mare, Alfred Noyes (who later joined the faculty), and Amy Lowell with her inevitable large cigar. I'll never forget Miss Lowell's reading of her verse *Patterns*, especially that last tragic line, 'Christ, what are patterns for?' Among others who came were General George Goethals, Cardinal Mercier of Belgium, and Vachel Lindsay. I began to buy good books —Unamuno, Hocking, Chesterton, Henry Adams, Henry Osborn Taylor, Rousseau, and Boswell.

"The richness of life at that time was so great I could not begin to absorb more than a fraction of it. There was just too darned much going on!"

In June, 1916, Sam wrote: "Our undergraduate days were at an end. I would have been sadder about it all were it not for the fact that I had decided to accept Tom Evans' offer and return as the executive secretary of the Philadelphian Society.

"I want to say that I think the greatest thing Princeton did for me was to give me a technique through which to express that within me which craved expression. This is why my work in English stands out so far beyond all else in its interest and inspiration that I scarcely remember anything else with such vividness. We can hardly overemphasize the tragedy of people with feeling, convictions, insights that they desperately long to express, but have no medium or instrument through which they can do it. We need this, not only in order to give to others whatever of truth or appreciation of beauty or faith about life we may have, but for our own sheer emotional relief.

"The spirit of Princeton, its soul, is a most mysterious, potent reality which makes returning here and coming up the steps of Blair Arch an exhilaration compared to which I know nothing.

"Princeton is, next to Burnside, the dearest place in the world to me."

The Road Ahead—
By Way of China   4

SAM FIRST FELT CONCERN REGARDING THE religious needs of school and college boys while he was still at St. George's. There they held chapel twice a day, and the boys learned the collects, hymns, psalms, and various Scripture passages by rote. Also there was a weekly exercise called Sacred Studies which, Sam recalled, was about as dry as could be. Sam was all for religion even then, and he did not rebel against the exercises but could not see that they had any relevance to the life the boys were living.

His interest in this direction was further spurred by attendance at a series of summer conferences, where he came in contact with some of the great spiritual leaders of the time. The first of these were held at Northfield, Massachusetts, in 1911 and 1912. Sam wrote: "In 1911 Dr. John R. Mott was there; Dr. Robert E. Speer and Dr. Sherwood Eddy came the following year. Mott and Speer were physical and spiritual giants and Eddy, smaller of figure, was a great spiritual power.

"It seemed to me that I had never heard men of such stature with such a message of the worldwide significance of Christianity. Dr. Mott, with his influence on the Student Movement, and the Student Volunteer Movement for foreign missions, the sounding of his great phrase, 'The evangelization of the world in this generation,' and his prodigious labors toward the dawning Ecumenical Movement half a century ago, was justly called the greatest layman of his generation. On the platform he was immensely impressive. Dr. Speer, also a layman, secretary of the Presbyterian Board of Missions, was probably the most powerful devotional speaker some of us had ever heard or will hear. Later I came to know Sherwood Eddy well, to work and travel with him, to work and pray with him.

"These three men left an indelible impression upon me. The Christian faith could never again be the small, parochial, denominational affair that it once had been. I had tasted a wider world, smelled its

clearer air, traveled a little to its roomier spaces. The Episcopal
Church would always be home base and we had our 'spiritual greats,'
but I could not hold myself away from this which I saw at Northfield."

In the summer of 1916 at the Blairstown, New Jersey, Conference, an appeal was made for men to serve the Y.M.C.A. in the
camps of the New York 7th, 12th, 69th, and 71st Regiments then in
training on the Texas border. Along with several others, Sam volunteered. A few months later came another call, from the "Y" hut at
Lympne, near Hythe, in Kent, England. He went. The men to whom
he ministered were fliers. One evening as the hut was being closed a
flier came up to him and asked if he could stay and pray a bit after
the others had gone. Sam learned that he had once been an active
church member but that when he had been ill in the hospital for
eighteen months, no one came to see him. He had thereupon drifted
away and lost interest in the church completely. That evening, hearing the men singing "Nearer My God to Thee" as he passed the hut,
he said, all the old, half-forgotten associations had come flowing
back and he simply had to pray.

"What went on between us," Sam wrote, "was of God's doing. I
just forgot myself and prayed for us two sinners. Almost anybody
could have won this fellow; he was like ripe fruit. I had little to say
to him about the next steps in going forward—prayer, the church,
fellowship, witness. But it was a first step, important for me as well
as for him."

Meanwhile Sam had drawn a high number in the draft, which
meant that he would not be called up for at least a year. Sherwood
Eddy, then in London, was scheduled to go to China to work for the
Princeton-in-Peking project and suggested that Sam go with him. The
Rt. Rev. John Gardner Murray, the Bishop of Maryland, favored
Sam's going, although I doubt if he sympathized with his pacifism.

Sam arrived in Peking on October 29, 1917. There was a wonderful welcome from the staff: Robert R. Gailey, who spoke Chinese as
though born to the language; Dwight W. Edwards; Stewart Burgess;
Chang Pei Chih, Y.M.C.A. General Secretary; and the younger
Americans, Donald Carruthers, Richard Ritter, Arthur Tyler, Lau-
rence Sears, and Walter Young. Sam's friend Sid Gamble was also
there and took Sam sightseeing to acquaint him with the city. At first
Sam lived in the East City, in Princeton Court, an ancient house of a
Manchu prince, where the young bachelors boarded with their Chi-

nese cook for about a dollar a day. But soon Mr. Gailey decided that Sam should move in with his family in the West City so that Sam could help him start a branch of the Y.M.C.A. there. The Gaileys had a room specially prepared for him. Sam put up some hangings he had acquired in Japan, which he had visited on the way to China, and some others he'd picked up in Peking. He settled down comfortably in his new quarters.

A lot was to happen to him in that room.

Sam was scheduled to teach insurance at Princeton-in-Peking—a subject about which he knew absolutely nothing. But since the Chinese boys whom he was to teach knew very little English, he had no trouble keeping ahead of them. He enjoyed the rickshaw ride twice a day to the East City. In the West City, Sam was given charge of two adult groups of inquirers into Christianity, most of whom were government officials. At that time Sam began to realize how great were his own spiritual needs. At one of the first meetings there were some twenty people, at the next twelve, and at the third only seven. His material was well prepared, but there was no experience mixed with it, so it became a mere swapping of ideas.

Then there occurred what Sam felt was the greatest turning point in his life. "On January 19, 1918, Frank Buchman and his party came for a personal-work campaign. I had met Frank Buchman and known about his work as Y secretary at Penn State, where he had been sent by Dr. Mott. From the fabulous number of Bible classes he had got going there, the way he brought in Christian fellows from all over the east to talk personally with men at Penn State, it was evident he was getting things done. But I recoiled from what sounded 'evangelistic' about it. Dr. Robert E. Speer, in one of his books, had said that the essence of the ethics of the Sermon on the Mount was the Four Absolutes: Honesty, Purity, Unselfishness, and Love. Frank rang the changes on these from the time he heard them. Many thought they were his own creation, but they were not. For thousands of young and not so young folk, fumbling and groping for a way of life, they became a sharp challenge—clear, demanding, giving a plain starting place. The Law came before Grace. Few could feel anything but guilt before any one of the Four Absolutes.

"As I tried to apply them to myself, I had not lied or stolen in any shocking fashion; but neither had I ever been honest about myself with any other human being.

"Absolute Purity means to find some all-consuming and high faith and purpose which takes up and uses one's energies. It is partly because Christ offers just such an all-engulfing program to anyone that He can call for such a high standard of living. As Seelye said, 'It takes a passion to conquer a passion.'

"Absolute Unselfishness—that catches us all in a hundred places, but for me the main place was in the whole matter of life-work. Almost as soon as I heard the phrase, I started saying to God, 'I am going into the ministry—what more do You want?' But I knew quite well what more He might want. He might want me to stay in China the rest of my days, not just for this short-term assignment. And I balked at that. I had to let go and say if God wanted me in China for life, I would come. For several months I thought He did, and many a lesser string did I have to cut in my imagination. I do not believe God wanted me to be in China for life, but I believe He wanted me to be willing to be in China for life. William James says, 'The crisis of self-surrender has always been and must always be regarded as the vital turning point of the religious life.' The crisis of self-surrender involves 'obedience' to what we understand of God's will, and who of us enjoys the prospect of a lifetime of obedience?

"And then Absolute Love. There were many minor irritations, but the cleavage between my father and me, due to our inability to communicate, was a deep one. I say in the diary, 'I wrote a letter to Father, a very hard one to write, saying I was sorry for anything hard I had said or thought of him.'

"It was a Saturday night. I just knew that basic dishonesty, impurity, selfishness, want of love, and withal a kind of pervasive inferiority, were holding me down. One by one I tried to release them like a lot of blackbirds out of a crate. There was no emotion or elation about it. I felt only a sense of release as I went to bed that cold, crisp January night. But—to change the figure—it was as if something that had been out of joint had slipped back again where it belonged. I felt forgiven and free. The ways seemed open to God through Christ.

"Can one evaluate such an experience with anything like honesty or correct analysis? How much is it a complete turning to something new and unknown? For years I have spoken of it as if it were this. How much is it an important step forward, a kind of lunge after delay, into a pool you knew from the first you must get into? Can any man know? Moreover, surrender does not always mean permanent victory—one hopes it will mean this, and in some areas it does and in some it does not. And when the Old Adversary comes back along some worn track, a special discouragement comes with him. When this occurs one attempts a 're-surrender,' but there will come a day when you realize that total victory over all sin would take you right out of the world; you must learn to expect some failures, be honest about them, with yourself, with God, and with any persons they concern when they come; and start trusting also those slower, steadier 'means of grace' by which we are forgiven, begin again, and grow. Yet without some decisive, comprehensive facing of ourselves and our sins at the outset, I do not think we ever make even a start of overcoming our sins. For me the best test has proved to be whether God could use me in the life of someone else.

"Next morning I wakened with an uneasy sense that I must go and talk to my young Chinese business friend, Mr. W. That afternoon I got into a rickshaw and drove over to the East City where he lived. I paced up and down outside his door, almost prayed he wouldn't be home, for I did not yet know what I would say to him. I don't know what would have happened if he had been out that day—but he wasn't! Crossing his threshold, I prayed God to tell me what to say. And it seemed to come to me, 'Tell him what happened to you last night.' My Chinese friend asked me to sit down, and in a pair of creaky wicker chairs we began to talk. 'I believe you have been interested in my class,' I began, 'but not satisfied with it. The fault has been mine. May I tell you something that happened to me last night?' He listened to my story intently and when I had finished surprised me with, 'I wish that could happen to me.' 'It can,' I replied, 'if you will let God in completely.' And that day he made his decision and found Christ. The person God uses is always blessed as well as the one with whom he is used, on the principle that a pipe carrying water gets wet itself on the inside.

"Frank Buchman knew, as do few spiritual leaders, the value of getting a young convert on his feet to begin witnessing about what has happened to him, and bringing him in contact with other persons on a team in action; and also of keeping in touch with him by letters. He wrote me dozens of them in the ensuing weeks and months. I hooked up again with him whenever he was within striking distance. In those days he sometimes called himself a 'missionary to the missionaries,' and heaven knows most of us needed one."

But the real excitement of the Peking days for Sam was relating his own new-found spiritual experience to the lives of the young men and boys around him.

In the spring Sam moved back to Princeton Court and the East City of Peking. This was more convenient, and it gave him opportunity to begin what he continued practically all the rest of the time he was there, namely, inviting a schoolboy to the house after school for tea and talk, and a young businessman for dinner or the evening. How could he talk with these fellows who had little if any English, and he still less Chinese? For one thing, he would find certain places in the Chinese Bible—the story of Nicodemus, Christ's teaching on prayer, the apostles' retort to the authorities that "we ought to obey God rather than men" (Acts 5:29)—and would offer these to them to read. Somehow with the little language they had, they pieced it out. In April he wrote, "I begin to think my mission in life is to be something like Frank Buchman's, to spread the gospel of personal evangelism. Would I might do it in my own Church throughout every land where she is at work!"

China was the laboratory in which he developed, with much help from Frank Buchman and his fellow workers, the principles of personal evangelism that strongly influenced his future ministry. These young Chinese were not very different from young people anywhere. Frank picked up an old Chinese proverb early and quoted it often, "Crows are black the whole world over."

The war terminated before Sam's draft number came up, so he remained in China until the summer of 1919.

Sam had every intention of heading directly for the General Theological Seminary in New York City upon his return from China. He was met at the dock, however, with a sheaf of letters from President Hibben of Princeton, Dr. Robert E. Speer, Dr. John McDowell, and others, urging him to come back to Princeton as executive secretary of the Philadelphian Society. He did not sleep much that night. But after discussing his dilemma with Bishop Murray and the family, he changed his plans and accepted.*

His associates in the work of the Philadelphian Society at Murray Dodge Hall were David Shotwell, class of 1918, and Henry P. Van Dusen, class of 1919, with Robert R. Gailey as Peking Secretary. Henry Van Dusen describes their partnership: "My friendship with Sam Shoemaker dates from my first evening as an undergraduate at Princeton in the autumn of 1915. The Philadelphian Society (Christian Association of the University) gave its annual reception for

---

* However, also with Bishop Murray's advice, he was ordained deacon in June, 1920. How this came about without previous seminary training is explained in Chapter 5.

entering students in Murray Dodge Hall and Sam, as President, was host. During that and the following years when, after graduation, Sam returned to Princeton as Executive Secretary of the Philadelphian Society, I came to know him quite well in connection with various aspects of the Christian program at Princeton.

"When I graduated in 1919, I agreed most reluctantly to follow in Sam's footsteps by serving the next year as Executive Secretary of the Philadelphian Society. However, the undergraduate delegation at the June Northfield Men's Conference came strongly under the influence of Frank Buchman who had just returned from China where he had come to know Sam. They dreamed of a far more vigorous Christian program on the Princeton campus under the leadership of three or four alumni and, with Frank Buchman's support, prevailed upon Sam when he arrived home from China to defer his first year of theological study at General Seminary and return to Princeton as Executive Secretary of the Philadelphian Society with me as his associate. Sam took a small, delightfully appointed apartment on Nassau Street, where I joined him for meals; thus we virtually lived together throughout that year of 1919-1920 and were partners in what was to prove one of the strongest and most effective religious programs ever known at Princeton, or perhaps at any other American college. Thus a friendship of peculiar intimacy and depth was forged."

In his first report to the Board of Directors of the Philadelphian Society in February, 1920, Sam said: "Radical and successful departures in the general policy of the work have been promised from time to time in the past by the various sets of men who have assumed charge of it. It may be questioned if in the eyes of the undergraduates much difference was to be noted. I think it may, however, be fairly said that this year we have struck out on a line of work which has not been largely tried in Princeton for at least a good many years. Individual evangelism has been given a place on the program every year, and little or nothing has been done. *This year it has been the program.*"

Sam began in the fall, very fortunately, with a staff that was unanimously of the opinion that individual work was what Princeton most needed. A group of undergraduates came to see eye to eye with them, and this number increased as the year went by. Probably the best work was done by the undergraduates themselves. The staff tried to bring students to fundamental decisions, through vital religious experiences, and to get them to share these with their friends. This

program differed radically from trying to get men to share a certain
set of intellectual views, or to cooperate in a piece of work. It raised
issues and drove wedges; there was risk in it, and the spiritually timid
were frightened by what they were pleased to call emotionalism or
excitement. But those who watched impartially saw a normal group
of men come through a normal experience. They saw unlikely men
brought into the Kingdom by their friends; men living defeated Christian lives awakened to a new power; men on the outside roused to an
unprecedented interest in religion. The group at the center was
drawn together in a bond of common experience and a joy of
conquest that had not been known in Princeton in years.

Some of the finest and strongest men of the class of 1920 wound
up in the Christian ministry, and the work done by Sam and others at
least helped a good many of them in their decision. Frank Buchman
made frequent visits, talking with men all hours of the day and night.
Sam remembered packing him up in a car with blankets wrapped
around him as he went off to Lakewood, New Jersey, to rest up after
three or four days of the most tireless giving of himself. He later went
in some directions where Sam couldn't follow him; but he saw the
needs of a place like Princeton with a great deal more clarity and
courage than most of those people who thought they knew it better.

Sam felt that if a man had any flare at all for college work he owed
it to himself to devote to it his best younger years, and perhaps some
of his mature ones as well. Therefore, although he had accepted the
position of executive director for only one academic year (1919-
1920), when the Board of Directors of the Philadelphian Society had
called him to return and take charge of the work at Princeton beginning in the fall of 1922, he gave it serious consideration. Most bishops
are inclined to steer their men into parochial work, but Bishop Murray wrote as follows: "After careful and prayerful consideration, my
judgment is that there is only one thing for you to do, and that is to
accept the call [to Princeton], your incumbency to become effective
at the fall opening of 1922." His authoritative word was backed by
dozens of informal ones from people whose advice Sam trusted, so
Sam accepted.

He wrote concerning this decision: "My heart is at Princeton—not
alone in those dear, beautiful halls and broad green lawns, but in that
pulsing young life that surges through there, so eager, so pliant, so
charming and light-hearted! Many are my dreams, of lives freed from

self, of men in definite Christian service, of the gap between school
and college somewhat bridged by visits to schools, of Princeton
Christianized. What a parish! And who is sufficient for these things?"

By this time Sam's work was becoming known in other places,
and there were many invitations to speak. He preached at St.
George's, Groton, Taft, St. Mark's the Episcopal Seminary in Cambridge, Dartmouth, Hotchkiss, Hill, Lawrenceville, Rutgers, St.
Paul's and was at conferences at Silver Bay, Northfield, and Mil-
brook. He also gave a series of lectures on personal evangelism at
Hartford Theological Seminary. These weekends were interesting,
but they were grueling, too; for besides the public speaking there was
always an unbroken series of interviews, occurring every half hour
for as long as he could stay. This went on in colleges for years
afterward. Sam felt some resentment toward the honorable D.D.s who
preached at eleven on Sundays, collected their fifty-dollar checks, and
took the two o'clock out of town. If anybody was stirred by what
they said, he had no opportunity to speak to them. Some of the
closest friends Sam ever made were lads he fished out of line filing
out of chapel or a meeting somewhere, and asked if they'd like to
come over and talk.

At first, a challenge that presents a kind of spiritual dare to all undergraduates is exciting, especially to those for whom all organized
religion has seemed irredeemably dull. Frank Buchman and various
of his associates, some from overseas, were with Sam quite often. He
knew undergraduates to place wagers that they could get in, talk with
Buchman, and get out without being converted. This was a very
healthy state of affairs, and for sheer edge it could seldom be repro-
duced in student work as generally known at that time. But as this
sort of challenge lingers and will not abate or go away, there tends to
cystallize studied indifference, criticism, resistance, hostility. Sam's
group, like all human groups, made mistakes; but the then current
criticism of open meetings with lurid confessions about sex was false
—he went to most of the meetings himself and never heard anything
said publicly that would have been improper for a sixteen-year-old
girl to hear. When one has been confronted with a blunt spiritual
challenge, he must either face it or find some good excuse why he did
not face it. If he can find some fault in the person who presented it,
or the way it was done (and he almost always can if he looks for it),
this gives him, as he thinks, a legitimate "out." It is not fashionable
to talk as people once did about "conviction of sin," but the fact of it

has by no means gone out of existence. Unless we understand this, we will never understand why it was that Jesus, Who made no mistakes, Whose knowledge of human nature was unerring, and Whose patient good will toward all men must have been evident to all, had within a space of three years brought about a coalition of hostility toward Himself of political and religious forces that brought Him to His Cross.

The laws governing this sort of reaction do not change a whit in the centuries. Religion is only mildly irritating when preachers announce the ideal from the pulpit, all goes along smoothly if they don't expect people to do anything about it. But as soon as they do, and as soon as they cut away from the crowd a few who try to meet this stiffer challenge, the thing becomes obnoxious. Dr. Nathan Pusey, president of Harvard, said recently, "The world has never wished to be bothered with the Gospel, and it does not wish to now. Yet it is our conviction that it is precisely in this hostility, or at least indifference, to the Lord—not in rampant population or underdevelopment or threat of war—that the world's most basic need is to be found—always and now."

At the end of the academic year 1922-1923, Sam had completed his term as executive secretary of the Philadelphian Society and he left Princeton.

II
THE NEW YORK MINISTRY

"A Young Man's View
of the Ministry" ▓ 5

IN JUNE, 1920, FOLLOWING HIS RETURN FROM
China, Sam was ordained deacon in the Episcopal Church, as
was mentioned in the previous chapter. How can a man be ordained
who has not gone to seminary? He must pass some examinations set
by a board of examining chaplains and also be passed by the Standing Committee of his diocese. John Gardner Murray, then Bishop of
Maryland, had himself been in the wholesale grocery business till he
was thirty-eight, and he was within a few years to be made Presiding
Bishop of the entire church. He well knew that there were other
experiences besides seminary that might help a man in the ministry.
It was arranged that a year of seminary would come after Sam's
ordination as deacon.

The ordination took place at Emmanuel Episcopal Church, Baltimore, on June 6, 1920. Sam recalled: "We had a houseful of
people at Burnside: Mrs. Randolph Williams, our great friend from
Richmond; the Sadhu Sundar Singh of India, who was like a piece of
the New Testament sent down for the occasion; Frank Buchman; and
Sam Harper. Early in the morning I went out and gathered armfuls of
pink peonies and hundred-leaf roses and filled the house with them.

"Sunday was the day of ordination. I woke with a wonderful sense
of joy, and wanted to go out alone under the wide, blue, sun-filled
sky. I walked up and down the road thinking what the next few hours
would bring. There came upon me a deep sense of unworthiness. I
put myself in His hands. And soon, as I walked, I felt a hand of
compulsion staying me. I stopped and something said, 'Be still and
know that I am God.' As I stood there breathing in the wild west
wind which blew all day, as though to remind us that 'so is everyone
that is born of the spirit'—strong, clean, free, unpredictable—there
came distinctly into my mind the verse, 'Ye have not chosen me, but
I have chosen you and ordained you that you should go and bring
forth fruit.' This was in a deep way my ordination. The laying on of
Episcopal hands was but the outward and visible sign of this inward

and spiritual command. That spot on the road will always be something approaching an altar to me. I can take you to it now; it is between trees directly opposite to each other on the first rise after you come in the front gate."

In the autumn of 1920 Sam was at the General Theological Seminary in Chelsea Square, New York City, for the academic year. Why the General? Why not Virginia? Sam's natural sympathies were with Virginia and he was delighted that later (1948) Virginia made him an honorary son by giving him a D.D. But somehow he felt that all his life he had been oriented to what was then "Maryland churchmanship," and it was on the whole "low." The Episcopal Church is a two-party church, as America's political system is a two-party one, and Sam thought it would be good to have some experience with the "other half." Not all, but many of the men there were Anglo-Catholic.

On many of the Sundays when Sam was in New York City, he went to Grace Episcopal Church. He had met the rector, Dr. Charles Lewis Slattery, when he was preaching at Princeton. Dr. Slattery had written asking him to join the staff of Grace Church when the time came, and Sam told him he would give it most serious consideration. Sam had been asked to go to St. Andrew's, Yonkers, New York, and to St. George's School, as chaplain. But he wanted training under a good all-round rector, and Dr. Slattery was such a man. In January the invitation was renewed, and Sam accepted for a year, starting August 1, 1921. The old church itself was, Sam thought, the most beautiful in New York and he came to love it.

On June 11, 1921, Sam was ordained priest, again by Bishop Murray and at Emmanuel, Baltimore, the Rev. Ralph B. Pomeroy, rector of Trinity Church, Princeton, preached, and Sam was presented by "Billy" De Vries, Canon of Washington Cathedral. Henry P. Van Dusen was with them again, as was the Rev. Donald Carruthers, Sam's colleague from China days, and Mrs. Field, longtime family friend. Sam celebrated Holy Communion for the first time at St. Thomas' Church, Garrison Forest, Maryland, next day. He was soon off for a conference at Silver Bay, New York, every free hour being taken up with interviews; he counseled with forty young men, and nearly every one of them made some kind of Christian decision.

Sam said of this summer, "By August I was on duty at Grace Church, New York. I shall not forget the move from the seminary. I hired a driver, horse, and dray to cart my stuff, and open to the world was my desk, my bed, my chairs, trunks, etc., myself topping the lot, and my straw hat topping me.

"Dr. Slattery, leaving for vacation, had left me six pages of specific instructions. One celebrated Holy Communion from the north end of the altar at Grace, and there were other rules that were strictly *de rigueur* as well. But the whole organization was so well-knit that one could hardly make a mistake. The rector told me he wanted me to make a hundred calls a month, in addition to all else, and I made a hundred calls for each of the twelve months I was there. I had one half-day off in twelve months. I wish some of the men coming out of seminaries today without knowing anything about the meaning of a day's work could have served under him. Each month we submitted a report on the number of our calls, Communion services, sermons, weddings, funerals or baptisms; I always put in one more count that was not on the list: how many interviews. I sometimes had to fight for it, but I sought to get in at least one good long talk with somebody on spiritual matters every day, and usually managed it. Frequently they were with men I had met somewhere speaking in colleges, who were now working in New York."

Sam did not see much of Dr. Slattery, except now and then when he would come steaming round the corner of the parish house, get into his vestments like a fire-engine horse into its harness, and appear at a service ten seconds later perfectly cool and collected.

It was at Grace Church that Sam met and saw much of Tom Langford, a fine young man from Williams College. Langford entered the ministry; when Sam went to Calvary Episcopal Church, Tom was his first assistant. During those days he also began seeing much of two persons who were to become his lifetime friends, Irving Harris and Leslie Glenn, and he saw them turn from promising careers elsewhere to the ministry.

During this winter he had his first contact with psychiatry and psychology at their best. In the congregation at Grace Church was a Miss Marion Webb, an intellectual and socially concerned person, who took it upon herself to interest Sam in learning something about the relation between psychology and religion. She persuaded him to take some courses at the New School in New York City and later introduced him to Dr. Edwin G. Zabriskie, head of the Neurological Institute. Dr. Zabriskie, Sam said, was one of the finest men and best doctors he ever knew. One day there came to Sam's study a young man of great potential, whom I shall call George. He was in deep depression. Sam asked Dr. Zakriskie to see him. The doctor reported that

George had nothing the matter with him physically but faced the possibility of spending the rest of his life on a hospital bed in an apathy from which he could only with difficulty be roused. Sam asked Zabriskie what on earth they could do. The doctor informed Sam that George needed constant companionship and a chance to air his difficulties again and again. "If you can make him hate you or love you, you will do him a service."

Sam had a tiny empty room in his apartment. He told George if he'd get himself some furniture he'd be glad to take him in. Every morning for months George would put his head in the door of Sam's study, then come in for half an hour of repetitious analysis of his feelings. After that, the two of them would pray together and he would go back to his books and cigarettes. Between what "Dr. Zab" did on the psychiatric side, and what Sam was able to do on the spiritual side, although it took some years, George finally came out of it. He blossomed into the finest maturity, married, took on a big business job, and made a success of it.

Sam had gone to Grace Church with the understanding that since his seminary course had been without homiletical instruction he might be free to attend some courses at Union Theological Seminary. Dr. Harry Emerson Fosdick and Dr. G. S. Johnston Ross were giving courses two days a week during successive hours, and Sam enrolled for them. It was a joy to Sam to get on top of one of the old open-top Fifth Avenue buses at 10th Street and ride the whole way in the open to Union at 120th Street. Everyone knows about Dr. Fosdick; not everyone knows about Dr. Ross. Ross was a delightful and witty Scotsman, brilliant as only Scotch Presbyterian preachers can be. He was a great friend of Dr. Albert Parker Fitch, a brilliant Presbyterian clergyman, and in some ways singularly like him.

Sam once said of himself, "I do not pretend to be in the class of those men as a preacher, of course, but I do know that I owe much of what little homiletical gift I have to their inspiration. No man can preach who is not excited about preaching, and these men made it exciting.

"I could write on and on about that rich year at Grace Church. I there learned something of the common pastoral problems of the ministry, much of the problems of middle and old age; of poverty, disappointment, suffering and sorrow; of the need for comfort as well as for exhortation (though most churches preach more comfort than they should and less real challenge). I found no incompatibility between the sort of intensive personal religious work which I most wanted to do, and the work of a parish, though the routine of a parish will steal all your time if you let it. Few clergymen do anything like what they should and could if they would give themselves to more personal dealing."

It was while he was at Grace Church that Sam wrote *A Young Man's View of the Ministry*. It has been reprinted many times and, as John Oliver Nelson says in a preface to the 1957 edition, "It influenced thousands of lives in that post-war generation, and well-worn copies of it are still found on the bookshelves of many a campus Christian Association. But by this time, its message has the enviable distinction of being corroborated and exemplified in a quarter-century of his own remarkable ministry. Thus it stands as a classic in presenting, with vigor and insight, the best challenge and excitement which comes to the committed minister."

Sam did not intend this book to be an exhaustive treatise. Such a book must have the authority of a long and successful ministry. It came as the cumulative result of his school, college, Peking, and Philadelphian Society experience at Princeton, as well as his first experience in a parish. It is the distilled essence of what he had learned in recruiting young men for the ministry up to that time.

He begins provocatively:

"How shall a man know whether or not he ought to go into the ministry? Is there anything like a sure way of finding out?

"Two factors must be taken into consideration when a man is deciding on his lifework: his own abilities and inclinations; the prevailing situation in the world.

"Most men want to serve, but they have not quite reached the point of being willing to give themselves entirely, without one eye on gain.

"Sometimes they are in duty bound to consider family obligations. A widowed mother, young brothers and sisters who have yet to be educated when the family income is small, reversals of family fortune —all such matters must be taken into consideration. God must see this and want us to make up our minds partly with reference to it.

"Now let us look at the other side of family hindrance. Here is a family of nice, reasonable church people, none too warm in their enthusiasm, but they pay their dues and come to church. Their son hears a stirring appeal regarding the ministry or the mission field. His family tells him to let somebody else's son go! So the young man is caught on the horns of a dilemma.

"That dilemma may be solved by taking some steps which, if they are faithfully and consistently followed, will usually bring a man into clear daylight:

"*1. Pray.* Prayer, mind you, is not an effort to affect the will of God but to discover it.

"*2. Think.* There is moral obligation to be intelligent. We want to look all the facts in the face. It must have our thought plus God's thought; our minds illuminated by the grace of God, which has a way of casting over men's minds a kind of colossal honesty which makes them play fair.

"*3. Talk to wise people* but do not regard their views as final.

"*4. Look out for your own bias and predilections* but do not be too much afraid of them. Do not think of His will as always in the line of the disagreeable. If He is plainly pointing where we do not want to go, let us rise up and follow—not because it is unpleasant, but because it is right.

"*5. Use your Bible.* The Bible is no answer-book to which a man can turn and have all his problems solved, but there is no book in the world which throws a clearer spotlight on life than this old Book with its searching emphasis on motive, its broad principles, and its plain commands. . . .

"The call, then, is a recognition of need and a willingness to meet that need if it be within our power. The reason most men hear no call is that they are not within calling distance, have not given their wills wholly to God, nor preoccupied their minds with these things.

"Now let me be personal and tell you of the very simple way my own call has come.

"I went through the usual period of intellectual adjustment, when the faith which my family had given me became my own faith, but I never seriously doubted that Jesus Christ was vastly superior to any whom I heard slurring Him, and the many whom I saw ignoring Him. He seemed to me, and has always seemed to me, the most altogether enchanting Person I have ever met. He seemed to know how to keep sweet, how to turn difficult corners, how to meet testy people and testy situations, how to get on and be happy in the midst of trouble, and to keep first things first no matter how pressing were other claims, as no one else I have ever heard of. And then I looked about me and saw a great many people who seemed to me to be failing miserably in the business of living; I was one of them. Some called themselves Christians and did not quite ring true; some of them did not, and they were all missing the mark.

"Then I happened to be thrown with some men whose service in

the Kingdom of God has been great, and they struck me as being the
most worthwhile men I had ever met. I wanted to be like them. They
were happy and unselfish and useful. People in trouble went to them
and were helped. They did not lose their tempers and they did not
lose their heads. They seemed to be propelled by a vast Power outside themselves. And I knew that I myself, and those whom I saw
missing the way, needed to be got into touch with that Power. And
when I tried it, and found peace and power in it, I said, 'This is too
good to keep!' and I went into the profession whose business it is to
keep people from missing the track in life, by showing them The Way.

"As I watch people, it seems to me that there emerge three spiritual hungers, comparable to the hungers of the body, which are
continually demanding satisfaction; three realms in which the soul of
man is on a still-hunt for reality. We want *explanation*, we want
inward peace, and we want *dynamic*.

"Now it is the supreme task of religion to deal with these great
needs in all their aspects, collective and individual.

"Science may make its contribution to the thought and comfort
and energy of the world, but science, because it deals with processes
and not with origins and destinies, can never give men final clues to
life; it cannot comfort them in their misery and cannot reach into
their lives with moral power. The ultimate things belong to religion.
And to think deeply and wisely and practically for and in behalf of
people; to heal and console and watch with them in the hours of
darkness, when there may be none else to watch; and to build up lives,
to put new incentive into them, and set them on their way rejoicing
and giving joy—this is the business of the ministry, and it takes the
best energy of the best men to make even a faint attempt to do it.

"Men in the ministry are set as Watchmen, to point to men the
way—the old, old and ever new way—of the Master, which old folks
love and children understand, and sophisticated people miss because
it is so plain. We are set as shepherds, to cheer and comfort, to be
always loving, always carrying their sorrows in our hearts close to
His joy, to give *all* of ourselves night and day for our people. And we
are set as prophets, to blaze where fire is wanted, to call where a
challenge is wanted, to speak the thrilling words of God to jaded
hearts in a jaded generation, to draw from men the heroic and Christ-
like, to scorch the evil and draw down the blessing of God upon the
good. And this, because men and women are of infinite value and
know that their hearts are never at rest until they rest in God. These
are eternal needs. They will last while men live. They have arisen as

the fundamental needs of every generation. And, more than any other work to which a man can give himself, the ministry busies itself with meeting these needs.

"And then I see a great fissure in the modern church which needs to be healed. On one side is a group of men vigorously holding to an old interpretation, fearing the dogmatism of science, reverencing the Bible, with a deep desire to preserve the essence of the evangelical experience and a rich piety and devotion to Christ. On the other side I see a group which is frankly scientific, intellectual in its approach, keen for social Christianity, a fuller program of religious education, modern, and possessed of almost as much sympathy with enlightened social workers as with the followers of Christ. Both these groups root strongly in Christ, and one is emphasizing one half of His teaching, the personal side, the other another half, the social side. And some enemy has been bedeviling our minds with the belief that these are irreconcilable positions, and there can be no peace between them. But I see no real opposition here. I do not see how any Christian with a "social conscience" intends to do without Christ; and I do not see how any disciple of His can fail to want the full blaze of His light to shine in every corner of our corporate life.

"To heal this apparent rift, we must raise up men of ripe spiritual experience, men with a vivid vision which lies parallel to a vivid personal Christ. We need scholarly men, who will not lose the sense of moral need in the world, and deep drivers against personal and social sin, who will fit themselves with the most rigidly accurate scholarship. We want neither the half-seeing exponent of social Christianity alone, nor the bigoted champion of personal religion alone. We need—God send them to us!—men who will brood seriously upon the mysteries of life and religion, face facts, and deal honestly with our minds: but men who have drunk deeply of the springs of life that are in Christ Jesus and who know that this involves them in a profound personal commitment to Him and also to a whole purpose to heal with His reconciling power, the hideous and wide cleavages among men.

"Thus, the ministry of the future must join together in holy wedlock all that is established in modern science with the eternal spiritual experience: the demand of the soul for a personal hold on God with the demand of collective men for a just social organization and the findings of psychology with that ancient and never-to-be-lost appeal to clear decision for Christ.

"All of this means that the Church wants for this work men of larger caliber and broader gauge than we have been getting. We must have men who cannot be stampeded by popular clamor to forsake Christ's message. We must have men who see farther than their generation and who do not fear to call back to their fellows, 'Come on!' We must have men who will preach a whole Gospel, in all its vivid beauty, and all its exhaustive demands upon men's lives.

"The Christian message is one of unconquerable joy and hope. He who is set to preach it is entrusted with the transmission to men of the greatest gift ever let down from heaven into earth. It is the most optimistic and fact-facing interpretation of life that the world has ever seen. It makes life dignified and valuable and happy as nothing else can. If Christianity is not true, life is devoid of rhyme or reason; all the perilous and costly ascent of man, and all the rolling of the restless spheres are alike as idle as the wind that blows the sands into senseless shapes upon an undiscovered beach. But if Christianity is true, if God is what Christ says that He is, then there is not a bird note in a woodland, nor a fleck of errant cloud in the sky, nor a holy hope in the heart of a savage, which is not brimful of tingling significance.

"And it is true. . . .

"And now I come to what is to my mind by far the most important work in all the ministry. And that is *Personal Work with Individuals.*

"I am convinced that unless a person is born again he cannot see the Kingdom. Let us be frank! Not more than a small portion of the church is converted or has ever surrendered. And while you may preach on it till the crack of doom, men will only rarely surrender until the matter is put to them in the form of an appeal. And because we have come to fear the hysterical in public evangelism, there is only one place to do that effectively; and it is with your people one at a time. The seminaries are little equipped to teach men to do this supremely important work, for only clinical experience is of much value; most theological professors are too busy digging out matters of research to care anything about evangelism. And year after year you are getting a lot of men out of seminaries, each of whom is comparable to a medical graduate who has heard lectures on surgery through all his course and into whose hands has now been thrust a whole set of instruments, faring forth to operate without ever having seen or taken part in an operation.

"We have *got* to know *how* religion takes hold of people by continual dealing with them spiritually if we are to begin to meet their needs. . . .

"Then there is . . . *The Uniqueness of the Work* of the ministry, which is . . . a considerable satisfaction. You are doing for people what absolutely nobody else even attempts to do. They know it is the greatest thing in their lives, the thing they want most. They will not turn to anyone else for the kind of help they expect from you. Incredible personal questions they will bring to you. You will live in the midst of the heavy burdens of others. It is by far the most wearing thing in the ministry to listen to story after story of tragedy and misfortune and folly and sin; to give yourself with sympathy and intelligence to each one, attempting to hew a way out for this distressed soul which cannot hew its own way out alone. But this, which draws the energy from you as though it were taking the blood from your veins, is the glory and the crowning joy of your work; either you will help that person, or he will go unhelped. The unchurched seldom try more than one minister. If one fails them, they are through. But if he can withdraw his wits from a dozen other preoccupations and give himself utterly to this person and his need, and if he can bring order and peace out of chaos and pain, then be it known to him in his innermost soul that he has done God's work that day and maybe saved a soul alive.

"Fellowship with other ministers is a rewarding experience. Some men will want to know what their associates in the ministry are like. To be sure, some of your brothers will be weak sisters. Dr. G. A. Johnston Ross remarked once that the trouble with about half the clergy is that they look as though they were descended from a long line of maiden aunts. Though there is the other side—men who by their industry and patience and love and sacrifice shame you and do you good. There will be men like this, the latchets of whose shoes you will not be worthy to touch. They are the lights of the world, and I tell you it is an honor to be their colleagues. To be thrown with them, and to work with them, is one of the very greatest joys of the ministry.

"Most of us will not be very long remembered after we are gone, and I, for one, prefer to make the investment of my life in the things that will not perish, in the immortal stuff of human character. And there are a whole lot of men, some of whom have yet to find it out, who just never will have as good a time anywhere else on earth as they will have in the ministry."

The Call to Calvary
Episcopal Church,
New York City　　🦢 6

LATE IN THE SUMMER OF 1923, SAM WENT to Europe with Tom Langford. Sam's artistic and spiritual enthusiasms were always enriched by visits to Europe. He described two of this summer's experiences as follows.

"At a conference in England we saw a good deal of the Oxford and Cambridge men. And never shall I forget coming round a corner one day to hear a crowd of them in a house with the windows open, singing a capella Vaughan Williams' then new tune to 'For all the Saints': it was one of the most thrilling things I ever heard." This same tune which he came to love so much was sung at his own funeral forty years later.

Later he and Tom spent two rich days in Venice; then to Ravenna with its marvelous mosaics. He wrote of the tomb of Galla Placidia, "I think it is, together with Chartres and the Taj Mahal, one of the nearest things to perfection ever created by the hand of man. The yellow light coming through the alabaster windows upon those ancient ivory-colored marble tombs, with the blue mosaics above— there is no way to finish that sentence."

Sam was in Egypt the winter of 1923-1924 traveling with Frank Buchman, when he received the cable and then the letter from Mr. Cornelius Zabriskie, the senior warden, asking him to become rector of Calvary Episcopal Church, New York City. Cables and letters from friends followed. One informed him that it was a preaching stand only, that there were no young people, and that the plant was run down. Another said it would break the wings of a man's creative imagination; another, that if Sam accepted, it should be on the condition of moving the church elsewhere. But one said that the situation "presents nearly every phase of distributed difficulty to be found in lower New York," and strongly urged that he "accept the distinct challenge which has come."

Calvary Church, once a great, fashionable, and missionary-minded church, was at this time distinctly a church in a changing inner-city neighborhood. Sam thanked the Vestry by letter for the honor they had done him and asked for time in which to study their invitation.

The last few days of 1924 he took two days apart to consider finally and make up his mind about Calvary Church, New York. He had his Bible, and Frank Buchman gave him a copy of Fitchett's *Life of John Wesley* to read. Sam prayed and read, read and prayed. He took a sheet of paper and put down on one side the reasons for accepting and on the other side the reasons against it. His reasons for accepting were as follows:

1. The financial situation, which removed any immediate worry about money for the work.

2. The very fact that the parish was rundown, which gave a chance to do something distinctive.

3. The fact that the Vestry saw the importance of preaching, and would not be so eager to move to another location if he could draw people to the present one.

4. The fact that New York was a center, accessible to all, a great crossroads.

5. The Vestry's emphasis on the need for vital personal religion as the only adequate basis for meeting social and community needs.

6. The possibilities of a growing staff life and of creating a training center for leaders.

On the basis of these considerations, which Sam felt came to him as a result of his meditation and prayer, he decided to accept the call and wrote the Vestry accordingly.

Calvary Church had come into being in November, 1835. At its inception New York was a city of 270,000 people, most of whom lived south of 14th Street.

The section of the city in which Calvary Church was built was almost wholly destitute of churches. From Eighth Avenue eastward to the river, and from 14th Street north to 34th Street, no church of any kind existed in 1835.

The first church—Calvary—was built near Broadway and 21st Street.

From its beginning Calvary was a missionary church. The Protestant Episcopal City Mission Society had four of the Calvary founders on its board. Also from the beginning, it was a young men's church.

Its most distinguished early rector was the Rev. Francis L. Hawks, the sixth rector of Calvary Church, who served from 1850 to 1862 and who was considered one of the great preachers of his time. He continued the missionary emphasis of the church and was the founder of what was known as the Missionary Association of Calvary Church. A chapel and a lodging house were erected on East 23rd Street, which Sam fell heir to when he became rector of Calvary Church.

Two dramatic events took place during the rectorship of Francis L. Hawks. He was responsible for the conversion of Lola Montez, the famous and notorious prosticute of Silver City fame, who sent for him when she lay dying in a lodging house nearby. The story of his counseling with her and her consequent conversion is dramatic.

The other event brought about Dr. Hawks's resignation. On Sunday, April 16, 1861, after the sounding of the first note of war from Fort Sumter, the people thronged Broadway. Dr. Hawks, who was a prominent citizen and known to be a southerner, refused to run the Union flag up the church flagpole, although threatened by a mob. He was forced to resign his rectorship; he left and went to Louisiana where he spent the rest of his life.

Another of the rectors was Henry Yates Satterlee, who came to Calvary in 1882. He stood out in Calvary's history as the great organizer.

In its early days, Calvary parish faced the almost constant possibility of either going out of existence or trying to become a protectorate of a stronger parish because of financial difficulties. Throughout its history more or less, it has faced the temptation to strike its tents and move to a less difficult field because of the changing nature of the neighborhood.

Under Dr. Satterlee, Calvary Church experienced its "halcyon days." The Galilee Mission was started to save needy men. The parish stood fourth in missionary giving among all parishes in the New York Diocese and continued almost as good a record for years to come. Prayer was the life of the parish, and literally hundreds of people prayed and worked daily for this center of Christian life. On December 27, 1895, Dr. Satterlee left Calvary to become Bishop of Washington.

A number of fine Churchmen succeeded Dr. Satterlee and in 1911, Dr. Theodore Sedgewick, called from the Church of St. John the Evangelist in St. Paul, Minnesota, came to Calvary and served until 1924.

Dr. Sedgewick established the habit of receiving in the porch of the church. This was such a natural way of meeting people that it has continued at Calvary ever since. Another innovation begun by Dr. Sedgewick and continued by my husband was the idea of going outside of the church with a fully vested choir before the service of evening prayer. Sam went a step further and had his choir proceed with trumpets to Madison Square Park on Sunday evenings, where a short service was held with lay speakers before returning to the church for evensong.

To aid in carrying out the missionary concern of Calvary Church, in 1914 the Rev. Dr. Francis Lister Hawks Pott, president of St. John's College, Shanghai, was made an associate minister of Calvary Church.

There is a strangely contemporary ring in these words of Dr. Sedgewick's, "Believing that no parish which lives to itself is justifying itself, and is fulfilling its duty, we have carried on with zeal the missionary spirit for which Calvary has been marked."

Dr. Sedgewick resigned from Calvary Church in 1924 because, as he said, "Commercial interests have slowly been pushing the people uptown, until Calvary has become a downtown church, and many of its members have left to go to the churches nearer at hand. A third of the congregation is present on Sunday, while two-thirds are invisible. I therefore believe the time has come when new talents, and new policies must be employed to create greater vigor, which will give promise of more efficient service. I hope the Vestry share with me the conviction that Calvary still has a mission to this great city and under commanding leadership the church may carry on its necessary and beneficent work."

After Dr. Sedgewick's resignation from Calvary Church, the Vestry consulted with the Rt. Rev. William Thomas Manning, then Bishop of New York. Cornelius Zabriskie, the senior warden, suggested that they pick someone, present the problem of Calvary Church in a changing neighborhood, and trust whomever they chose to lead them. He thereupon took the matter to Bishop Manning who gave them his support, saying, "This experiment must not be for your geographical limits alone. You must make it for our whole diocese."

Mr. Zabriskie and the Vestry committee began their search. They had never seen Sam but they had contacts who recommended him. These people were enthusiastic about the idea that it would take a man with great creative imagination and courage to make this experiment a success.

Cornelius Zabriskie was for many years one of the most eminent laymen in the Episcopal Church; his voice was always listened to with respect in any council. One of his great works was his ceaseless labor for the reunion of the churches upon a sound ecclesiastical and theological basis. Sam came to love him deeply.

Sam arrived in New York on May 15, 1925, and went immediately to inspect the parish of which he was to be rector for twenty-six years. He says, "I shall never forget looking for the first time into the rather gloomy old interior of the church, and the spacious old rectory.

Gramercy Park itself was a real neighborhood, rather more charming then than later, because La Guardia's "white wings" really kept the streets clean in those days. It is one of the few private parks in existence, being actually the front yard held in common by the members of the Gramercy Park Association, only to be entered with a key given to them—theoretically undemocratic, practically a godsend as a place to put children or sit quietly in the sun. It was a "community" in the vast spaces of Manhattan. The old rectory, not quite on the park, but at its northwest corner, was of sandstone, the same as the church, with a large and handsome living room, a dark hallway, a good-sized dining room, and a big study surrounded with glassed-in bookcases. There were four bedrooms on each floor above. Sam's old friend, the Rev. Henry Pitney Van Dusen, spent one winter there with him, and they rattled around as bachelors in lots of space.

During the first year at Calvary, Sam began to assemble a staff of workers. A casual remark once made to Sam by an English friend was of great help to him: "You have two ears and one mouth. Why don't you listen twice as much as you speak?" Sam took this advice seriously. In praying about the choice of a staff he also tried to do some listening to the Holy Spirit. Then he kept his eyes open.

The first clergyman to accept the office of assistant minister was Sam's friend Tom Langford. He was a man's man with growing power as a preacher and a tenderness which would have made him a great pastor. He helped untold numbers of individuals. He took charge of the children's work. One Friday night in March following his appointment, he took a service when he was gravely ill, pneumonia developed, and within a week his body lay just where he had spoken to the children seven days earlier.

The other assistant clergyman who joined them was the Rev.

Cornelius P. Trowbridge, a friend of Sam's since Princeton days. He took hold of the *Calvary Evangel,* the old parish newsletter, and made of it a force which carried far beyond the borders of the parish, raising its circulation over 400 per cent in two years.

One thing that Sam as a churchman had always felt to be of vital importance was the music. He inherited a superb choirmaster at Calvary Church in the person of John Bland, who conducted one of the most beautiful mixed choirs I have ever heard. The renowned Christmas Eve carol services, known throughout the city, were his creation.

The first lay persons to join the staff after Sam became rector were two Bryn Mawr graduates, the son of a bishop, a young Jewish businessman in deep trouble who became a Christian, and the daughter of a first family of Boston, among others. They were housed in three adjoining brownstones on East 22nd Street and had to put up with many inconveniences.

The furniture had seen better days. The beds had broken springs and in the corner of the dining room was a closet which contained a two-burner stove. This became the kitchen. None of the workers seemed to mind the inconvenience of this rather haphazard living because the pace was so fast-moving and exciting.

I have already mentioned the Galilee Mission for needy men which Dr. Satterlee had established on East 23rd Street. Under succeeding rectors it underwent several changes and was finally closed. One morning of that first summer at Calvary, Sam walked down East 23rd Street past this dilapidated property and the lodging house alongside it, both of which buildings still belonged to Calvary Church —and he had an inspiration. The story of the exciting results of that inspiration is told in Chapter 24, "A Rescue Mission and Alcoholics Anonymous."

Bishop Manning remained Bishop of New York throughout Sam's early years at Calvary. Sam thought him one of the greatest of bishops. Some said, "You cannot serve God and Manning." What was Sam's own experience? He found him uniformly just and courteous and never had the slighest misunderstanding with him. Surely Sam was going in a direction that was neither personally nor ecclesiastically congenial to Bishop Manning, yet the bishop never questioned him. He once welcomed a huge Oxford Group crowd in the ballroom of the Waldorf-Astoria Hotel and often said good things of the parish work at Calvary.

Most of the Sunday mornings that summer of 1925 Sam preached about changed lives, giving the actual histories of men known to him who had found God and learned the secret of sharing Him with others. He heard only one negative remark about that series of sermons. A very old woman met him in the aisle one day, and with arm and cane upraised, declared emphatically, "I don't want to hear anything more about those men—I come here to hear a good evangelical sermon!"

As another innovation Sam had some simple cards printed and placed in the vestibule of the church for distribution. They read as follows:

CALVARY CHURCH
Fourth Avenue and 21st Street
REV. S. M. SHOEMAKER, JR., Rector

Personal Religion   Straight Preaching
Good Music   A Friendly Atmosphere

The staff of Calvary Church like to talk with
people in search of vital religious experience.

When a new member of the congregation, with large advertising interests, offered the church 175 car-card spaces in the Fourth Avenue, Lexington Avenue, and 23rd Street trolley cars, Sam accepted, and the notice was the same as these smaller cards. It was this notice in the streetcars which caught the eye of a new neighbor, Miss Olive M. Jones, recently president of the National Education Association and pioneer and founder of the first school for delinquent boys in New York. She came to the church to see what kind of people had imagination enough to advertise religion in the streetcars. She began coming to services throughout that summer and the following winter. In the spring of 1927 she made her decision for Christ with a member of the Calvary Church staff.

That October (1925) Sam wrote in the "Rector's Comment" in the *Calvary Evangel*: "My days have been filled with personal interviews, sometimes three or four a day, and lasting from half an hour to several hours. Some have been our own people, some have been visitors who came to the church and wanted to talk personally, some were sent to me by my friends outside. If I could tell you something of the confidences which have been shared with me in the study at the Rectory this summer, and some of the lives which have been transformed by the power of the living Christ, your hearts would thrill. I say this to every member of this church—it is not for your clergy alone to do this work—you touch some whom they do not touch—Christ wants you to be fishers of men."

There were many conversions that summer. These conversions included persons as wide apart in background and interest as a sidewalk newsboy and a charming woman in her late fifties who had attended church all her life.

JUNE 1, 1927, WOULD MARK THE END OF the second year since Sam came to Calvalry Church. In his acceptance, he had said that he favored a two-year trial of his arrangement with the Vestry. Accordingly, he now sent this letter:

Calvary Church
May 10, 1927

My dear Mr. Zabriskie:

When I accepted the Rectorship of Calvary Church, I did so on the basis that if, after two years of experiment in the work, either the Vestry or I should feel that if we cared to terminate our agreement, we should be at liberty to do so.

For myself, these past two years have been full of adventure and happiness and reward; and there has been sufficient response from the people to make me feel hopeful of the future if the Vestry wishes me to continue as Rector of the Church.

Very faithfully yours,
S. M. Shoemaker, Jr.

Two days later Sam had their kind reply:

23 Gramercy Park,
12 May 1927

Dear Mr. Shoemaker:

When you accepted our call to be Rector of Calvary Church, you had but small acquaintance either with us or with the parish; and you had not been Rector of any other parish previously. You thought it reasonable that if, after an experiment of two years, you came to the conclusion that you and this parish were not fitted to go on together, you should feel free to give it up, and we recognized the generosity of your sentiments in proposing like liberty for us. If clergymen when called to a spiritual cure would always take thought to leave the way open to both sides to retreat it would conduce to the contentment of both sides.

During these two years you have discerned the weaknesses of this parish, and you have employed your unusual gifts to strengthen it where it needed to be built up. A bishop from the most distant continental diocese of the Episcopal Church, who was in the congregation last Sunday evening, remarked to one of us: "Things are certainly happening in this parish." The Vestry realize the elating truth of this remark. You have done great things for us.

Beyond this, you have become dear to us all, congregation and Vestry; we know that you love us; we are certain that we love you.

Thus we receive with joy your decision to stay here, and to continue your fruitful ministry in Calvary Church.

Faithfully yours,
Cornelius Zabriskie

So Sam stayed.

In the summer of 1927 he began holding outdoor services in nearby Madison Square. A parishioner, Amelia S. Reynolds, describes it graphically in her book *New Lives for Old*:*

"Each Sunday night in summer the cross over the door of Calvary Church is lighted an hour before the evening service begins. Young men are carrying signs that read, 'The Church has come to you. Will you come to the Church?' The clergy and a robed volunteer choir march out to Madison Square. A trumpeter, playing familiar hymns, and the clergy, reckless of their voices, lead the singing.

"Friendly police hold up traffic on Twenty-third Street, the service in the square is for the men on the benches and the passers-by. One who attended them recalls, 'On this special Sunday I saw standing in the crowd a Western bishop, the acting rector of a fashionable New York parish, several youngbloods, and what a bum called "a couple o' gents in dog collars." There was also a woman who came all the way from Tennessee.'

"During the singing of 'Jesus Calls Us,' two men shared a leaflet on which the words of the hymn were printed. One was an old fellow with broken shoes and no hat, the other a bronzed young giant. They sang so lustily, with such abandon, that I wondered when they had sung that tune before, so evidently familiar to them. . . .

"Mr. Shoemaker was the last speaker. A reporter for the New York *Herald-Tribune* quoted him in the news columns on August 20:

" 'We fix flats,' he said, 'or rather Christ fixes them. If any of you are flat tires running on your own rims, come with us and Christ, and let us help you pray.' "

It was to one of these outdoor services that a young rector from Emporia, Kansas, who was filling in at St. James's Church in upper Manhattan, came incognito in a dark suit and sporting a red tie. He followed the rather straggly crowd back to the church for evensong, and was so taken with what he saw and heard that he came to

* Westwood, N.J.: Fleming H. Revell, 1929; pp. 35-38.

counsel with Sam and took a leap forward spiritually himself. He soon joined our staff as an assistant, and subsequently became associate rector. His name was Jack Smith.

In the fall and winter of 1927-1928 Sam turned his attention to transforming the church school.

Until this time Sam had not quite known how to translate the Christian message into terms of teaching and practice that children could fully understand. Many of the changed parents had shared with their children their own new faith; but as yet there was no one who could transform the church school and fill it with the new spirit which their parents had found. Then Miss Olive Jones came along. Sam asked her to direct the school, which she most willingly undertook in May, 1928. She quietly set about enlisting the services of teachers with a vital experience of Christ and training them to teach the children in their classes the naturalness of "listening prayer," of open sharing with one another of the problems and victories in their lives, and of the availability of God to the problems of anyone, child or adult, who would put Him first. As soon as she was able, Miss Jones established a system whereby there were two teachers for every class, both to be present every Sunday. Despite the double demand, almost from the beginning there was a double supply.

"What are you teaching my daughter?" asked the mother of a ten-year-old girl one day. "She gets up early every morning and writes things in a special notebook. She doesn't fib to me any more about what happens in school, and she hasn't put her feet on the sofa since I asked her not to."

In such fashion, Calvary Church School built up a quality of character in its children that was calculated to forestall the kind of division, defeat, and doubt that we meet so often in the adults who turn to ministers for help. The principles Miss Jones established were followed scrupulously in all of Calvary's Christian education work during the 1930s.

In 1928 Sam wrote, "I am always really happier when at my own work, be it desk or interviews or working on sermons, than in any of the other hundred happy places where I go. Life is so good, the zest of it so unbroken, and the growing richness of it so satisfying, that I wonder sometimes how or whether this can last. Somehow I feel the need of more sorrow, suffering, and illness before I shall know all God wants me to know, or half of Christ's sufficiency. But again sometimes I think God gives me this to keep my emotional life occupied. I am eager for love and marriage, and have long been. It seems as far off as ever. Maybe He doesn't mean to give it at all, maybe He is saying, 'Isn't the joy of this work enough without your asking for human love and children as well?' The girls I have cared most for don't seem to share the spiritual convictions which alone could make them happy living my kind of life with me—the others don't have much of a pull."

Sam now had his hands full. He noted in the summer of 1929, "My telephone often begins when I'm at breakfast at 8:30, and my day seldom stops before 11:00. In between it is constant 'phone' calls, interviews, writing, visiting the sick, conferring with the staff. I believe I have cut executive routine to the minimum. Now nearly every contact is spiritually productive. I love my life!"

The average size of the Sunday morning congregation had increased by about one hundred persons during Sam's first year at Calvary, and by about one hundred more the second year. Like former rectors, Sam was sure the location of the church ought to be kept where it was, for distances are nothing in New York if people want what is at the other end of them. He had made hundreds of calls on his own parish families and talked with hundreds of individuals in his study. The staff members were as busy as he. They were reaching out into the city. But the work was outgrowing the plant. What were they going to do?

Sam said of it, "Here was the situation: We owned the church building on the corner, the gymnasium (the old chapel) next door to it, the rectory at 103 East 21st Street, and five houses back of it on 22nd Street, three of which, 102, 104, and 106, had doors cut between them which threw them into the semblance of a parish house.

"We did as much of the parish work as possible in the rectory. But one morning when the staff was assembled there, one member casually suggested we move back into the study, and a few minutes later a circle of the ceiling about ten feet around fell with a sickening thud right on the chair where that person had been sitting; and we realized that the old place needed serious repairs. It was so like an old English rectory on a London Square, that we all resisted the thought of removing it.

"Yet the obviously sensible thing seemed to be to sell the five lots, one hundred feet square, which we owned on 22nd Street, and build a high parish house on the site of the old rectory. Sentimental voices were heard which seemed more concerned with the past than with the present or future. Discouraging voices were heard too, even in the Vestry, about the financial problem involved in such a large building. Some seven thousand dollars only lay in the so-called parish house fund. The property on 22nd Street was not even sold. We were no longer a wealthy parish."

After much discussion, the old rectory began to be razed in the summer of 1927. Buildings were rented at 135 and 138 East 22nd Street as a kind of parish house annex for staff members to live and work in, and Sam took an apartment nearby. Calvary House was building.

The story of the giving toward the building of Calvary House is a remarkable one. The Christmas offering in 1927 was $78,118—all for the parish house. People gave family jewelry, Liberty bonds, silver and gold. Contributions came from all sides. There were two or three very large gifts, but all the rest was given by people in moderate circumstances. The 22nd Street property was sold in January, 1929, and the proceeds, $195,000 minus a small sum belonging to the endowments, went into the new parish house. They employed no professional money-raiser; personal letters went out from Sam's office to the people and interested friends. He did not spend the time of three whole days' work on it. By January they had in hand $270,-460. As Sam said afterward, "We had prayed it into possibility; we prayed it into actuality. I have always considered it a miracle in the material."

Calvary House was very attractive when it was first built and opened. I first came there late in the year of its opening, when it still looked fresh and charming. Sam, himself, had impeccable taste, and the Great Hall was particularly handsome with a stage at one end, stone-colored walls, and four apertures on one side which held beautiful copies of the Cluny tapestries. The second floor looked out on the Great Hall through windows that could be folded back, to form a kind of balcony. This floor was exquisitely furnished with carvings and tapestries and works of art which Sam brought back from Europe.

The third floor contained the dining room, a small sewing room for the Woman's Auxiliary, and a large living-room.

The fourth floor contained offices, rooms for parish organizations, and bedrooms. On the fifth and sixth floors were the apartment of the assistant rector and more bedrooms. On the seventh was an apartment for the organist and his wife, and in the front a duplex apartment for the rector. All of the rooms and offices were simply but attractively furnished.

The autumn of 1928 saw the opening of Calvary House. The day of dedication was a memorable one. Sam said on this occasion, "Calvary House is an expression of something already created, a new life pulsing all through the parish, manifesting the adventure of living religion; and this should always be the case—the life first, and then the new form in which it expresses itself.

"The house gathered all the staff conveniently under one roof where they were now in constant touch with each other, and is the solution to the problem of parish workers getting off into holes and pockets, doing good work, but not integrating it and keeping it in the midstream of God's will. It may be that some future generation in Calvary Church will censure those who decided to put living quarters and workrooms in the same building, so that the workers literally live 'on top of the work'; but it seemed wisest to plan a building which was economical, which would both manifest and increase the spirit of teamwork, and which would best serve in furthering the work at that present time. None connected with it ever regretted it. This building with its extra rooms allowed also for another great opportunity: that of taking in from time to time guests and visitors who might want the fellowship of this house and come to learn the secret of what was happening there."

Miss Olive Jones became the first director of Calvary House shortly after its opening, and when I arrived to join the staff of Calvary Church in the latter part of December, 1928, all the girls on the staff were living on the sixth floor under her benign eye. As the parish house was largely a residence for the purpose of training the laity, people came to stay a week or two and some stayed as long as a year. Many future clergy got their start at the midweek meetings on Thursday evenings in the Great Hall and while they were in seminary came for training for longer or shorter periods of time. An informal permanent conference was continually going on at Calvary House throughout the entire twenty-three years of my residence there.

In those days various organizations met in the church, such as the Committee of the Church Women's League for Patriotic Service, the Woman's Auxiliary, the Women's Benevolent Society, the Church Periodical Club, and others. We also held regular weekly Bible classes which were very well attended.

The building was often called a Spiritual Power House, and increasing numbers of visitors from all over the world thought of it in such terms. They came in 1932 and 1933 and throughout the years thereafter from every part of the world—America, Canada, Mexico, England, Scotland, Holland, France, Germany, Turkey, Greece, Egypt, South Africa, India, Burma, China—many already with a genuine experience of Christ, which had transformed their lives, to learn how to make that experience available to others, and how to relate it intelligently to the needs of the people whom they touched. "They learned by doing."

Calvary House had three main functions. It was, of course, the center for all the activities and meetings of the parish; second, it was a home for most of the members of the staff and their familes; and third, it was a training center for spiritual leadership. Many people lived in Calvary House and participated in the fellowship and the work, fitting in wherever they were needed.

On Sunday evenings, eighty to one hundred young people gathered at the church. First, services of evening prayer were held at 6:00; these were followed by a supper in Calvary Hall and a meeting at 8:00. On Monday nights professional and business women met. They were led by Miss Cornelia Lyne, who was then with the Hoover Commission and later was to become an executive with the Child Labor Commission. Just recently I received a note from Miss Lyne in which she said, "I was not at Calvary at the start of Sam's ministry but I saw it fairly early and I do well remember how it grew and flourished and how much I always enjoyed seeing Sam at the door after services. These were great days and I'll never forget them. Sam and Calvary meant so much to me. When I foolishly lost a lot of the money I had saved up on the stock exchange, and my job evaporated about the same time, Calvary came to me at the time of great need and I got back again the faith and understanding I had lost. I was literally born an Episcopalian, but I never saw an Episcopal Church like Calvary."

The leadership in all these activities was interchangeable and the growth in number and quality of leaders was one of the great contributions of these groups. Late on Tuesday afternoons, sixty to eighty men would meet in Calvary Hall for fellowship and prayer while the girls' group met in the Guild room.

In the summer of 1929 a group of seminarians joined in fellowship. Jack Smith, who was in charge of training them, attached an amplifying system to a record player in the church basement which was then placed in an open basement window and boomed out "The Bells of St. Mary's" in order to attract the hurrying noonday throngs. At the proper moment a seminarian would mount a soapbox in the corner of the churchyard behind the high iron fence surrounding it and get a workout in street preaching, good for his ego as well as his powers of persuasion. Surprisingly enough, large numbers of passers-by paused, listened, and were sufficiently intrigued to come into the church for noonday prayers.

In the spring of 1930 a rash of weddings took place. The seminarians and the clergy were the grooms and staff members were the brides. Among these were Sam and myself and Jack and Alys Smith. Alys was one of the Bryn Mawr girls who first joined the staff.

When Sam came to Calvary there were no groups whatever of this kind. He had a vision that there might be some day, but he did not go about creating them by setting up the forms which they eventually were to take. The new life came first, demanding channels for its expression, and the gradual growth and multiplication of these groups provided those channels. The natural order was: change lives first; then provide groups for their fellowship and training so that the message could be spread.

The Pastor Takes a Wife   🏵 8

I FIRST MET SAM SHOEMAKER IN THE FALL of 1919 when I was sixteen and he was almost twenty-five. We had just moved to Princeton. My father, H. Alexander Smith, had been asked to become the Executive Secretary of Princeton University in the reorganization following World War I.

We had a small house on Library Place, and one weekend a charming lady from Baltimore, Miss Annie Penett, who had been for a time a companion to my grandmother in New York, visited us. Mother discovered that a Sam Shoemaker was a distant cousin of Miss Penett's. He was living in Princeton, serving as the Executive Secretary of the Philadelphian Society, so my mother invited him to tea.

I was a gawky teenager who didn't have the least inkling how to talk to a man of twenty-four. On this auspicious afternoon, however, my mother put me in charge of the tea table. I was to bring it in at the proper moment and remain in the room while Miss Penett and the handsome young man who, I had been told, was in some kind of religious work, chatted together.

I did what I was asked. The tea table was set up to perfection— my mother was and is a perfectionist. I remember the afternoon vividly. I was totally unequal to the occasion. After wheeling in the tea, I retired to the other end of the room and sat down, hoping I would not be noticed. Miss Penett and Sam carried on a typically vivacious Baltimore conversation, which consists to this day of swapping stories about mutual relatives and acquaintances. They had a wonderful time of it and many, many years afterward I reminded my husband that I had been present on this occasion. He lifted his eyebrows in complete surprise and said, "I don't remember you at all."

Our interests were poles apart. My sister and I were busy enjoying the Princeton undergraduate body socially; Sam was occupied in enlisting them spiritually. In fact, from that time until I was twenty-three I never met Sam again, though Princeton was a rather small

town. I heard of him sometimes, of course, but I was not in the least
interested in religion, for I was completely absorbed in all the excite-
ments of being a "flapper" in the Roaring Twenties.

In 1925 we were living in the house that is now occupied by the
Dean of the Chapel. Many young seniors came that year to spend
Sunday afternoons in our living room. The boys came to call on my
parents as much as they did on us, since my mother and father
thoroughly enjoyed the undergraduates and always made them welcome in our various expandable homes.

I remember a particular Sunday afternoon following a chapel service at which Sam had been the preacher. I had never heard him
before, although I had been told that he was a dynamic and aggres-
sive preacher. That morning I was sitting in the gallery of Alexander
Hall, which at that time was used as the chapel, when out onto the
stage that served as a sanctuary came Mr. Shoemaker. I thought him
extraordinarily handsome, with wavy gold hair and strong, chiseled
features. There was something dynamic and magnetic about his personality that made the blood race. But it was what he said and the
way he said it that really captivated me. He was on his mettle that
day and his sermon was both challenging and searching in describing
the sins, delinquencies, and needs of the undergraduate body.

Having had some opportunity to observe this group at first hand, I
agreed with him completely in everything that he accused them of
being and everything that he challenged them to become.

That afternoon a violent discussion broke out over Sam between
two groups gathered in our living room. We were evenly divided—
ten pro, ten con. The pros said passionately that the sermon was
timely, to the point, and long overdue. The cons said that he was far
too judging, exaggerating both the sins and needs of the undergraduate body, and they found him demagogic.

I was at that time very much in love with a senior, and the course
of that particular true love was going far from smoothly. As a result,
for the first time in my life, I began to feel the need for some spiritual
security and a personal faith. My sister was in love with another
senior, who had come under Sam's influence and who had made a
decision to give his life to God and to whatever Christian work God
called him.

My sister and I were very close; anyone who loved her became
automatically a friend of mine. But this was a most unusual and

exciting friend. He was willing to sit down with me and tell me very simply that I needed to find the same kind of faith that he had found. He went on to describe to me how he had found it. I was fascinated by his recital. I had always heard that religious people were dull, elderly, and wore low-heeled shoes and unbecoming hats. When he asked me to go to a weekend conference which would be attended by others who were also searching, I accepted with alacrity.

I shall never forget that conference. The surroundings could not have been more drab. It was held in a shabby conference center in a little town near New York. Since this was a gathering of students from various universities—with a few older people thrown in for good measure—many of the conferees were far from drab.

Sam was one of the leaders, and again I had an opportunity to admire his confidence, his magnetism, and his salesmanship. I was so captivated by all this that before the conference was over, I had taken my first very small steps forward into the Christian life. Of all the talks at that conference, a sentence of Sam's was the most gripping thing I remember. "All you need to do is to see sin as anything that separates you from God or anything that separates you from other people." Immediately there flashed into my mind my resentment toward an older member of my family, and my jealousy of a younger member. It had never crossed my mind before that these could be sins, but if what Sam said was true, then these things could be considered such. Also I realized that I had in me a total scorn for so-called "religious people." There was one very pious old lady at the conference who talked enthusiastically about how tracts could be used to interest people in the Christian faith. This to me seemed the acme of bad taste. Nice people simply did not do things like this and my whole pseudo-sophisticated soul revolted against the thought.

A much larger issue, however, was involved. I remember having an acute and painful tussle with myself over this question. I had to sit down with my mentor, my sister's fiancé, to work it out. I realized that what separated me from God was my fear of what He might ask me to do for Him that I might not wish to do, and I was soon enlightened. I found that I would be asked to do anything for Him that He wished. I had not heard in those days of the word "obedience," the word "commitment," the word "mission." But, of course, all of these great words with their connotations were involved in the decision that I made at that time.

I saw Sam again the following autumn when he was training a

group of students and seminarians for an evangelistic assault on a small New England city. We met in a most uncomfortable and unattractive Y.M.C.A. camp outside the city. The camp was situated in a hay field. Sam, alas, was afflicted by hay fever. In the midst of earth-shattering sneezes he attempted to prepare about one hundred and fifty eager beavers for their part in taking the unsuspecting New England city for Christ. Again, I was impressed, in spite of the hay fever, with his magnetism and spiritual power.

I don't remember seeing him again until some time after my sister's wedding. Sam performed the service, but I was far too concerned with comforting my sister's former beaux and enjoying my present beaux to interest myself in him. Shortly after the wedding the whole Smith family accompanied the bride and groom to England, on their honeymoon. My brother-in-law was to study at Oxford as a Rhodes Scholar. I cannot to this day understand how the long-suffering couple ever put up with having the whole family along; nor did it occur to anyone that this was a rather peculiar thing to do. We spent the winter there. While my brother-in-law attended Balliol College, the rest of us intermittently did conference work with the Oxford Group, as the movement started by Dr. Frank Buchman was known at that time.

The following spring Sam came to England to lead a conference at Keswick. One afternoon he invited me take a walk with him. This was the first time that I'd had any intimate conversation with him, although we had corresponded the year before in a rather desultory fashion about some mutual friends whom we hoped to be able to interest in the Oxford Group. During the walk Sam asked me shyly if I would be interested in coming to work on his staff at Calvary Church in New York. I was of course very much flattered, but I was also alerted to the possibility that he had other things in mind besides inviting me onto his staff. I remember putting down this unworthy thought and discussing what membership on his staff would involve. He assured me that he wanted just such a girl as myself to take on the large number of young women who were then attending his midweek meetings at Calvary Church and for whom he had no shepherdess. This sounded intriguing as I had done a good deal of work with young women in England in connection with Oxford Group conferences and I did know something about how to reach them. Later Sam came to see me at our hotel in Queensgate, London. I'll admit to being in quite a flutter. That afternoon I prepared tea very carefully. I appeared in a green twill dress with leopard collar and cuffs which I greatly fancied. I don't know whether he fancied it or not. He was again exceedingly shy and we stuck strictly to business, but I was again aware that behind the very businesslike conversation in which we engaged there were thoughts going through his mind of an appraising nature.

Once Sam had made up his mind that he wanted something to happen he saw to it that it did happen. I began to receive letters urging me to accept his invitation. I was to let him know as soon as I could, since the Church year began the following September. I was not as impatient as he was. I wrote him that this was a matter in which I would have to ask God for direction. So I went off with my sister and brother-in-law to a resort in Switzerland for a vacation. One day, while I was sitting on a flower-covered hillside and drinking in the glorious view, I put down all the pros and cons on a piece of paper, then prayed to be shown what to do about Sam's invitation. It seemed to me that I should accept, but not until the following December, as there were certain conferences in Europe that I wished to attend the earlier part of the year.

It never occurred to me that this decision might inconvenience the rector of Calvary Church, or interfere with his plans for opening the year with a full staff. I knew very little about churches at that time. I wrote him accordingly and I expect he decided that something was better than nothing and replied that he would be very glad to have me come when I felt that it was right to do so.

So I went. I have very little recollection of whether or not I was in the least effective. I know that a group of girls met with me weekly and we had interesting discussions and prayer together. I don't believe that I was sufficiently trained to give them very much leadership. I know, however, that from participating in Sam's midweek meetings, attending the church services—which I was supposed to do—and going to the weekly meetings at Calvary Mission, a great deal of indirect know-how began to work its way into my rather obtuse subconscious as to the duties of a committed Christian working in the church.

It wasn't until the fall of 1929 that I began to be aware of a deeper relationship developing. There were several other girls on the Calvary Church staff also working as volunteers. Sam had a way of escaping to his apartment on the top two floors of Calvary House with someone he wanted to interview as soon as meetings were over, so that we rarely saw him. He had the same fascinating way of escaping from the porch of the church on Sundays as soon as people had shaken hands with him. We girls who lived on the floor below his apartment rarely had an opportunity to see anything but his coattails.

And then all of a sudden he invited two of us for dinner in his apartment. We accepted, and I remember writing a ridiculous poem and slipping it under the door of the apartment the day before. After this dinner he took me on a date. I could hardly believe that such a thing could happen. Things developed at a somewhat accelerated pace after that and we became engaged at an Oxford Group house party at Briarcliff Manor, Briarcliff, New York, on the first of January, 1930.

It was a very cold day and Sam asked me to take a walk with him around the frozen golf course. We sat down on the edge of the ninth hole, and there he proposed. Because of the cold atmosphere, not of the proposal but the weather, we quickly decided that it would be better to finish plighting our troth within the manor house itself, and we made our way back into a little turret room and became engaged. The excitement among the leaders of the Oxford Group was tremendous. Sam was then thirty-six and I was twenty-eight. We set our wedding date for April 26.

We were married in Princeton. I have always insisted that it was the first warm day after a dreadfully cold and unpleasant spring, which I considered a good augury. Sam disagreed with me about its being a warm day and up until the time of his death insisted that it was a very cold day. However, that was the day of our marriage and a marvelous occasion it was. Again Sam had won. He had a considerably stronger nature than I had. I had feebly suggested that we have a small intimate wedding to which he replied, "Nonsense! I only expect to be married once and I want everyone I ever knew to be present." As a result, his congregation at Calvary Church in New York as well as a vast number of friends of my parents and his parents and all of our Oxford Group connections were invited.

We were married in the University Chapel, which was newly completed and very beautiful but somewhat austere. Sam imported the whole Calvary Church choir for the occasion.

I shall never forget the exquisitely meaningful Communion Service which was celebrated for the wedding party in the chancel of the Chapel early in the morning of our wedding day. We all sat in the choir stalls and at the time of the post-Communion, when we were kneeling quietly, Sam slipped me a small envelope. We had agreed not to give each other expensive wedding presents and I had given him a gold locket with my picture etched in it to hang on his watch chain. Much was my amazement and total delight when I opened the envelope and in it found a most exquisite circle pin of pearls and diamonds accompanied by a note saying, "To my darling Helen on our day, April 26, 1930," and quoting some lines from a Shelley poem, "The day is come, and thou wilt fly with me, to what so ere of dull mortality is mine, remain a vestal sister still; to the intense, the deep, the imperishable not mine but me, henceforth be thou united even as a bride, delighting and delighted."

And so we were prepared for our marriage, sharing together our Lord's precious gift of Himself at His altar before we took our vows. This was a deep and lasting symbol of the way it had to be for us. He became again unalterably then and always our first commitment, our first love, our first loyalty. My husband in describing marriage on many occasions afterward likened it to a triangle, with God at the apex and the man and the woman at the base, and this understanding of it was deeply engraved in both our hearts and souls that day. John Coburn, Dean of the Episcopal Theological Seminary in Cambridge, Massachusetts, wrote me when Sam died, "There is a mystery in a wife's being able to free a husband for his work in the world and I believe that you have lived very close to the heart of this mystery."

I did not know it at the time, but there were to be many occasions during our nearly thirty-four years of marriage when with varying degrees of anguish I found it necessary to give Sam to God all over again. In such subtle ways does an affectionate woman, craving affection, try to possess the man that she loves. I did not realize when I married how deeply I wanted to be the center of my husband's stage. Over and over again I had to understand that a priest of the Church of Christ has a holy and sacred duty to serve, first, his Lord and Master with all his heart and soul and mind and strength, and second, the people whom his Lord and Master has committed to him. Then, and then only, can he give his time and attention to his wife and children. This was the hard demand made on me, and it was made over and over.

Sam believed passionately in the ministry of the laity, enlisting and training them. Consequently, he could hardly fail to train his wife as the first layman in his life. Sam's vocation was evangelism; my vocation was prayer. Sam agreed that perhaps the work that I was able to do with him later on in the field of prayer was a valuable supplement to his own endeavors in the field of evangelism. Sam always said that "we should believe the incredible and tackle the impossible." This we tried to do throughout our years together.

Our first child, Sally Falls, was born on December 11, 1931. She was a love child in every respect. Sam had wanted a son to carry on his name, but he soon forgot his disappointment. I was so desperately ill when she was born that the whole church and all our friends spent most of their time for six weeks on their knees praying for my recovery. Poor Sam had to carry on a full ministry with a wife slowly convalescing for almost two years.

One may get some idea of what our life was like from Sam's own description of a typical day:

"What was a weekday like? It is difficult to describe. I would wake up, say my prayers, take a look at my datebook and find it clear of appointments, and by about 11:30 A.M. find there was hardly a niche in it anywhere. In general after breakfast I would go into the study, open the mail and dictate till it was cleaned up—all but the letters that had to wait, often in an accumulating, disorderly pile at the right of the desk, for further consultation with somebody. A couple of mornings a week took up the sermon. I kept my typewriter conveniently near, so that I could wheel round in my desk chair and put down whatever was 'coming' at that time—sermon, aphorism, idea. I kept at the left side of my desk four little three-by-five boxes, one for sermon ideas, one for quotes, one for 'the next book,' and one for people—names and addresses and phone numbers of those I wanted to keep in touch with currently. Then would come lunch, at home or with someone outside. I tried to make calls on everyone in the parish once a year and never quite managed it, as I recall. There were usually interviews, sometimes several, in the afternoon with people in the parish or coming sometimes from far outside, for our 'wider Calvary family' never seemed to shrink. I sought to get in a couple of miles of walk every day and always slept better when I did. At about [age] fifty-five I began taking a real rest, half to three-quarters of an hour, clothes and shoes off, stretched on the bed. Then dinner at home or an evening appointment, and so to bed. This was exacting, but there were always some evenings to be with the family, and Friday afternoons till Saturday afternoons I sought to get in my day off. It would be a good plan if clergy took Saturday off rather than Monday; they would be fresher for Sunday, and would look forward to what they might say tomorrow rather than backward to what they might have said yesterday. Such a schedule as this does not leave much time for reading. One could manage the papers and magazines more or less on the run, but bigger and more important books usually had to wait till vacation, though I usually had one at hand to dip into if I had an hour."

Through the years Sam recorded in his diary what he considered the most important family events. In January, 1942, he wrote: "Mary Sims ('Mamie') has come to live with us and cook for us. I had called up my old friend, the Rev. Willard Monroe in Harlem, and told him what we needed. 'I've got just the person for you,' he said, 'And Mamie Sims is well saved.' He spoke the truth. For over twenty years she has been an indispensable part of our household, and Helen and I depend on her loyalty, her good sense, and her graciousness with people personally and over the telephone, more than we can acknowledge. She is a good cook, but she is also responsible and wise and a good companion, our friend and fellow worker in God's service. It does not fall to the lot of many families to have a James and then a Mamie. Oddly enough, they both came from the same part of Virginia."

Mamie has been and continues to be right beside us in all the great events of our lives: Helen's birth, Sally's wedding, our move to Pittsburgh, our retirement to Burnside, Sam's illness and death, Helen's marriage. Now when my children have scattered to their work in the world, Mamie remains to give me that thing priceless beyond "the price of rubies"—her sustaining loyalty and love. And how she can still cook!

On May 16, 1942, Sam entered in his diary, "Our little Helen Dominick came this morning at 1:58 A.M. at the Doctors' Hospital in New York where Sally Falls was born. There were no signs of her early approaching advent so I went on to Bedford [our country hideaway] yesterday afternoon and about 2:30 A.M. Jack Smith arrived in his car, there was no telephone in the house and he didn't want to waken the neighbors next door, so he drove all the way—just like him. By the time we got in the baby had been born for more than an hour and a half."

Sam expressed his love for her well in a tender poem that he wrote when she was two years old:

To H. D. S.—Aged Two
June 7, 1944

She's gone away to the country,
My daughter whose summers are two;
I look through her door in the morning
As I am accustomed to do;
There are the blocks in the wagon,
Waiting to go for a ride;
And the shabby old calico cat,
And the brown woolly dog on his side.
I turn away from the doorway
Feeling the place is bereft:
For what in the world is so lonely
As a room that a baby has left?

That gay little voice is calling
Out there in the trees and the flowers;
Where she runs in the soft green grasses
Through the long and wonderful hours,
With all the surprises of summer,
The sky and the birds and the light,
Hers to enjoy in the daytime,
And hers to dream at night.
But I'm closing the door of the nursery
Until the summer is done;
For what room in the world is as empty
As the one whence a baby has gone?

Somewhere in the other green gardens,
Or at play in another pen,
There's a little masculine toddler
Who's meant to be hers—and when
He asks her to leave our roof-tree
And with him to spend her days,
We shall love the little robber
In spite of his taking ways . . .
These are the thoughts that linger
Long in her father's mind,
When that mite of a person's departure
Leaves such a big hole behind!

The "little robber" read this poem at the wedding dinner the night before their marriage on December 27, 1963. It was just two months after Sam's death, and I had a lump in my throat as I listened.

Sam loved his children dearly and was very tender with them. I expect that we spoiled them both, because we never spanked either one of them and they were always completely included in everything that we did. Perhaps it was the right way to raise these two, because they "have done us proud," to use one of Sam's favorite expressions.

Many people may wonder how a man as singleminded about his ministry as Sam could have been a successful father. And yet he was. He never concerned himself much with the details of his children's welfare; he left that largely to me. But I think his love for them is best highlighted by two or three incidents that are etched in our memories.

The first was when Sally was about two and a half years old. Sam and I had decided that she was old enough to say her prayers with us, so we knelt down by her crib and Sam explained gently that if she was very quiet for a few minutes Jesus would put His thoughts into her mind. As we knelt she put her curly, golden head solemnly down on her fat, pink hands. In a very short time up popped her head and her round, dark blue eyes were shining like stars. Sam said, "Sally Falls, did Jesus say anything to you?" To which she replied, "Yes, Daddy, He said 'Sally Falls.' He knowed my name."

We never made our children the center of our attention. In the first place we did not believe this was good for them. In the second place we were far too busy with the work that we felt God had called us to do. So we included them. They were very much a part of our total life. When we had to leave them to go abroad for conferences or trips, we always told them why this was, so that they never felt rejected from our hearts or from our lives. There were times when I felt, particularly with Sally, who for the first ten years of her life was our only child, that I left her too often. But I was young and ardent and deeply in love with my husband and our work. And in the long haul Sally did not much suffer from it.

There was always excitement in our home: people coming and going, all kinds of people, all kinds of occasions, all kinds of color. We lived on the top two floors of our parish house in New York and through its doors at one time or another trouped alcoholics, visitors from other lands, people in all kinds of need, people of various kinds of distinction and with no distinction. The children saw all these people, in fact they could hardly miss them because in order to gain the privacy of our own home we had to come in through the parish house doors, and in the front hall of the parish house there was always sitting an oddly assorted group waiting to see my husband.

Sam would often say that Sally was just like a Shoemaker. She was rather shy and reserved, as all Shoemakers were, and as Sam was himself in deep and unexpected ways. He was brought up to have perfect manners but not to show his feelings, and Sally was very much the same.

In January, 1948, Sam wrote, "Sally Falls is home from Chatham Hall—her prep school—for her vacation. Much more grown up and daily growing more beautiful. She has had quite a gay vacation. The little one is a personality all to herself, very positive and definite, a wonderful sense of humor and of music. They are very different.

"Helen works too hard, but I know no answer for it. Her book *Prayer and You* came out this year and has brought an additional lot of people who seek her out day after day. She is really almost as much in demand as I am, speaks well, greatly helps people. I don't know what I would do without her in the business of my life. Our home is too often invaded by our work, yet we both love it and love doing it together and when the whole thing is totaled up, I'm not sure it's not just what we believe God wanted for our marriage and our home. It has been a spiritual partnership from the first and never closer than now."

At the age of eighteen, at a parish house dance, Sally met her future husband, Court Robinson, who was studying medicine at the College of Physicians and Surgeons, New York City. He was the son of a Presbyterian minister, and it was a case of love at first sight. She never looked at anyone else after that. Sam was a bit jealous of the young men who dated our daughters, and this was no exception. He was quite perturbed because Court did not see fit to come and ask him for her hand. Court and Sally went to him together and told him that they were engaged. Sam, having been brought up in the early part of the century when it was customary for the young man to wait upon the father and ask for his permission to steal his daughter, could never become accustomed to the modern, casual manner of young people just coming and announcing their plans. However, he quite forgave him, because he discovered that Court was an ingenious and imaginative husband and father. Whenever he and Sally visited us at Burnside after their marriage and during his internship at Presbyterian Hospital, New York, he would turn-to with Sam in the carpenter's shop and repair all kinds of items in the house that needed repairing. Sam remarked to me admiringly, "That fellow certainly knows how to use his hands."

By the time of Sally's marriage, in 1953, we had left New York and were serving another Calvary Episcopal Church—in Pittsburgh,

Pennsylvania. March 31, 1953, Sam entered in his diary, "It's been almost exactly a year since we came to Pittsburgh. It may be well to use a fairly full evening in Holy Week to set down some impressions. Sally and Court were married at St. Thomas' Church, Garrison Forest, Maryland, on January 3. Stewart Robinson, Court's father, took the betrothal; Phil Jensen, the opening sentences; I, the marriage; and Noble Powell, the Bishop of Maryland, the benediction. The old church still had its Christmas decorations, and we added a few more exquisite flowers and many candles in the sanctuary. Sally wore Mother's wedding gown, and looked truly regal. The Senator, [my father, H. Alexander Smith], who had to give her away, had to dress in his cutaway for the opening of Congress, which took place at noon that very same day, and come up behind a police escort with open sirens all the way from Washington, but he made it and was there in good time to escort her down the aisle. It was a lovely, meaningful service. The reception was at Burnside. We had had the house painted without and papered within and it was shining clean. Helen and I spent all morning decorating it with greens and great sprays of magnolia so that it looked beautiful. Mother stood it all surprisingly well, blessed old Aunt Sue came, and it was the last function she attended. Court was very handsome and the whole thing old-fashioned and satisfying in every way. We couldn't be more delighted with our son-in-law."

There were no more diary entries about family affairs until September 29 of that same year when Sam recorded, "We had left the house to go to Bishop Thomas' consecration [the Rt. Rev. William Thomas, Suffragan Bishop of Pittsburgh] when the phone rang that Sally had gone to the hospital to have her first baby. I got the message, had Helen paged out of the huge congregation in the Cathedral. She came home at once and took the 2:00 plane and was in New York at 4:30. At 6:30 Samuel Shoemaker Robinson put in his appearance at the Medical Center where Court is interning in Ob-Gyn. All has gone very well."

Sam had a special feeling for this first grandson, who was named for him, and he expressed it in a tender poem, written in 1957, entitled "My Grandson":

> He takes my hand, my little boy
> And feels as safe as safe can be;
> Talking as we walk along,
> I with him, and he with me.

I take my Father's hand in faith,
Though where He leads, I may not see;
My hand is given into His
I trust Him as my child trusts me.

In January, 1954, Sam wrote: "On December 25 we celebrated Mother's 90th birthday. We had in all her old friends who were living and the first and second generation of family. The Rt. Rev. Noble C. Powell, Bishop of Maryland, came and read a lovely scroll that the Woman's Auxiliary of the Diocese of Maryland had prepared for her. The old house was, as ever, ready to have a lot of guests. Ma sat in the parlor and held court and enjoyed it immensely. Earlier in the afternoon, I had a photographer come and take some pictures of the four generations: herself, myself, Sally, and Sam, Jr. In one we included all my family and James.

"On Easter Even, 1954, my cousin Edwin Poe called me to say that Mother was in another of her attacks, and Dr. Williams was there and it looked very serious. While he was talking to me they told me she had just died. I knew that I must stay in Pittsburgh and see through my Easter services. The services went wonderfully; I was sustained by many prayers. I thought the Communion Service would be especially difficult and 'we bless Thy name for all Thy servants departed this life in Thy faith and fear,' but I was able to keep up. Few heard of it 'til we'd left. I wondered how I would feel entering that old house with Mother not there. Turning in the Burnside gate we saw James had left the shutters open to make the house bright with all the lights on. Sally had come down a little earlier by train. After we had settled in a little James and I went into her room. She lay fully dressed in her bed looking younger than she had for some time. I put my hand on her cold brow and felt neither anything of horror nor even of grief. 'He is not here, He is risen,' was in my mind. She and I were very close, and this was the loss I felt most of any I had ever experienced."

On January 20, 1958, another family event took place. Sam says of it, "Helen and I are just about to fly down to Baltimore for James's funeral. He had a stroke last week and went yesterday without gaining consciousness. I don't know when anything has hit me harder. He has been a part of my life since I was four years old, and I was sixty-four last December 27. During the past three or four years since Mother's death he has been my manager at Burnside, and we've had a wonderful relationship. I never had a deeper, truer, or more loyal friend. He kept up his work throughout the summer when the house was pretty full. He looked after us when we were all here just after New Year's and had the annual family Christmas Party, with the four generations present. It was the last expression of the old Burnside, and James was in his element. Little did we know he would never again take care of us in that house and dining room, every inch of which will speak of him to us as long as we live."

When Sam learned that Sally and Court had accepted the call to go to Korea with the Presbyterian Church, Sam accepted it too as any Christian father should, and in many ways proud that they had chosen to serve God in this way. He hid even from me the anguish of heart that he felt over parting with them and their three little boys. Our final evening with them in Pittsburgh in late February, 1960, was unforgettable. They had come to us for a last visit before their departure. We knew that they were going for five years before their first furlough; we knew that there was a possibility that we would not see them during that interim. Sam hid his feelings over parting with this dearly loved little family until the very last moment. We laughed and joked at the dinner table. Then came time for our final prayers together when our dear Mamie and Jean [Mamie's great-neice who has lived with us since she was ten years old] came into the room to join us, Sally holding the wee baby on her lap, the two little boys sitting on either side of their grandfather.

Sam opened the Book of Common Prayer to the wonderful prayer for those we love. Then he read the prayer for missionaries: "Almighty God, who hast willed in the fullness of time to gather up all things in Christ, bless we pray Thee Thy witnesses and servants in every land especially in the hour of trial and danger. Strengthen and deliver them, that they may powerfully set forth Thy glory before the world; through Jesus Christ our Lord." And finally the prayer for those absent from us, which he changed a little bit to suit the occasion: "O God, whose fatherly care reaches to the uttermost part of the earth; we humbly beseech Thee graciously to behold and bless those whom we love, now leaving us. Defend them from all dangers of soul and body; and grant that both they and we, drawing nearer to Thee, may be bound together by Thy love in the communion of Thy Holy Spirit and in the fellowship of Thy Saints; through Jesus Christ our Lord, Amen." Then he closed with his blessing, and we gathered ourselves together to say the final goodbys.

When Sam and I returned to the house after seeing them off, and I found a small crushed celluloid Indian lying on my dressing table along with two or three scribbled little drawings made by our little boys before their departure and we knelt down to say our evening prayers together, Sam—for the first time that I had ever seen him— broke down and wept.

The last entry in Sam's diary is a poignant one—and it is the entry he made that night in February, 1960, after we had seen Sally and her family off: "Helen and I have just put Sally and Court and the three boys on the train en route to Korea for a five-year assignment under the Presbyterian Board. He at Severance Hospital, Seoul. They have been with us here for three happy days. We have been cherishing every hour with them all. They feel a call to go and we are reminded of the great hymn which we sing so frequently, "Give of Thy Sons to Bear the Message Glorious," so how could we hold them back. Besides which you can't talk, as Helen and I have always done, about the needs of the underprivileged people of the world and then when your own flesh and blood feel a call to go, not be proud of them and give them willingly. But I tell you it was hard to come back to this big house and hear a stillness where those gay young voices had been chattering only an hour ago. Sambo [the grandson] has been sleeping with me. Roughhousing him yesterday I said, 'Sambo, I love you.' He said, 'Big Sam, you love all of us.' And 'tis true. It was terribly hard saying goodby to Sal. She is our first-born and she has been so wonderful in all ways. We can only be thankful for her marrying such a sterling fellow whom we love and for those three adorable boys, Sambo, Corkey, and Alex. I guess one feels these things more as he gets on the shady side of the sixties which I still cannot believe is my age."

Strange that in this part of Sam's personal journal he should have recorded these three poignant family events coming so close together. And how could he know when he wrote this last entry that he would never in this world see this family again. Perhaps he did know, because Sam was gifted with considerable pre-vision.

After their departure, Sam more and more centered the love of his heart on our younger daughter, Helen, whom we called "Nickie." These two had a most extraordinarily intimate relationship. Her humor never ceased to delight him, and many were the hours they whiled away reading Hilaire Belloc, Edward Lear, Ogden Nash, and other foolishness. Recently I ran across some of her seven- and eight-

year-old prayers and a diary she kept when she was nine and a half
years old. They are deliciously typical:

"Dear God, help Stalin to look up and see your face," she prayed
in April, 1949. "Help him to have a vision of you so that he'll stop
being so bad."

"And help Elizabeth's grandmother to get well in her nerves so
that she won't go nuts and Elizabeth won't go nuts with her. Amen."

"Oh God!"

"Help Jane not to be ornery and me too. Not this year or the next
or the next. Amen."

And in the summer of 1951, she wrote in her diary: "If I had to
choose between being a great woman and a lot of things I would
choose to be a great woman." She signed it "Helen D. Shoemaker,
aged 9½."

Nickie says of her father: "He always called me 'Rabbit,' and my
earliest recollection of him is one of warmth and protection. More
than most fathers are to little girls, my father was to me. We were
exceptionally close and remained so until his death.

"The earliest recollection I have of thinking about or believing
that there was a God were the nights when I was sick. I remember
one particular time when I had a dreadful earache, and called for
Dad, and he came in and put his hands on my ear and prayed that it
would get well. I calmed all down inside, and went to sleep, wondering what it was that happened when Daddy put his hands on me like
that. He didn't *have* to tell me there was a God when I was a little
girl. He *believed in Him himself* and practiced that around me, and I
caught it. Children know when parents are phoney. My parents have
never been phoney with me.

"If I could pinpoint what it was that made me love him so: I
suppose, perhaps, it was his amazing capacity to accept me *as I was*,
and as a person in my own right. When I was at my very worst (and
knew it) and was driving my teachers crazy, not to mention my poor
mother, my father remained quiet, loving, unruffled by my antics.
When you're that age, all the world is spinning around you because
you're growing so fast, and everyone reacts to you because you act so
foolish. Dad never reacted to me, rather he acted *toward* me.

"At the end, a phenomenon occurred which must happen in many
families when a parent becomes ill. The man on whom I had de-
pended so completely came to depend, in part, on me. His illness was
so severe as to demand some pretty constant care on the part of my

mother and Mamie and myself, and my greatest joy (although it was a constant sorrow that he needed it at all) was to be able to return a little of the tremendous amount that he put into me. We sat and talked for hours and hours that last summer, and I took care of him alone for a bit when my mother had an important church obligation to fulfill. He trusted me completely with his health during that time, to give him his medication, and most of all just to be there to talk to. I've never forgotten that. I felt I had the responsibility of taking care of the most important person in the world.

"More than all the rest, I must say that for me my father is very far from dead. His memory is crystal-clear in my mind, the things he said, the belly laugh, the twinkley eye, and the sickness. But more than that, he is around every corner I turn. For everywhere I go I meet people, all sorts of people, endless numbers of them its seems, that he has helped. They have read his books, he led them to Christ, he got them into the ministry. How could a man be dead who helped so many people? And also I find that as I wend my way forward in the Christian life, I turn more and more toward the *way* he did it. Eminently practical, this father of mine. It works, by gum, it works. It is contagious, and the same sort of religion he devoted his life to selling, and I never feel far from him because I want to sell it, too. And so, in many ways for us, 'death has no more dominion.' "

A Missionary Parish ❁ 9

Tʜᴇ ᴘʀᴇᴄᴇᴅɪɴɢ ᴄʜᴀᴘᴛᴇʀ ᴡᴀs ɪɴ ᴀ sᴇɴsᴇ ᴀ flash ahead, chronicling our life together as a family. Actually we left Sam's career, at the close of Chapter 7, at the beginning of the 1930s.

Early in July, 1932, the members of Calvary Episcopal Church received a two-page letter from the Vestry. It read in part as follows:

"We must all realize that the work which has been characteristic of Calvary Parish for the past few years is part of a much larger movement which is making a tremendous spiritual contribution in many countries today. A First-Century Christian Fellowship, or the Oxford Group, has been called by the Archbishop of York* one of the main movements of the Spirit in our time.'

"The evident need of our country and the world for spiritual awakening . . . lays a special obligation upon us all at Calvary to share with others what has helped us.

"When, therefore, the Rector asked us to come to a special meeting of the Vestry on June 15th, and proposed to us that he be released for a six-months' sabbatical leave, during which time he should devote himself entirely to the furtherance of this important work [with the International Team of the Oxford Group] throughout America, we felt that this was a call which neither he nor we could disregard. Further, we wanted him to go as our representative.

"We freely acknowledge that our expansion in equipment, gifts and influence, has been due to a new lease of spiritual life. This we believe to be the answer to the Church's depression; and a revitalized Church has the answer to the world's depression, through reaching individuals one by one."

The Vestry's quick understanding and cooperation had had no small part in this revitalization of the church's work. Mr. Henry Parrish, who had succeeded Cornelius Zabriskie as senior warden, told Sam that he believed less and less in large institutions and more and more in personal contact between individuals as vehicles for the

* William Temple, later the Archbishop of Canterbury.

spreading of the gospel. Mr. Parrish's unfailing enthusiasm for this kind of work, together with that of other members of the Vestry, had been largely responsible for the obliteration of the usual line drawn between clergy and laymen, and made both groups primarily life-giving Christians. Thus the rector's projected six months with the International Team of the Oxford Group was seen as a true expression of the missionary fervor which has characterized Calvary Church since its founding in 1835.

On September 15, 1932, Sam's leave began. For a month the emphasis was preparation. The American leaders of the Oxford Group gathered to make themselves of maximum effectiveness to the International Team, which was expected from England in mid-October. Sam met with his American teammates in a series of leadership-training conferences.

In Montreal, Sam had his first taste of a citywide campaign, an experience that was to be repeated with more or less variation in its details in a dozen cities across the country before his return to Calvary in March, 1933.

"On Sunday we spoke in forty of the city pulpits, including the most outstanding churches of the Protestant communions. I was at the Cathedral in the morning, and at St. James's United in the evening. (This is the church of which the minister is Dr. Lloyd C. Douglas, author of *The Magnificent Obsession*). The daily papers were filled with news about the Group. There were several editorials which praised the work. On Monday began the open meetings in the Ritz Carlton. The first night the ballroom was filled, with about eight hundred people. The Bishop, and the Rev. Dr. Leslie Pidgeon, one of the great forces of the United Church of Canada, gave us the welcome: and then followed such a group meeting as we all know, with sparkling witness from diverse members of the team."

On November 8, the whole team had the honor of being invited to luncheon by the Prime Minister of Canada, with his entire cabinet and their wives, and of hearing from him a remarkable statement of his own religious convictions and of his expectations of the work of the Oxford Group.

Later, in Detroit, Sam wrote, "More American members of the team were arriving by the hour, till there were some fifty of them. Our team meetings were as large as our largest open meetings used to be. I felt that one of the outstanding contributions made at Detroit, where, of course, the business and economic situation is most grave, came from our American businessmen, several of whom, by the way, had been changed during the past year and had a very fresh and vital message for men in business, some of whom were in utter despair and at the point of suicide. It made a profound impression to hear men whose business situations were as precarious as their own speak of their condition with calm faith in God, and say that He alone was keeping them from worry and rebellion."

Refreshed and fortified with new vision, Sam was in the east in January, and it was then that many Calvary people caught their first glimpse of the overseas team. There was a great meeting in New York, in the Waldorf-Astoria, the night of January 2nd, and then a ten-day house party at Briarcliff Manor, Briarcliff, New York, where hundreds of New Yorkers and others gathered.

The six-month trip wound up in California, from where Sam wrote: "I am enjoying something which is better than even the beauty of this sun-filled southern California weather; and it is a conviction that we are beginning to see the first red streaks of dawn above the darkness of the general discouragement of the present hour. I may be too optimistic, but it seemed to me that I felt in the great meeting at the Waldorf, and I think that I have been feeling ever since, a growing wistfulness in our American people which lies very near to humility, and not very far from a revival of faith in God and His righteousness.

"The turn which is coming is *not* born alone of economic insecurity, as the cynics would have us believe. There is widespread search for a realer meaning in life and, wherever the Gospel is forcefully and practically presented, an extraordinary willingness to face its rigorous demands and meet them. I have said before that I believe God is waiting yonder above us with another great grant of His Holy Spirit to the world. I believe now that we are beginning to see the world's hands stretched upwards toward Him, in asking mood."

A team under the leadership of Jack Smith, Alys, and myself, together with the Vestry and staff kept Calvary House functioning during Sam's absence.

Sam was back in his regular place in the chancel of Calvary Church on the third Sunday in Lent, March 17, 1933. On that day, Bishop Manning confirmed or received fifty-one people into the church, the largest confirmation class at Calvary in fifteen years. The Holy Spirit had not confined His activity and benediction to Canada and the west!

Iden protest

In addition to the regular activities of the parish, which continued unabated during Sam's absence, some new enterprises were particularly noteworthy. One was the Advent Mission of Personal Witness. Every night during the first week in Advent six or eight lay people told at a simple service held in the church the story of their own experience of Christ, relating it to the larger problems of the world in such a way as to show how new individuals are the only possible foundation for a new world. Those who came to hear the evidence (and there were two to three hundred every night) saw instanced in the lives of those who spoke many of their own problems and the solution of them, and some passed that week from a religion of aspiration to one of possession. Excerpts from what was said may bring out some of the quality of this witness. One man said, "Surrender costs you something; and since I thought a whole lot of myself, it cost me a whole lot." "Religion is like a talent," said another; "if you don't use it, you lose it. I find that I have to keep witnessing to people I meet every day." One woman confessed that the summer before she had "unbuckled the whole armor of God, and just relaxed." Another declared she had found that "sin was not just an inconvenience to me, but an insult to God." And so it went.

Then, in February, there was the Mission house-party,* when the men of Calvary Church and Calvary Mission met "down in the Gas-House District" on East 23rd Street over a weekend packed with the kind of fellowship that flows from a mutual recognition that sin is sin, and Christ the only Cure, whether one comes from Park Avenue or a park bench, "whether he's in jail or in Yale."

As for the large confirmation class previously referred to, it was significant for several reasons. A number of the people who had found God inwardly through that fall and winter wanted to identify themselves outwardly with His Church and thus have access to the sustaining and vitalizing grace of the sacraments and other ministrations found there. It was the normal next step. But the interesting feature is that the work of bringing people to the Lord Jesus Christ and His Body, the Church, was not left entirely to the clergy. They did, of course, share in the work, in the winning and in the final training of the candidates. But the majority of those confirmed were interested first, and then won, through the counseling activity of lay workers such as myself and many others—the fulfillment of the ideal Sam had envisioned from the beginning of his rectorship. It was

---

* This refers to the rescue mission described on pages 188–193.

simply the inevitable expression of normal, living Christianity.

"The butcher, the baker and the candlestick-maker have been out- *up* done by the variety in the confirmation class," said the *Calvary Evangel* account. "Among this group of pilgrims are found: a former lumberjack, an ex-millionaire, an accountant, a long-time notorious criminal, a retired headmaster, a champion long-distance swimmer, a medical scientist, a physician, a commercial artist, a Bryn Mawr sophomore, a nurse, a lawyer's wife, a salesgirl, and other business people. Harvard, industry, Park Avenue, prison, medicine, mission, Germany, and Jewry have been caught in the strongest of bonds— the integrating spirit of an ex-carpenter, Revealer of God."

It was a demonstration of the fact that true, rounded Christianity has two sides to it, an inner and an outer. There is the life within—a personal, intimate, vital force—and then there is the tangible form which sustains, protects, and enriches that life. Those who were confirmed were assuring themselves of both emphases.

As Sam's homecoming drew nearer I began to be concerned about his getting enough rest before he undertook his arduous duties at Calvary once more. So followed a letter with wifely advice: "I have had some thought about you and your health. That was, in your times of rest to really try and relax completely. Don't write letters or copy sermons or make up back work. I feel that your tendency is to do something else just as hard as what you have been doing, and that isn't relaxation, it's distraction. You're not a spring chicken. A real relaxation and flopping occasionally wouldn't hurt you.

"My feeling now is that we need a group of us to get together when you get back to hear your vision and give you ours, not only as to the work to be done but where we can relieve you by taking some things off you and generally being bulwarks for you."

I want to say a special word here about the relationship that had begun to develop and continued to develop between the Smiths and the Shoemakers—a relationship which has lasted for almost forty years. We had known each other, of course, before we were married, and Alys and I had served together on the early staff of which she was a member when I came in 1928, and which Jack joined in 1929. Alys and I shared our romantic hopes and dreams and went through many ups and downs together in regard to them. Some of these are exceedingly humorous as we look back on them. To make a long story short, we both "landed" our men, and I have already referred to the rash of marriages that took place in early 1930.

Jack had many of the abilities that Sam did not have, and Sam was smart enough to know it. Jack had business experience and was a fine administrator. As assistant treasurer he kept all the books for the parish, Calvary House, and the Olive Tree Inn—the East Side lodging house which had been started by Bishop Satterlee in the 1880s, and which had continued to charge twenty-five cents a night for the poor bums on the East Side who had the twenty-five cents to invest in a bed. This lodging house was connected with the Mission. Sam had complete confidence in Jack Smith in regard to all these matters, and Jack, in turn, had complete confidence in Sam's salesmanship and endless creative imagination.

As I have mentioned before, Sam's great interest was in enlisting people for Christ—and he never saw fewer than three people a day from the time he began his personal counseling when he was a very young man until the time he retired from Calvary Church, Pittsburgh, in 1961. Jack, Alys, and I added up the number of people he must have seen in the thirty-three years of his ministry, and we discovered to our amazement that it came to about 35,000 people, most of whom were brought to a living faith as a result. But to go back to my story. Alys in those early days took on the presidency of the Woman's Auxiliary, which she was well qualified to do, having been a staff member at church headquarters next door for some time. She instituted the practice of opening prayers, which had not been one of the customs of the women of Calvary Church and which afterward led into our much more ambitious opening worship programs and eventually into our whole prayer-group movement, which I developed more specifically in later years.

Sam was home in time for Good Friday to conduct the three-hour service, and this Good Friday was especially wonderful. There was always something special about Good Friday at Calvary Church—it was tremendous in power and depth. Sam knew how to drive its full meaning home in his interpretation of the Seven Last Words. The church was always filled, with people quietly coming and going during the three hours. Because we were an inner-city parish in the center of the suit-and-garment district, hundreds of salesgirls, clerks, stenographers, and messenger boys slipped in and out in an unending stream. So many came just this once, and Sam yearned with all his heart and soul to be used by his Lord to reveal to them what He had done for them and what He held out to them in the way of forgiveness and release and victory and fulfillment and power. Sam made not only the manner but the meaning of His death so important that there was always a long line of people waiting to talk to him afterward. Hundreds discovered God for the first time or rediscovered Him in new and wonderful ways on those great days.

Sam was always exhausted after each Good Friday service. I had sandwiches and tea waiting for him when he returned to the apartment, and his first query would be, "Mummy, how was it? Do you think they got it? I'm glad, I'm wrung out. It's so litttle to do for Him when He's done so much for me. So little."

On Holy Saturday he helped to decorate the church. He loved it. It reminded him of the wonderful Easter Saturdays when as a child he rode in the flower-filled wagons from Burnside to Emmanuel in Baltimore. He wanted our equally homely old church at Fourth Avenue and 21st Street to look as radiant as Emmanuel used to look.

Easter morning was always vividly joyous, and this particular Easter of 1933 was no exception. There was something quiet and expectant in the old church made so beautiful with lilies and smilax and great banks of pink geraniums on either side of the pulpit and lectern, with the figure of Christ with outstretched arms and standing behind the altar and the cross of lilies over the sanctuary. The smell of those lilies and hyacinths as we tiptoed in for the early Communion was always for me an experience of "minor ecstasy." Sam celebrated at the early service and at the Festival Service at 11:00, and I always knew, especially at Easter, that when he said in the prayer of oblation "and here we offer a present unto Thee ourselves, our souls and bodies to be a reasonable Holy and living sacrifice unto Thee," he meant it with every fiber of his being.

Sam's poem "Easter Even" sums up his whole response to Easter:

I stood, and called and called
But there was no answer.
My little surroundings lengthened out into the universe itself.
I was calling within it,
And it became like a vast, empty corridor—
An empty corridor with great rounded shoulder-arches
That seemed to enclose infinite space.
But it was all empty, and cold—
With that emptiness that has been empty for years,
For centuries, for aeons. . . .

It was a space that called to be filled.
An emptiness that was cavernous with vacancy.

I called and called
But there was no answer, save the echo of my own voice
Coming back to mock itself.
It was like the reflectors by the side of the road,
Which have no light in themselves, but only send back
The light of your own headlights.
It was vast and cold and empty.

And I waited. I had to wait.
I had to wait until Easter Even. . . .
And then suddenly Voices began to come.
They burst out that morning in a chorus. . . .
They couldn't hold back until Easter Day, they unleashed themselves
Like unmanageable steeds, they poured out like cataracts of great water.
The stars called out, and the planets, and the sun and moon,
And all the inter-stellar space caught up their sound in a mighty echo,
Till the whole universe was sounding with Voices. . . .
All of them said the same thing, said it in deafening chorus,
Said it coming at me in such mass and quantity,
Said it so many ways and so insistently,
Said it so that my heart heard it unmistakably,
And I knew it was the universe's delayed answer to me.

And the burden of the song of the spheres
Was caught up by the mountains and the seas,
And it flowed with the rivers, and it spoke out of the skies.
It kept leaping out from the inwardness of things,
And pointed itself at me like a million million
Little spiritual rapiers, pointed right at me
Who had called into the empty corridors.
And the song they all sang
Was a hymn I had loved since my childhood,
Loved more than I ever loved any hymn . . .
And it went
"Jesus Christ is risen today . . . Alleluia!"

The Festival Service at 11:00 A.M. was a triumph of glorious
praise to his risen Lord. To him, the Easter music was the perfect
medium of praise. Our adult choir was perfection. I always slipped in
early so as not to miss the overture with trumpets, cymbals, and
violins assisting the organ, and I shall never forget the choir sweep-
ing down the aisle, singing "Welcome, Happy Morning," and the
radiant joy on Sam's face as he followed them. We always sang the
"Hallelujah Chorus" as the offertory anthem, and Sam would throw
his head back and look up when the climax shook the rafters with
"Lord of lords and King of kings, Lord of lords, King of kings, And

He shall reign forever and ever." The angel choirs seemed to have joined our human choir, and when our people sang Gounod's "Sanctus" during the Communion the angels seemed literally to come down into the church to join us in our prayer and rise back again into heaven at its close.

On Easter afternoon, we began what became an Easter ritual for us. We took a walk before our children's service and slipped into the other churches in our area to see and smell their flowers, not without drawing some comparisons—so easily do Christians slip into complacent self-congratulation.

The children loved Sam. His best-loved children's talk was about the cocoon and the butterfly, comparing them to our natural bodies and our resurrection bodies. The little children always crowded up to look at the cocoon and the butterfly, and I've often wondered how many of them remembered the meaning of the simile as they grew up.

In some ways, for Sam the tenderest of all the Easter services was what we called the Emmaus Service on Easter evening; again he started this service on this particular Easter of 1933. He read to us and then interpreted the story of the two disciples walking sadly to the village of Emmaus and how Jesus in His risen body joined them and questioned them about the past three sad days, and interpreted the Scriptures to them, and then revealed Himself to them in the breaking of bread, and vanished. Sam somehow made us feel the tingling excitement of these two disciples as they literally ran the seven miles back to Jerusalem and burst in upon the others with the stupendous news, only to hear that Peter had seen Him too, and then suddenly Jesus was with them. What an experience!

On several later warm Easter evenings after the service was over we walked up Fourth Avenue in New York and imagined together how we'd feel if we had been those two disciples, and Jesus had come and joined us in His resurrected body as He had joined them. Then we would fall silent and just walk, remembering all the glowing impressions of that glorious day—Easter. How Sam loved Easter and how he reflected the wonder and the promise of it to thousands and thousands of people through the years! As one young seminarian wrote to me after his death, "He interpreted for me the meaning of the resurrection."

As the War Clouds Gather ⬚ 10

IT WAS DURING THE SUMMER OF 1938, AFTER participation in the Moral Rearmament Assembly in Oxford ("Moral Rearmament" was the new name for the former "Oxford Group"), that Sam came home and wrote his passionate and prophetic book, *The Church Can Save the World*. Hitler was gobbling up Austria and Czechoslovakia; statesmen and churchmen were aghast and helpless, and no one seemed to heed the warnings.

In his book Sam said, "I believe that what we need more than anything else is a spiritual mass-movement: millions of men and women in personal touch with God, and united in a spiritual army which God can mobilize.

"I believe we can get it.

"I believe that the churches are the natural place (though by no means the only place) to look for this kind of force: and that there are within them tons of spiritual dynamite, in moral and spiritual conviction, waiting for some fire to set it off.

"I believe there are thousands outside who wait for the church to give the world a clear spiritual lead, who will join us in an effective warfare to restore the values for which Christianity alone stands.

"I believe that the marching of 'a mighty army' of the Spirit is the only answer and cure for the marching of the mighty armies of war: if God's army were vigilant and victorious, there would be no occasion for men to slay their brothers."

July 3, 1939, Sam recorded, "This has been an exceptionally interesting day. I had the day fixed up with dates, some of them important, but it became increasingly clear to me that I ought to drive Helen Hitchcock and her sister, Mrs. Walker, up to Hyde Park to get Mrs. James Roosevelt's signature on twenty-six letters going to British mothers in England. So I cleared my desk and went. Mrs. James Roosevelt was there to greet us, couldn't have been sweeter or more cordial and said at once, 'Who do you think is here, the President!' Then we went into the big study at the south end of the house and she and Helen and Lil Walker and I had about ten minutes. She said,

'I think it's so fine the way you've stuck in your church and worked all this out there.' Then it was announced that lunch was ready and the President was there, so we went into the dining room. The table was set for a family lunch. The President seated at the head of the table in a seersucker suit and comfortable shirt. He greeted us most cordially. The President asked me to say grace. Then we fell to talking about some local interest. After that he got on the possibility of war, which he said was fifty-fifty within fourteen months. He then told us what would happen if Hitler and Mussolini won, which he called another fifty-fifty chance. He believed with Europe conquered they would begin on the Americas. Argentina would come first with economic throttles that would force them into line, then up through South and Central America into Mexico. He said a congressman from Kansas was in to see him the other day and said he hadn't any fear about war in Kansas. 'Haven't you?' said the President, 'I think I'd be safer in Hyde Park than you would be in Kansas. Kansas is only two hours by air from Mexico.' And he said it gave the congressman quite a new idea. Two other interesting things from the conversation were his saying that he expected to return and live here soon again, as if to let us know that he was not thinking of a third term and didn't want us to think that he was.

"I got an impression of him today that I have not had before. It was an impression of simple sincerity and goodness, though political sense we all know he had, apparent financial recklessness he seems to be quite guilty of and going into greater and greater debt. But today it was not those things, nor the almost fatal glibness or domination of the situation. He seemed to me very courageous and sound and a solid citizen. I was impressed with how little he did to impress us. The President gets his personal charm directly from his mother and is very much like her. She is so informal and yet dignified. Feel the old-fashioned lady there every inch. I spoke to her of what an ideal place it was in which to be brought up. The President evidently loved it. She took us in to see the drawing room, small, Victorian, gorgeous Dresden candlesticks and chandelier and the piano literally covered with photographs of royalty; all the Scandinavians as well as the King and Queen of England, Queen Mary, King George. She showed us an ivory box which the Maharaja of Kapurthala had recently given her. She so simply and unaffectedly enjoys these things and her devotion to F.D.R. is as touching as is his to her."

We Part with
Moral Rearmament ❈ 11

parted with the Oxford Group (i.e., Moral Rearmament) after so many years of active participation. Here are his reasons in his own words:

"If there was so much of power and of good in the Oxford Group, why did some of us find ourselves one day outside it? Something happened to the Group about 1936. That year Buchman was in Germany. It was while walking in the Black Forest that the idea of 'Moral Rearmament' came to him. He came back with a broader base and a new name for his movement that he thought would include more people in it, and give what was needed for a world-wide advance. Some of us thought at first that this was a great new inspiration, and went along with it.

"I should like to say several things about this: F.B. [Buchman] hated Communism with everything in him; he believed in freedom and the democratic way of life, feeling it to be basically an expression of Christianity. But he was also profoundly aware of the softness, selfishness, and materialism that were increasingly fastening upon the whole of the west. He was seeking to create a force that would bring the west to its senses by bringing it to its knees.

"F.B. was a strong authoritarian. He was clear-headed and competent, he knew just where he was going, and just where he wanted his movement to go. As his work grew, the element of authoritarianism in his nature increased. He could no longer see all the people personally that wanted to see him; much more must be delegated. The movement which prided itself on little organization developed a very complete organization."

In 1936 the International Team of the Oxford Group spent some time in Geneva, and Sam and I were with them. These were the sad days when the League of Nations was showing itself increasingly ineffectual in preventing Mussolini's depradations against Ethiopia. Upon our return to Calvary, Sam wrote:

"Frank [Buchman] came to stay with us when he returned to New York. Everything else really stops when he comes, and the household revolves around him. I managed to preach each Sunday but all my actions centered in preparation for the Norwegian Premier, Carl Hambro's coming to the United States and giving him the largest opportunity. [Carl Hambro was at that time the Premier of Norway and an active member of the old League of Nations.]

"He came down here early on his visit and allowed Dr. Buchman to manage his visit in America, although he was officially the guest of the American-Scandinavian Foundation. We had a magnificent luncheon for him at the Bankers' Club. On that evening he and Frank Buchman were the main speakers at a great meeting in the Metropolitan Opera House, which I led. He made a profound impression every place he went and added to the deepened respect which is increasing on all sides for the Oxford Group."

An assembly was held in Richmond, Virginia, and later a leadership conference in West Point. On April 27, 1936, Sam recorded in his diary, "More and more I came to feel that I could not alone meet the demands of leadership in the American work, and at Richmond I said this to Frank Buchman and the Inner Team. I said it was a group movement. In no other country is there one national leader as I have been here, and I believe a group should carry it. Through the winter that team has been emerging. I worked with that smaller team in complete harmony but the decisions are not mine, they are ours. The leadership is not invested in me but in us. The guidance we follow is the guidance of the group."

In the spring of 1937 the whole American team went through a process of self-evaluation. Sam said of it: "What I saw at the time of this self-evaluation was that my call to the ministry tended to come into conflict with the great conversion experience which I had undergone in China and which also set my feet in the path of personal evangelism and counseling. I shared this conflict with the others, but it was not resolved."

Meanwhile, the activity of the international members of the Oxford Group was taking over more and more of Calvary House and pushing our commitment to our parish into the background. This was a contributing factor to the final parting with the Oxford Group three years later.

There is no further reference in Sam's diary to the Oxford Group and its activities until May 7, 1939, when Sam wrote: "Everything we've got has been going into Moral Rearmament Week and the big Madison Square Garden meeting a week from tonight. Frank Buchman has been back from Florida since just after Easter and has been staying in our guest room.

"Calvary House has really become the center of the Group life in the country. Books, plans, and living quarters are centered here. Frank is pretty consistently critical of the Church, with plenty of justice. They should have been glad for his advice, and they have almost consistently denied him approval, let alone assistance and cooperation. I believe he's right; that the men of practical concerns, politics, and business will be the first to grasp the practicalness of the Group, and 'moral rearmament' in the Church will follow along afterward. This hurts me and I'm not always above it emotionally. I happen to love the organized church in spite of its timidity and ineffectiveness, and I wish that she would lead instead of following. I deeply believe in both and want to incorporate and incarnate both in my own life and ministry. I cannot deny my orders. Nearly all my significant national contacts and opportunities are related in some way to my ministry as well as to my connection with the Group."

The conflict in Sam was growing.

Sam continued: "In early July [1939] we went to California for the Hollywood Bowl meeting July 19, and the second world assembly for Moral Rearmament on the Monterey Peninsula. We took a special train from New York with twenty-two cars and three hundred people. Helen and I were supposed to be in charge of the crowd as we traveled out and it was a very constant job. The Bowl meeting the night after we arrived was magnificent; thirty thousand there and ten thousand turned away. Frank Buchman was in great form."

Later, "Frank came in last week to prepare for and carry through the big Moral Rearmament weekend of December 2-3, 1939, with broadcasts as wide and as many as we could secure. Frank believes immensely in the general statement which contains adequate thinking about the world and its problems. I favor much more for America the concrete answer to the problems that people meet every day. I am sure it is the only way America will grasp our message."

In the early summer of 1940 Sam recorded again: "As time wore on I became more and more aware that Calvary House was no longer in any sense a parish house. It was a national headquarters for Moral Rearmament. Many of our Calvary people began to feel unwanted and not needed."

On the night of June 7, 1941, matters were rapidly approaching a climax in Sam's mind. There was a small meeting in the living room of our rectory which I shall never forget, because it was in the nature of a luminous spiritual experience that came first to Sam and was reflected to us. He recorded: "On Saturday night, June 7, the inner crowd were up in our living room seeking to find a unity of spirit which had become lost. Somewhere in the situation it seemed to me we were acting as if Christ was dead and not alive. Then He simply came right in and began giving me very clear direction, which seemed to give me a curious leadership amongst the rest of them which I had never before had and which gave us a remarkable emotional unity. As I look back on it, I see some of the subsequent events which have not been in the direction of unity curiously presaged in it. My guidance that night was this: 'Jesus, I come to Thee not to obey a fellowship but to try to love and serve Thee, my Lord and my God. Frank may go, MRA may die, the body of Christ never dies because He wears it. God make me simple, open. There is great truth in the fellowship. Why don't you talk more about Jesus Christ and Him crucified? Be simple, Christ-centered. Jesus is the head of this fellowship; not Frank Buchman or anyone else.'

"Next day was in radiant power. I preached the sermon I had prepared, but there was a superhuman element in it. My leading that day was: 'Keep freedom in Christ, where His spirit is, there is liberty. You have a cause but you have a life first, and that is Christ. Your people are all starved for Him. Stop calling the Church down, call them out and introduce them to Christ.' This kind of a spirit could win America, for this is sheer spiritual power in every life."

Later that month Jack and Alys, and Sam and I attended a houseparty on Cape Cod, which was the beginning of the end of our continuing participation in Moral Rearmament. Sam said of it: "After four days Jack and I pulled out, and there began coming to me the real meaning of my guidance of some previous weeks. We spent July writing out a statement of the things we believed. We said that unless we felt that the things where we disagreed with MRA could be resolved, Calvary House could no longer be the Moral Rearmament headquarters in this country. We offered to see Frank Buchman, but he would not see us when in the city—only in Maine where he was having a training group, and we said frankly we could not leave our work to come so far. Finally we had to give him a deadline when everything that belonged to Moral Rearmament should be taken from the house. On November 1, 1941, we sent a letter to the parish under that date: 'Many members of the parish share with us a deep gratitude to Dr. Buchman and other leaders of the movement from whom we have learned great truths, and with whom we have enjoyed real fellowship. The Group has made a great contribution to the life of this parish. When the Oxford Group was, by its own definition, a movement of vital personal religion working within the churches to make the principles of the New Testament practical as a working force today, we fully identified ourselves with it. Certain policies and points of view, however, have arisen in the development of Moral Rearmament about which we have had increasing misgivings. With this in mind and also because it has become increasingly difficult to function as a parish church when the facilities of Calvary House were largely taken up by its use as the national headquarters for Moral Rearmament, it has seemed advisable to us after careful thought and prayer that this house should cease to be used in this way as of this date.' " This statement was not made without the full concurrence of Sam's Vestry.

Unfortunately, the statement had to be read from the pulpit of Calvary Church on a Sunday morning, and the newspapers picked it up. Considerable publicity ensued, which we all deeply deplored.

It is only fair to say that Alys Smith and I—the wives in this case—were not as convinced as our husbands that the time had come to make a break. To sever relations with the people who had meant most to me through fifteen years of my adult life was one of the most anguishing experiences I had ever suffered. We both knew that if we chose to go with our husbands, as of course we did—not only in loyalty to them but to our deepest conviction—these people would no longer continue to be our closest intimates. We made the decision —although not without great cost—and we have never regretted it. We have had moments in our life and work, however, when we missed intensely those dear friends who had traveled the road with us for so long and who now found it impossible to see our point of view.

For us, we knew that God's call in the future was to work within the framework of the established church and yet at the same time to honor the convictions of those who felt called to work differently.

Therefore, I, myself, have always felt that those committed to Moral Rearmament had every right to follow the light as they saw it, while at the same time giving us the same right. At the time of the "great harvest" God will judge whether our devotion to Him and our work for Him is acceptable.

Faith and Freedom   🏵 12

After moral rearmament left Calvary House it was natural that reorganization and re-evaluation should ensue. It was decided that Sam would reach out once more into the colleges, and that we would concentrate more strongly on Christian fellowship within the parish, but without the participation of the international Moral Rearmament people.

In June, 1942, just after the birth of Helen, Jr. ("Nickie"), Sam was again down at Burnside where he was working on a Christmas "Forward Day by Day" that he had been asked to write. It was at this time, while Sam was in Maryland, that his dear friend and senior warden, Henry Parrish, died. Sam wrote in his diary, "Dear old man, how I loved him. He had been like an uncle to me and such a support in all of our work at Calvary. I went up early next morning and went straight to their house. I found Mrs. Roosevelt there. [Eleanor Roosevelt was related to the Parrishes.] Mrs. Roosevelt was wonderful with Mrs. Parrish. No daughter could have been more loving, more tender, or more devoted. The church was full for the funeral service. How many loved that dear old man! I drove up afterward to Tiverly, New York, in the Parrishes' car with Mrs. Roosevelt. We talked much with Mrs. Roosevelt about today and the problems we face. We had lunch at her cottage at Kill van Kull, after driving up with her in her gray roadster. She couldn't have been nicer. It was an interesting hour driving through Dutchess County in an open roadster with the First Lady. I find her humanistic, scarcely understanding spiritual ideas except in terms of human relationships, kindly wise in many approaches, erring on the generous side toward human beings, shrewd in handling most people, not easy to get on the inside of, very conscious of the greatness of her responsibility and yet strangely lacking, outwardly at least, in the consciousness of her position. I was with her in all nearly eight hours today. We laid Mr. Parrish to rest under a pine tree in the yard of that baronial church of the Livingstons in Tiverly.

"Yesterday I spoke of Mr. Parrish at the services and my sermon was strangely appropriate, for I spoke of Christian qualities which he vividly exemplified. His influence was so pervasive, yet so quiet—so constant, so unassuming—that we shall probably miss him more and more as time goes by."

Sam continued, "I was here at Calvary throughout July and carried a daily hour or two of welding of fellowship for the twenty-five or thirty people who were here for this purpose. Some in Calvary House, some coming in by the day.

"Jack Smith has been on vacation in Los Angeles, preaching every Sunday in St. John's Church. While there, the Vestry of All Saints, Beverly Hills, came in to hear him and called him. He came back here early in August to decide it, but it seemed right to all of us that he should accept. I feel the time has come for him to have his own work. We have never had a winter of such close fellowship as we four have enjoyed this past year. It will be a real personal loss to have them go. Their decision seemed to be complicated by the fact that early in June, when I was with the College of Preachers in Washington for a meeting with the Presiding Bishop about preaching missions, Bishop Freeman took me aside one night and said, 'Barney Phillips' [the Dean of the Cathedral's] death is a great loss to us; would it interest you to come here?' I talked with him considerably about it. There are many and great difficulties in the situation there, yet it also has very great possibilities. But if a call should come, what is to happen at Calvary would be a problem. Jack knew that this was in the wind and that if I ever was called to Washington he would, of course, be made rector. But he had a yen for California and he felt that he should accept Beverly Hills; so did we all; it will force us to turn somewhere to find a man to carry on here. The Washington call may never come."

On October 20, 1942, Sam wrote, "This afternoon we saw off Jack and Alys, their sons Peter and David, and their friend Helen Zabo on the train for California. I don't know when anything has hit me harder in my emotions. I simply cannot realize that the daily, hourly intimacy and fellowship which has been ours for so long, and this so heightened and intensified for the past sixteen months, is at an end. They are a part of our lives as Sally Falls is—an organic, living part. We miss them already, almost unbearably. This house will never seem itself without them; dear, loyal, steady, effective, devoted friends that they are. My eyes are full of tears as I write."

Thanksgiving Day, 1942: "Day before yesterday I went to Washington. Bishop Freeman had written that he wanted to have a good long talk, so I met him at his house and had lunch with him. He went fully into the different conception of American and English cathedrals. In the latter a bishop has only his throne but no say whatever, while here it is the bishop's church. He made it clear that in Washington the Dean is the Bishop's vicar. He told me much of Bishop Satterlee's vision for it. I asked him about two things. One was the pastoral evangelistic opportunity to touch the many who come to the Cathedral and who have no other church affiliation. He said that it was an almost untouched field which he hoped I would work to its fullest capacity. And we touched on the question of when I should preach. It was a very satisfactory talk; we ended with prayer in the Bishop's chapel. I came away happy. It ended nearly six months of great uncertainty."

On June 13, 1943, Sam wrote again: "The winter and spring have come and gone. When Bishop Freeman sent for me last December he was ill, but did not take his own illness seriously and said he was postponing my nomination until January at least. By the time he mentioned my name to the chapter his illness had progressed very far. Serious opposition had developed in the chapter itself. Things dragged on and finally in the spring the Bishop wrote me he must tell me that an opposition had developed which he couldn't overcome and that I would come to a divided house. His letter was a blow; it seemed to close the door. I was a bit cast down by it in my heart. It leaves a hole when you pull a Cathedral out of your heart! A week ago he died, and on Wednesday I went down for the funeral. I thought sure that the opportunity for me ever to go to the Cathedral died with him. But on the train a talk with Dr. William Adams Brown and Dr. John R. Mott showed me how many wished me to go there. A luncheon recently in Philadelphia with Senator George Wharton Pepper revealed his conviction that I should be there. Ten days ago Bishop Tucker [the Rt. Rev. Henry St. George Tucker] came in to ask if I were really interested in the Washington Cathedral, saying that he didn't think it would interest me except as a great evangelistic opportunity."

In August, 1942, Sam wrote, "Recently a Diocesan Convention in Washington decided not to elect a Bishop until after General Convention. Some weeks ago I had a rare, very fruitful conversation with Bishop Matthews [the Rt. Rev. Paul Matthews] on the report of the committee of General Convention on the Presiding Bishop's seat.

That committee and one of the Cathedral chapters met to find common ground for the future. The outline seems to be that the Presiding Bishop should resign his Diocese as soon as elected and reside officially in Washington, the Bishop of Washington really to be the Bishop of the Diocese and give his chief attention to it, the Presiding Bishop to nominate the Dean to the Cathedral so that he might be the Dean and not the Vicar of the Bishop of Washington as is now the case. It seems to be all to the good. There is a simply magnificent opportunity there which excites me more than any known to me on this continent. Maybe I'm not up to meeting it and God sees I need the discipline of keeping on where I am. He must and will settle it."

On July 15, 1943, Sam wrote, "This has been I think the blackest day in my life emotionally." The first cause was the concern about his mother, who at that time appeared to be seriously ill. She rallied from this illness and, as I have recorded earlier, she lived to be ninety years old and did not die until Sam was halfway through his ministry in Pittsburgh. Sam continued in his diary: "The other situation remains. There is an undeniable ache in my heart. The spiritual opportunity of that place in Washington is without parallel on this continent. Bishop Dun [the Rt. Rev. Angus Dun] has appointed Dr. [John Wallace] Suter Dean of the Cathedral. There are black spots to be lived through and this is one of them. Like pain after an operation there is nothing for them but to endure them. One knows that God brings us through these times and that we are shown the reasons why later, but they are crucifixion while they are going on." / yes

The winter of 1945 was difficult. God brought us through it with our flags flying. In January both children had chicken pox, and Sam came down with it while preaching a mission in the Moravian Church in Bethlehem, Pennsylvania. After seeing that the children were cared for, I had to go to Bethlehem and bring Sam home. A more forlorn looking creature I have never seen. Poor Sam, who didn't really appreciate quite how ill he was, fortunately had a very fine local doctor. We bundled him up and brought him home in the car, which might not have been wise as it left him with a rather bad aftermath of lumbago. As Sam himself said, however, "but how personal and trivial do all these things seem in the light of great events."

Because of my father's interest in statecraft, his election to the United States Senate in 1944, and our very close relationship as a family, Sam became more and more interested in the world situation. In order to express this concern, Sam wrote the following books and pamphlets during this era: *Christ and This Crisis; National Awakening; And Now to Build the Peace; Total Defense for Freedom; National Moral Defense; God and Peace; God and You.*

On August 12, 1945, Sam recorded in his diary, "We are hourly awaiting the final announcement of peace."

The following year, 1946, Sam recorded, "Yesterday I went to Washington. Helen was already with the Smiths [my parents] there. This morning Frank Laubach came and at 10:00 he, Alex [my father], and I saw President Truman for twenty minutes in re: Frank Laubach's plan "The Christian Answer to the Atomic Bomb," which envisioned a massive program of technical aid to underprivileged nations. It was a general talk but an open and friendly one, and I believe more will come of it. On the train coming up, Alex and I met Felix Morley [then president of Haverford College] and had a long talk with him. He was frankly interested in the idea. We explored the possibilities of Herbert Hoover becoming a kind of special adviser to the president for World Service, coordinating the various government and private agencies that are out to better mankind."

It was shortly after this that President Harry Truman announced his technical aid program, popularly known as Point Four, and who knows but what this conversation may have had something to do with influencing it. And Mr. Hoover's talents were used in the program.

After another summer at Burnside, Sam described the contrast between our quiet sylvan family life in that serene old place and the world turmoil swirling around us everywhere. "So we go along, a family community with astonishingly little change in this topsy-turvy world. I record this glimpse into our life because the world outside is so entirely revolutionized and in such chaos.

"Families, family homes, family traditions, family memories, family religion, family associations—in the midst of wars and tumults and revolutions and tragedy and death, there are still millions of families who are moving into the future through their children and their grandchildren and their descendants. It looks as if there is a stabilizing force here, intangible, unpublicized, enduring, that is God-given and worth preserving."

In August, 1949, Sam wrote, "I am utterly burned up about the mess in China. I felt at the time that General [George C.] Marshall had been influenced by some reds in the State Department when he went out there and asked the Communists and Nationalists to get together. It was impossible and part of the strategy of confusion and delay. The left-wing influence is everywhere and doing all it can to buy security for the masses at the expense of liberty. Sound Christian faith would check this, much as we know that Christianity has not said nor done enough about the material things in the world."

Following this was the tragedy of the Korean War and the even greater tragedy of America's vacillating policy in the State Department, regarding the support of General Douglas MacArthur as commanding general. Sam always felt that it was left-wing influence in the State Department that caused the order to General MacArthur not to cross the Yalu River, with all of its proliferating consequences.

All through the 1930s and continuing through the 1940s, Sam became more and more exercised over the relation of Christian faith to freedom as we know it in the Western world and in Western civilization. In 1949 he wrote a book entitled *Freedom and Faith*. The subtitle is "America's Choice: Christ or Tyranny," and Sam dedicated it to my father, who was then in the United States Senate, with this touching sentence: "To H. Alexander Smith, valiant warrior for freedom and faith in the Senate of the United States."

In the book he said, "It is my profound conviction that if we want to keep our freedom we must preserve our faith from which it arose. Christianity is the mother of freedom. Faith alone gives men courage to throw off slavery, and faith alone gives them the self-control to use freedom aright.

"I am not urging people to 'use' God and faith in order to achieve a humanly desired end, even freedom; but I deeply believe that, when all is said and done, Christianity is the only thing that is to be found in the end on the side of man, devoted to his real interests."

November, 1947: "We are in one of the most strenuous years of work that I remember. All the churches seem to be waking up to the need for evangelism and all of them are finding that they need someone who is doing it. So many doors open to me now, I turn down about an invitation a day. Can't begin to meet them all. This seems to be my year. I was called to St. Paul's, Richmond, in June, the first parish in that great old diocese. Helen and I went down early in July and had a most wonderful time with Mr. Randolph Williams who was senior warden, and we met the Vestry and the women but at no time did I see or feel myself there. Bishop Tucker and others were cordiality itself and it has a great opportunity, but it was not for me. When I went to Bishop Gilbert [the Rt. Rev. Charles Kendall Gilbert, the Bishop of New York] about what to do before I went to Richmond, he said to me, 'We need you in this diocese. I have had some inspiration about you in the Cathedral. There are some difficulties which will have to be straightened out first.' He wants to give me a considerable place in a conference of clergy on evangelism early next month. Western New York sniffed at me for Bishop. Bishop Louttit [the Rt. Rev. Henry Irving Louttit] was elected. I ran about two-thirds of his votes in both houses; he has declined."

Moving On   ▓ **13**

THE YEAR 1948 WAS ONE OF GREAT OPPOR-
tunities. On June 12, Sam wrote, "This year we formed a Manhattan convocation. I could have had the deanship of it if I had not
nominated Louis Pitt [rector of Grace Episcopal Church] who, I
thought, deserved it. I'm glad to say he was elected. I am on the
council. At Diocesan Convention last month I was elected to the
standing committee. Then two weeks ago I was given my D.D. by the
Seminary at Alexandria June 3, and next day an S.T.D. by Berkeley
Seminary at New Haven."

Sam wrote just before Watch Night Service, the last day of the
year, "My work has taken on considerably more importance in the
Church. I have been almost swamped with invitations to speak on
evangelism, and between them and counseling it has been hard to
find much time for parish work. The work has grown so definitely
evangelistic that it is harder and harder to confine it to a parish at all,
though up to date the parish has been the testing place. Bishop
Sherrill [Henry Knox Sherrill] chose my book *Revive Thy Church—
Beginning with Me* as the Presiding Bishop's book for Lent. In the
spring, Bishop Gilbert [Charles Kendall Gilbert] told me he wanted
me to be Dean of St. John the Divine [New York City]. He had
spoken of this to me more than a year before, but he waited to see if
he could get unanimous support for it from the Trustees, and this
gave time for those who did not want me to form a determined
opposition, and I was not asked to serve."

During the winter of 1949 a particularly fine young-married group
met in the rectory on Sunday nights for Bible study, discussion, and
prayer. Most of our couples would leave New York after two or
three years, and these couples were no exception. Of this particular
group, every one have given a splendid Christian witness in their new
community and new church.

One of these couples, the Frank Davises, who moved to Hollywood
where he later became vice-president for the George Stevens Productions, wrote me describing their experience:

"Our introduction to the couples' meetings commenced on our first visit to Calvary. We had just moved into the neighborhood, and we went to Calvary just because it was near; we knew nothing about Calvary or its rector, Sam Shoemaker.

"We were tremendously impressed with Sam immediately, but nevertheless we were prepared after the service to duck out—from our seats near the rear of the church—and to go away satisfied that we had made the effort to be there at all. But we obviously didn't know Sam Shoemaker!

"It was a cold day, and Sam had his cape slung over his shoulders, the wind blowing it back. There he stood in the doorway, blocking it against anyone who would slip through. Before we knew it, Virginia and I had been forced—most graciously—to divulge the vital statistics, names and phone number and all sorts of other information, including where we were born and where we had gone to school. Immediately these little associations connecting us with Calvary began to appear: Sam was from Maryland, so was I; Virginia had gone to college in Spartanburg, South Carolina, so had a parishioner. And then—'You must come to our young couples' group tonight.' That was it.

"Later in the day, reflecting on the meeting in the vestibule of the church, I didn't look forward to joining any young people's group. It had seemed like a good idea when we had said we'd be there, but now we wondered why we had committed ourselves to go 'back to church' that night. Nevertheless, we arrived at the Rectory as scheduled, at 7:30.

"Sam Shoemaker was a dynamic man in the pulpit. In his home and even with a small group he was no less so. There we were with Sam and Helen responding to us as if we were friends of long standing and introducing us to a group of interesting and vital people, busy people who were starting, or in some cases, well on the way to important careers in many diverse fields—accountants, lawyers, and even a successful fashion model.

"For several hours that evening we shared dessert and coffee, but most importantly, we shared the experience, with Sam's easy prodding, of giving to each other an insight into what the morning's service had meant and in truth how all those Sunday morning services related to all of the other hours in all of the other days. The meeting that night with Sam and Helen and that group of young people gave us some answers and raised some questions which made us go back again and again for more answers—and more questions.

"These were for us never social occasions—they were much more meaningful. In our particular case, although we were both from out of town, we were not 'strangers in a big city' seeking to find friends and a social life. The meetings were significant in themselves."

In 1964, fifteen years later, I attended the General Convention of the Episcopal Church in St. Louis and was astonished to receive a note from Virginia and Frank Davis asking if they might see me for a few moments before they caught their plane. They were eager to tell me how the Holy Spirit had led them into their life work and to express their gratitude for the personal experience in New York so many years ago which showed them the way.

Frank had addressed the dinner meeting of the Department of Promotion of the Executive Council the evening before, and what he said there was a splendid illustration of the application of Christian faith and principles in his chosen vocation—the motion picture industry:

"I would like to examine the role which motion pictures can play in promoting the interests of the church.

"It is significant, I believe, that religious bodies throughout the world are coming more and more to recognize and to utilize the tremendous power and effective means of mass media to spread the word of their faiths.

"As one associated with this fascinating medium of communication and art, I am in awe of its power for evil.

"You may be sure that at least some of the enemies of the Church are fully mindful of the power motion pictures have, and that they use that power to advance their beliefs and to destroy ours. They are not just discovering that power; they have recognized it and utilized it over the years. Lenin declared, 'Of all the arts, the most important one is the cinema.' Stalin expressed it even more strongly when he stated, 'If I could control the medium of American motion pictures, I would need no help in order to convert the entire world to Communism in a very few years.' "*

---

* From an address by Frank I. Davis, vice president of George Stevens Productions, Inc., before the Department of Promotion of the Executive Council of the Episcopal Church at the General Convention St. Louis, Missouri, October 15, 1964.

From 1948 to 1951 Sam enjoyed a meaningful fellowship with some members of the Episcopal Evangelical Fellowship in the Diocese of New York.

The whole vision for a great Episcopal Mission in the Diocese of New York to be held in the Cathedral of St. John the Divine in December of 1950 began to evolve, and Canon Green (Bryan Green) was invited to be the missioner. There was very little time for organization as most of these busy clergy went away for the summer; in fact no organization was even thought of until September when they returned from their summer vacations. However, there was time for a great deal of prayer, and I remember that I was asked to mobilize the women's groups throughout the diocese, of which there were some ninety at that time, to support the Mission with our prayers and to pray through the summer that the Holy Spirit would be poured out in great power on the whole Diocese of New York during that one great week in December.

Nobody knew what would happen. The parishes throughout the diocese were notified that the Mission was being held; they were invited to bring their people; they were invited to pray for it. I shall not forget the opening evening of the Mission, sitting in the huge nave in which two thousand chairs had been placed and watching my husband and Jack Mulligan, rector of the Church of St. Michael and All Angels, pacing restlessly about in their cassocks with, I am sure, many butterflies inside as to whether anyone would turn up to hear their missioner.

The result of all the prayer and the care which had gone into it was astoundingly rewarded, because when the doors were opened people came in such droves that Canon West (Edward West) had to be hastily sought for more chairs, the crowd was five thousand strong on a rainy, sleety Monday night in early December.

The crowd continued increasingly throughout the week until on the final evening, which was dedicated to young people, there must have been ten thousand people squeezed into every nook and cranny of that vast cathedral nave singing the gospel hymns lustily and listening with their ears straining to Canon Green's message. That night I was sitting in a corner near a pillar, with two prominent laymen. When Bryan Green gave the altar call for the young people to come forward, it was an impressive sight to watch. Two or three thousand of them surged forward to take the altar call.

Canon Green's Mission in the Cathedral, with forty-two thousand people over eight successive nights, showed what the cathedral might be—the place became human, even intimate.

In Sam's evaluation of the Mission he made these observations: "Like all other churches in this startling time, there is a widespread feeling in the Episcopal Church that we certainly need 'something.' For three months previous to this Mission, we had gathered about once a fortnight to prepare spiritually for the Mission. The Bishop had asked me to lead these gatherings, which met usually at the Church of St. Mary the Virgin. All sorts came—High and Low, big and little, Negro and white. Men opened their hearts and mouths as they seldom had a chance to do in clerical gatherings, except to debate something in convention. One day, Dr. Leicester Lewis, a vigorous High Churchman and a fine scholar, said musingly aloud words to this effect: 'We terribly need a new spiritual movement in the Church today. We have had three—the Wesleyan movement, with the Evangelical emphasis; the Oxford Movement, with the emphasis on open-mindedness, scholarship and social application. But we need a new one. I wonder whether this is it.'

"We all wondered. Some of us hoped and prayed deeply. I believe, myself, that this might have been the beginning of spiritual awakening that could have swept the Episcopal Church. After all, New York is a tough situation, and when you can get forty-two thousand people to go to the Cathedral during a week to hear simple, dynamic preaching of the gospel, you have a seed and a root that is alive, and anything can happen. Why didn't it? Because the effort at follow-up consisted mainly in a clergy 'committee' which, after a while, just stopped meeting at all; and in a few parish missions conducted by clergy themselves, but lacking not alone the power of the great Mission, but also the power they might have had if the clergy themselves had even acknowledged their own need to be further converted. There were not half a dozen parishes prepared to follow-up the results of the Mission at the cathedral by anything except making these new converts into just the kind of people we had already. I do submit in all frankness that if we multiplied our two million Episcopalians by twenty, unless there occurred a spiritual change as great as the numerical, America and the world would not be a very different place. A Mission produces a few spiritual cut flowers: a revival (which is what we desperately need) would strike a root and grow. Our leadership was too timid, too easily deflected back into the uninspired channels, too ready to think that the only purpose of a mission was to increase the number of Confirmation candidates. So this did not produce what we had hoped for, not because Green himself was not magnificent, or because the Holy Spirit was not there in power, for He was, but because the mission began only with the enlistment and cooperation, not with the conversion, of the clergy. I hear bishops lament the need of the clergy for conversion: I see mighty few of them wrestling with their men and producing it. It is so cheap for bishops and clergy to 'talk spiritual.' "*

During the spring of 1950 there came a call to Sam to be rector of Emmanuel Church, Baltimore. Sam went to Baltimore and talked with the Vestry and looked over the situation very carefully. He told the Vestry that some of his friends in New York had made up their minds to put him up for election as Suffragan Bishop, and were working hard in that direction; he felt obligated to be loyal to their hopes, and Emmanuel said they would wait for his decision until after the New York election. Dr. Paull Sargeant of St. Bartholomew's was in charge of the "strategy," and Dr. Arthur Lee Kinsolving of St. James's made a most generous nominating speech; but Dr. Fred Fleming of Trinity had organized an unbeatable phalanx of high churchmen, and from the first Sam thought his election most improbable. In fact, he thought honestly it was more the convictions of his friends than his own that caused him to "run" at all. He was defeated. Walking home with his senior warden, Ed Cabaniss, Sam said to him, "Ed, I feel this is about three-tenths rebuff and seven-tenths relief. There is an aspect of it that hurts. Three times I have been considered for high office in the church; dean of Washington Cathedral, dean of St. John the Divine, Suffragan Bishop of New York, and three times been rejected.

"But then I reflect that I am called to a rather special kind of ministry and maybe any of the three would have required an amount of diplomatic compromise and consideration and might have made any free work under the Spirit difficult if not impossible. So it is not hard to feel the hand of God still at work in my life, perhaps saving me from great unhappiness. Helen feels this too."

The night after the election, Sam called the Vestry together, told them of the call to Baltimore, and asked for their frank opinion. He had, he reminded them, been at Calvary twenty-five years, and perhaps they thought that it would be better for Calvary to have a new man. He had opened the question with the Vestry long ago, after a

* Samuel M. Shoemaker, *By the Power of God* (New York: Harper & Row, 1954), pp. 119-121.

two-year trial, he recalled, and now he wanted to do the same again with them. Somehow Sam could never feel that Emmanuel was the right place for him, in spite of his love for it and its being always for him in some sense "his parish" more than any other would ever be. He had to write them accordingly, and we set out for what looked like the last dozen years of his ministry at Calvary, New York.

Then came the twenty-fifth anniversary celebration at Calvary on Whitsunday, 1950, and the people were wonderful. We had our annual Calvary family gathering over Whitsunday weekend. (Whitsunday was always, next to Easter, Sam's favorite Sunday of the year because he believed so deeply in the present living power of the Holy Spirit and wished to dramatize it.) Many people had come from all over the country. We centered the Whitsunday weekend around the four sides of living evangelism: conversion, prayer, fellowship, and witness. Sunday night there was a great service. We had clergy in procession; they sang all the Calvary music—including the hymn Sam had written for Calvary's centennial and various anthems dedicated to him—Norman Vincent Peale, Louis Pitts, and young Bob MacLean from Yale, speaking for the undergraduates, his friends Sherry Day and Quintin Warner were there. We were very thankful for it all; it was beautiful and in wonderful spirit, 750 people in the church.

During the autumn of this same year Bishop Block (the Rt. Rev. Karl Morgan Block) of California asked Sam if he would be interested in becoming the dean of the San Francisco Cathedral. But Sam did not feel that this was for him, and he declined.

Calvary Church was situated in New York with only a very small residential area surrounding it, and we were such a close parish family that we were able to recognize any strangers or visitors who came through our doors on a Sunday morning. I was always among the greeters, but one group of visitors entirely escaped my notice. This was a visiting delegation from Pittsburgh, including a member of the Vestry and a woman member of the committee. They came on several occasions, heard Sam preach, mingled with us in the coffee hour; I didn't even know they were there.

One morning, in late November of 1951, Sam called me into the study and told me that he had received a call from Calvary Episcopal Church, Pittsburgh, to become rector. Our old friend, Sally McClenahan, daughter of the former dean of the Washington Cathedral and always a warm admirer of Sam's, had followed up the official call with a personal call (she being a member of the pulpit committee), urging him to accept. He also heard from the Bishop of Pittsburgh.

The call was intriguing. Sam had been at Calvary Church, New York, for twenty-six years. I felt deeply that there comes a time in the affairs of men when you have done all that you can do and it is better for both you and your people to move on if the opportunity offers itself. I felt that such a time had come for us. Sam, a second-thought man, wasn't so sure. Besides his beloved Calvary Church, which he had done so much to build up and develop, he had increasingly exciting opportunities through radio preaching and in connection with college work all the way up and down the eastern seaboard (see pp. 151–155; 161–168).

Sam was well aware—as I wasn't—that if he moved to Pittsburgh, which was really the gateway to the middle west, he would quite naturally be required to give almost total time in the first year or two there to consolidating his position with his new parish and giving his full attention to his new parishioners. He felt that it might be a mistake to leave the opportunity that the growing eastern seaboard college work presented to him as well as the tremendous opening that he had in the field of radio.

One of Sam's close friends was Dr. Frank Goodman who pioneered religious radio for the then Federal Council of Churches. In 1946 he offered Sam a five-minute daily spot called "Gems for Thought" on station WJZ.

This was so successful that in 1948-1951 Sam did a Sunday half-hour broadcast over station WOR.

Dr. Frank Goodman and his son Wesley then proceeded to schedule Sam on another Sunday half-hour program with the title "Faith in Our Time." So one of Sam's reasons for hesitating about leaving New York was the growing scope of his radio ministry. As it turned out, however, after going to Pittsburgh, he was invited to resume his broadcasts under the title "Faith That Works."

I pressured Sam pretty hard on the Pittsburgh decision, and I don't deny that I did because something deep and instinctive inside me told me that this was it and we should move. We accordingly agreed to compromise, and we accepted an invitation of the Calvary Vestry to make an all-day visit to Pittsburgh.

I shall never forget the evening we started out. I had contracted an intestinal flu germ of some kind and couldn't have felt worse. When the train pulled into Pittsburgh on a dismal, sleety, gray morning at the small suburban station of East Liberty in the residential area in which Calvary Church was situated and we got out and looked at the gray skies, the prospect was anything but pleasing. Nevertheless, I immediately sensed the dynamic atmosphere of the city itself. We were whisked to Calvary Church by the senior warden, Mr. Lucius Robinson, a dear and wonderful person.

The church is an exquisitely beautiful example of Ralph Adams Cram's best effort at perpendicular Gothic. The outside is a gem of symmetry and beauty and the inside is equal to it. In spite of the fact that it needed renovating, we were transported by the beauty of it all.

The parish house had been an afterthought. The outside of it matched in symmetrical beauty the outside of the church, but the interior was not too functional. One thing caught my eye and that was the lovely new stainless steel kitchen. And the idea of a paid kitchen staff for parish organizational functions was to me a luxury beyond my wildest dreams. The housekeeping side of my soul responded.

Next we inspected our possible future rectory. Two wonderful Methodist women, the Misses Carnahan, had lived in a truly beautiful Victorian Gothic house catty-corner across from the church for many years, and this house was to become the rectory. It was surrounded by a large expanse of green and an old-fashioned wrought-iron picket fence. The moment we stepped inside the door, Sam and I fell head over heels in love with it.

A large house did not alarm us in the least. Sam had been brought up in a large house, and he had always loved space around him. I fell in love with the parquet floors, which needed a great deal of doing over, the funny stained-glass window panels around the doors, the glorious fifteen-foot ceilings, the beautiful hand-carved marble mantels, and the inside shutters in every window.

After our return home Sam needed a few more days in which to think it over. Sitting alone in his study one morning, asking the leading of the Holy Spirit in regard to this call, he seemed to see, in his mind's eye, the vision of a door closing and another opening. This was the guidance for which he had been looking, and he wired the Vestry of Calvary Episcopal Church, Pittsburgh, that he would accept the call.

There was great consternation in our New York parish. Yet I believe that many of our people felt that the time had come for a change all around.

Sam announced his acceptance of the call at the time of our last

Christmas Eve carol service. That occasion is filled with poignant memory. Perhaps it wasn't the best time in the world to announce such a decision to a congregation. Yet in another way it was, because we had always considered Christmas Eve—next to Good Friday and Easter—the great occasion of Calvary's year. This marvelous candle-lit carol service was never more exquisitely meaningful or beautiful than it was on that night, our last at Calvary Church, New York.

The time between Sam's announcement of his acceptance of the call to Pittsburgh and our departure for Calvary Church, Pittsburgh, was a frantic one. So little time and so much to do.

This change in our life came just at the time of our daughter Sally's engagement, and it seemed to us a fine opportunity both to announce Sally and Court's engagement and to say farewell to our New York friends before our departure. Accordingly we planned for February, 1951, our last and greatest affair at Calvary House, where so many great occasions of our lives had taken place: our own engagement reception way back in 1929, the launching of our Sunday coffee hours (among the first in New York City), the place of the midweek Thursday night meetings, the farewell reception for Jack and Alys Smith. Here too our wonderful and exciting twenty-fifth anniversary reception had been held and our various annual church benefits, which we inaugurated during the 1940s. Now this as a grand climax.

Hundreds of people turned up to wish the engaged couple well and to say goodby to us. The food ran out, but everybody had a good time and it was a most heartwarming, although in some ways a rather sad, occasion.

Sam recorded of the following weeks, "I wound up the confirmation classes and there was planned a delayed theological education Sunday where our nine candidates for the ministry who were going from Calvary to be ordained that year spoke briefly." This was also a fitting farewell to New York. The New York *Herald-Tribune* records of this occasion: "Nine theology and pre-theology students explained at the 11:00 A.M. service yesterday at Calvary Protestant Episcopal Church, Fourth Avenue and Twenty-first Street, why they had elected to join the ministry. The students, all but two in their early twenties, are all Calvary Church parishioners."

We left for Pittsburgh in our maroon Ford the last week of March, 1952: our beloved Mamie; Edith Winter, Sam's secretary; Nickie; and our canary bird, all surrounded by bags and boxes, were in the back seat; Sam and myself in the front. Sam did not know then, nor did I, that he would never enter those doors again in this life. He was invited back to the anniversary of the dedication of Calvary House in 1958, but unfortunately he was ill and could not go. The poignant words of Alfred de Musset are so true—"Partir c'est mourir un peu, c'est mourir à ce qu'on aime."

Sam the Churchman ❀ 14

THERE ARE NUMEROUS INCORRECT IMAGES of Sam Shoemaker in the minds of many people, and I should like this opportunity to set them right. Some think of him as a maverick who broke all the rules in order to establish what he considered his particular emphasis; some think of him as a totally unique personality and that God broke the mold after He had created him. Some think of him entirely in terms of evangelism or counseling. Some have been critical of him and accused him of being pietistic in his emphasis. Some think of him as a prophet, a man way before his time. He has been evaluated, criticized, scandalized, and eulogized variously. Few think of him as a convinced and dedicated parish priest.

He had a deep-seated belief in the Established Church and the parish unit as an essential part of God's plan for the Established Church. This belief contributed largely to the break with Moral Rearmament, but at the same time enabled him to put many of the principles which he had learned through his participation successfully to work in and through a local parish.

I am grateful for the material in this chapter to a Vestryman of Calvary Church, New York, Mr. Kenneth Kenneth-Smith, who became junior warden and then senior warden of Calvary Church between the years 1929 and 1955.

Mr. Kenneth-Smith went over the yearbooks of the old parish of Calvary Church and revealed the significance that lay behind the statistical records. There was a recognizable background of attitudes and loyalties which explain Sam's method of operating. He showed that it is possible to maintain all the essential functions of a parish church while at the same time reaching out to those who ordinarily were beyond the sound of its voice.

The message and techniques which Sam employed are applicable to any parish now. The prerequisite for these methods lies in the deep commitment of the rector and all lay leaders under the guidance of the Holy Spirit to both the established format of the Church and to the Church as mission. In other words, the gathered Church and the scattered Church.

Sam loved and was committed to the parish church—its members, program, and regular functions; and he was also committed to those who had not yet been reached by the message of the church—the self-satisfied pagans, the needy, the lost. In his writings in the *Calvary Evangel*, some of his books, and many of his sermons, we see these convictions clearly stated.

Sam believed that the Church was soul and body just as people are. "It is both organic and institutional," said Sam. "It is spiritual force and the channel of that force. It is wine and cup. It is sap and bark. It is inwardness and outwardness. It is unseen and visible. It is effectiveness and authority. It is anticipation and attainment."

He often said, "Outside the Church there is no salvation. What God hath chosen and cleansed, that call not thou common. The Church is His creation, His plan, and His hope."

Both Calvary Churches of which he was rector were essentially to him not stones and arches and foundations. They were essentially the people of years gone by, and of today and of tomorrow, who are part and parcel of these households of faith.

Sam had strong convictions about the church's worship services. He felt that worship was a means of grace, and he said in a sermon on April 7, 1940: "The Church long ago realized that more people would be helped if the service was ordered and prepared beforehand. So she developed a liturgy to safeguard services from the failures of spiritual leaders. Sometimes our spirits are aflame, and we find in the words of the service the vehicle of our aspiration. Sometimes our spirits are dull, and may catch only a word here and there that 'speaks' to us. Nevertheless, the impact of the service is always there, and makes its impression on our subconscious even when not on our conscious minds."

How are we to reach people and bring them into this ordered atmosphere of worship? This was a constant preoccupation of Sam's whole ministry because he felt so deeply, with Walter Carey, the Anglo-Catholic Bishop of Bloomfontein that "Unless conversion has taken place, there is no reason why anyone should wish to use the Sacraments or liturgical worship in the church, for God does not help us against our wills. But if we decide that we mean to live the life that Christ wants us to live, then we shall find more and more the grace that is in the Sacrament of Baptism, Holy Communion, and the ordered liturgical forms of worship in the established church." All meaningfulness in worship, Sam felt, hinged therefore on conversion.

He believed all prayer is a means of grace, that it is open to us at all times, and is probably the oldest of all the means of grace. He felt that solitary prayer as well as prayer with small groups of people were powerful and necessary kinds of prayer. At the same time he believed that for general week-by-week, year-by-year impact and use, liturgical prayer is necessary. Therefore, the marvelous order of prayer outlined for us in the Book of Common Prayer is essential if we are to understand and participate in worship which is the source of healthy emotion.

Sam felt deeply about the sacraments and said of them: "The two sacraments of Baptism and Holy Communion take of life's most natural and common things—water and food and drink—and by offering them to God with special intent, and by using them to transmit His grace, these natural things become the holiest things in the world."

Sam believed that worship ought to be attended with everything that rightly awakens and feeds while yet it controls the emotions. He felt that nothing brings us back to our elementary selves, and digs so deep down into our emotions as music, especially music that has become associated with great words and sentiments, music in which you can share and take part, like hymns, which can be the means of present joy and of better living.

He felt too that the beauty which the eye can see, of line, of carving, of painting, of stained glass, feeds the souls of people with joyous, satisfying emotion, and contributes to the totality of worship, especially when this is attended by the stately, well-ordered, sometimes quaint and old-fashioned words of our liturgy which are beautiful at all times, and on occasion become charged with emotion, depending on our subjective needs or the collective state of mind of the congregation, or perhaps some great event that is in the minds of all the people in the congregation at that particular time.

Sam also saw the necessity for organization. He believed that business done haphazardly is no glory to God, but also that meetings run as if the Holy Spirit did not exist simply have no place in the church. He felt it a great pity if some groups in the church regarded themselves as "practical" while others thought of themselves as "spiritual." With regard to the women, he felt it of vital importance that the Martha and Mary elements in all of them be stirred up and put to work for the glory of God.

Because Sam believed so deeply in the importance of the established ways, which through the years had been proved the best way for a particular parish to function, he was a great believer in the vital statistics of a parish. He liked parish yearbooks because he felt it important to inform the parishioners and other interested persons about the work of the parish as well as to preserve valuable records for the future.

The annual parish year book of Calvary, New York, always contained the Rector's Foreword, an account of the administration, of the corporation, the staff, the parish register, a prayer for the parish, accounts of the hours of service, the choir, the church school, the *Calvary Evangel* (which was the printed word), the Woman's Auxiliary, the Church Periodical Club, the Women's Benevolent Society, the Altar Guild, the memorial rooms and beds, and the financial reports.

As their spiritual leader, Sam never allowed the ministry to the local membership of the parish to be minimized or neglected or to be used merely as a base or cover for new experiments. Each new development as it emerged in his experiments was submitted to the Vestry for their information and approval. Sam thus was very careful not to abuse the wide latitude granted him by the Vestry in furthering or developing an experiment. His senior warden told me, for instance, that when Sam was making up his mind whether to break his formal ties with Moral Rearmament he polled every member of his Vestry personally for his opinion.

The experiment in outreach, therefore, or rather the mission activities of the church, became a team effort of Vestry and staff, with the Vestry serving as a buffer between the local parishioners and those drawn to Calvary by its outreach work. In time, about one-third of the Vestry were stanch parish members who were first drawn to Calvary by this same outreach work. (Some of these outreach activities are described in the section on "The Laity in Action," pp. 171–208.)

To deny that there were clashes between the conventional, traditional members of the parish and those experimenting in these wider and more daring fields would be to deny the facts of life. The whole structure, however, for both the local and the outreach work, or rather the gathered and scattered parish, was solidly laid throughout Sam's ministry, and laid so solidly that it could take any possible strains.

On several occasions the Vestry found it wise to trace the financial support of the parish by source. It turned out that about one-half of the church budget and most of the church on mission, or outreach, costs came from other than the purely local parish members. Furthermore, about one-third of the church membership came through the outreach.

Sam conceived of his role as threefold. He saw himself as a *pastor*, as a *priest*, and as a *preacher.*

As a pastor, he felt he must know his people, visit them, help them with their troubles and sorrows, and lead them in their united work for Christ. He knew that he would be called upon by many people not just his own parishioners, and that he must always be reaching out and drawing new people into the parish family.

As a priest, he realized all too well that as he stood before the altar and celebrated Holy Communion, he was God's ordained servant, charged with responsibility to "rightly and duly administer the Holy Sacraments," that he was the people's representative before God, offering these services to God with them and in their behalf. Looking toward the people, the priest acts and speaks for God. Looking toward God, the priest acts and speaks for the people. Here the office is greater than the man. When the priest stands before the altar, it is time for the people to forget him as a person and think of the holy office which he is charged with performing, the great gift which God is giving through human hands. He felt deeply that no higher spiritual privilege could come to any man than to be a priest in the Church of Christ.

Sam had deep convictions about the discipline of priesthood. He believed that all clergy should really begin with a rule of life that included at least a half hour of personal devotion at the beginning of the day, and he felt that all discipline started there and succeeded or failed there.

Sam sensed that people are often much more moved than we imagine by preaching and that there should be a strong element of teaching in our modern preaching, for people are spiritually illiterate, and preaching must have in mind the balance of the Christian message. He believed that all preaching today should be fundamentally evangelistic in intent and that this "Good News" must be presented with conviction, and with clarity, with passion and compassion. He deplored the modern tendency of educated people to become frightened of emotion and, therefore, to emphasize that everything must be under severe control, very submerged—especially everything that has to do with religion.

He used the simple simile of two young people falling in love and asked us to imagine whether this is possible without emotion. He believed that we have done great wrong to the gospel in insisting that religious expression should be kept under the severest control, and he felt strongly that this is the reason why our traditional churches today are not getting the masses, because we tend to hear sociological liberal sermons or academically conceived sermons rather than sermons that are meant to reach the heart of the hearer and bring him to conviction and conversion.

Sam often quoted Phillips Brooks, who used to say that preaching is "truth mediated through personality." A man is committed to some general truths which he ought to set forth: the basic truths and doctrines of our faith which are presented in a rounded fashion through what we call the "Church year." If he is a real man, though, he has deep convictions of his own, and it will be inevitable that some of the truths of Christianity will appeal to him and burn in his heart more than others. He felt that if a man had a message, he was bound to come back and emphasize the main points of that message again and again, that while a priest's work is in a sense impersonal the preacher's work is always personal. Talking to many, he is always talking to one. He speaks of the needs he knows in his own heart and in the hearts of others and of the way Christ meets and satisfies those needs. He knows that he is talking about needs that exist in all hearts, and of Christ's power to satisfy everyone.

Sam could see that the Church is not an end but a means. It was not the Church which "God so loved that He gave His only begotten Son," but the world. The Church is the company of those who, having heard the message of Christ, respond, discover the meaning of life in Him, and henceforth have but one aim, to reach all men for Him. The "means of grace" with which the Church is endowed are not satisfactions for the comfort of the "ins," so much as gifts for their equipment and empowering as they seek to reach the "outs." The early apostolic Christian did not think of the Church as merely a place for the shepherding of believers. Sam recognized that we are intended to receive training, knowledge, absolution, fellowship, and inspiration in the Church; but that these are for strengthening in the battle to win the world for Christ. He loved to quote Dr. Emil Brunner's great saying, "The Church exists by mission as fire exists by burning." And he went on to say that, "Any church that is putting its emphasis today anywhere else than on getting people into touch with the living God is frankly looking down the wrong hole, out of date, and blind alike to the danger and to the unparalleled opportunity of the present day."

III
THE PITTSBURGH
MINISTRY

A New Challenge 🔲 15

SAM TRIED TO BRING TO FULL FLOWER IN PITTS-
burgh all the distilled experience of New York—to a parish in a
changing neighborhood.

The history of Pittsburgh's Calvary Church has been illustrious.
The first Episcopal service held in the village of East Liberty, Pittsburgh, took place on the first Sunday in January, 1855. The Rev.
William H. Paddock, a missionary of the church, officiated. The
original church was a small brick Georgian building with a square
wooden bell tower and was called the Little Church Behind the
Mill.

For some time this little church had a rocky time financially. None
of the rectors remained very long, until the incumbency of the Rev.
Boyd Vincent. During the sixteen years of Dr. Vincent's rectorship
the parish got solidly on its feet. By this time the site of the church
had been moved to Penn Avenue, Pittsburgh.

By the time the twenty-fifth anniversary of the parish took place
on January 23, 1880, the number of communicants had grown from
thirteen to 238. The following year the rector's salary was increased
to three thousand dollars.

After Dr. Vincent was consecrated Bishop of Ohio in 1889, he
was succeeded by the Rev. George Hodges. During Dr. Hodges' five
years of leadership various ecumenical social programs were under-
taken in Pittsburgh. One such enterprise was Kingsley House, the
social service center organized by Calvary's Church Guild. Kingsley
House continues to serve Pittsburgh today under the guidance of the
daughters and granddaughters of its original members.

In 1893 Dr. Hodges was elected dean of the Episcopal Theological School in Cambridge, Massachusetts. When he left Pittsburgh a
year later, this energetic clergyman was considered the most influen-
tial and admired minister in western Pennsylvania.

The Rev. James Hall McIlvaine became rector of Calvary Church
in 1900. The Calvary church building that now stands in Pittsburgh
was built during his rectorship. The cornerstone of the present struc-

ture was laid on June 16, 1906, and the tower and spire were completed by the end of November. Parish records reveal that in the early morning hours of that somber fall day, during a snowstorm, Dr. McIlvaine clambered up through the maze of scaffolding to the top of the spire and there, with his own hands, placed the cross.

Designed by Ralph Adams Cram, Pittsburgh's Calvary Church is considered one of the most beautiful Gothic buildings in America. Cram based his plan on the architectural concepts of the Cistercians as represented in Netley and Tintern abbeys in England.

The symbolism contained in both the stone and the wood carvings, as well as that in the stained-glass windows, is elaborate and subtle. What Sam said about the importance of beauty in church architecture was amply borne out here. This was one of the reasons we were so strongly attracted to Calvary Church in Pittsburgh.

I never entered Calvary—in the early hours of morning, in the late afternoon, or at any other time of day—without a feeling of joy and gratitude for the wonderful colors, warmth, and symmetry that are combined in the interior of this architectural gem.

It was with the deepest regret that the Vestry of Calvary Church had to accept Dr. McIlvaine's letter of resignation in the summer of 1916. At his final sermon, on the last Sunday of October, the beloved minister gently admonished his packed congregation to prepare a warm spot in their hearts for their new rector while keeping a tender place for their old one.

In December, 1916, the first festival of the combined Episcopal choirs of Pittsburgh was held in Calvary Church. Ten choirs, made up of four hundred voices, participated in the impressive service. The entire festival was directed by Harvey Gaul. During his thirty-five years at Calvary, Dr. Gaul conducted a number of magnificent choir festivals and achieved wide recognition.

During Sam's rectorship, the choir festivals were revived under the superb leadership of Donald G. Wilkins, the present choirmaster of Calvary Church and Dr. Gaul's most outstanding pupil.

The Rev. Edwin J. van Etten succeeded Dr. McIlvaine as rector of Calvary in 1917. After a colorful and effective period of service, Dr. van Etten resigned in 1940 to become dean of St. Paul's Cathedral in Boston. A noteworthy event of Dr. van Etten's rectorship was the first radio service ever broadcast from a church in America.

Dean Arthur B. Kinsolving of the Garden City (New York) Cathedral was called to Calvary in 1940. On the eve of World War

II he made the statement that "the world in revolution is a church in resurrection. Faith and prayer have been the prelude to the greatest action—they can be again."

In February, 1945, Dr. Kinsolving was elected to the Missionary Bishopric of Arizona. His consecration took place in Calvary Church in May, and he was succeeded by Lauriston Scaife, who was installed as the tenth rector of Calvary Church in April, 1946. St. Michael's Chapel, a beautiful World War II memorial, was built while Dr. Scaife was at Calvary.

In January, 1948, Dr. Scaife was elected Bishop of Western New York, becoming the sixth member of the Calvary Church clergy to be elevated to this high office.

The lay members of Calvary Church were continuously taking civic action and responsibility in the city of Pittsburgh. Calvary was the "mother" of many missions and other churches in the Diocese of Pittsburgh.

It was to this distinguished parish that my husband was called in 1952. At the invitation of the Vestry, we visited Pittsburgh, as I mentioned earlier (see p. 109), and within a few days of the visit made the decision to accept the call.

Accompanied by three vestrymen's wives, I paid a second visit to Calvary in early January, 1952, to make plans for the refurbishing of the rectory. It was a cold, dismal day and the rectory was empty and unheated. The four of us stood around in our fur coats and galoshes trying to make up our minds about the right wallpaper for the various rooms. We grew colder and colder and more and more undecided. Suddenly the doorbell rang and there was Dean Emerson, former dean of the cathedral in Cleveland and Calvary's pro-tem rector, who had been observing us through binoculars from the Kenmore Hotel across the street. Without the slightest hesitation and with unerring taste, the dean marched from room to room, choosing the appropriate wallpaper for each. Our problem was solved. In March, when Sam, Nickie, Mamie, the canary, and I moved in, all the cleaning and redecorating had been completed, and there was an entirely new kitchen that surpassed my wildest dreams.

Sam preached his first sermon at Calvary Church on Passion Sunday. We had debated whether it would be wise to start immediately a coffee hour similar to the one that had become such an important part of the fellowship at Calvary Church in New York. Sam had some misgivings lest this new parish resent such an innovation, but I pressed him to do it. It turned out to be a most pleasant way to become acquainted with the parish, and became an integral part of the life of Calvary. On that first Passion Sunday I think we shook hands with at least a thousand people!

I shall never forget our first Easter Sunday—a dark, rainy day. There was a tradition at Calvary that after their own service in the afternoon, all the children would proceed with the choir to the Memorial Peace Cross in the churchyard. There, while the choir sang a special hymn, the children would release from their crates a flock of carrier pigeons and let them fly home, symbolizing the soul's return to God on release from the body. This symbol of resurrection had been instituted by Dean van Etten, and the children probably enjoyed it more than any other church occasion. Unfortunately, on that particular Easter Sunday, it was not possible to gather at the Peace Cross because of the rain. So the pigeons were released in the parish house dining room. Picture the bedlam when several hundred youngsters let fly some fifty terrified pigeons in the low-ceilinged room! Although the windows had been opened to enable the birds to escape they flew round and round in frantic anxiety, depositing their droppings on many Easter bonnets.

On May 2, 1952, I was asked to speak at the annual meeting of the Woman's Auxiliary of Calvary Church. It was a delightful occasion. Mrs. Lowell Innis, then president of the Auxiliary, had arranged a beautiful dinner, and Mrs. Thomas Hartley sent great bunches of lilacs from her own garden with which to decorate the tables.

I chose prayer as the subject for my talk, and the women were enthusiastic enough to ask if I would speak further on this subject at a later date. Accordingly, I held my first School of Prayer in Calvary Church the following autumn for six consecutive weeks. The women of the parish then started eight separate prayer study groups under their own leadership. Sam and I were both pleased with this development and it seemed that the women were ready for our whole small-group emphasis. They only needed such an impetus to draw them into the small living fellowships that would underlie and support all their other projects. The occasion arises at certain times in the life of a parish, and in the life of the whole church, when particular emphases are both needed and desired, and the Holy Spirit raises up those people who can make these emphases possible.

This first experiment with schools of prayer in Pittsburgh led us into ever widening circles with the same idea, and eventually evolved into what is now known as the Anglican Fellowship of Prayer.

I had asked the bishop when we went to Calvary what he would like me to do in his diocese and in the city, as I had had considerable experience speaking before groups of women of all denominations and had held a number of official positions in the church while we were in New York. One of the principal roles of a woman is to nurture what a man initiates. Prayer is the handmaid of evangelism; Sam's principal emphasis was evangelism, mine was and is prayer.

The bishop told me to go ahead and accept every invitation to speak that came my way, and I suspect that he himself quietly opened many doors to me, which I knew nothing about.

The first School of Prayer was followed by seven others, which became increasingly interdenominational as the result of my speaking to at least five hundred churches and groups in the area during the years that we lived in Pittsburgh.

In 1953 Sam recorded in his diary, that the School of Prayer attracted 1,600 women representing more than 150 prayer groups in the city. As a result of all this activity and the new prayer groups coming into being, it seemed to us that it would be appropriate to begin to hold a prayer group reunion dinner each September so that all the prayer groups might come together to receive inspiration for the year ahead. Accordingly, we started the Annual Prayer Group Reunions, which began with a dinner and ended in a worship service with a speaker.

The prayer study-group movement was established all over and way beyond the city of Pittsburgh. Although it was originally—and still is—organized within the Anglican Communion, it has become interdenominational and international. We have a Statement of Purpose, an Advisory Board of Bishops and Clergy which includes the Presiding Bishop of the Episcopal Church and the Archbishop of York. We have an International Executive Committee headed by the retired Bishop of Toronto, Bishop Wilkinson, with Bishop Pardue, Bishop Lichtenberger, Bishop Wright and Mr. Walker Taylor of The Commission on Mutual Responsibility and Interdependence as members. We have held nine international annual prayer group conferences, eight of them at Calvary Church, Pittsburgh, and one in Detroit.

There are Field Representatives of the Anglican Fellowship of Prayer in thirty-five dioceses of the Episcopal church. We are cosponsoring a prayer groups conference in 1967 at Notre Dame, Indiana, with a prayer group movement in the Roman Catholic Church. We have become a clearing house of information and inspiration for thousands of prayer groups in the Anglican Communion and beyond it who are praying unitedly for world peace, racial reconciliation, and the unity of Christendom.

All this has flowered because the women of Calvary Church, on May 2, 1952, asked me to come and speak to them about prayer, and eagerly formed themselves into groups to pray.

One of the miracles of history is the constantly renewing, revitalizing small and large streams of power that keep pouring out of small and large churches into the life of a community and a nation, because a person here and a person there has been "waked up."

By late May, 1952, the Pittsburgh rectory was in sufficiently good shape to allow us to have a two-day housewarming. Again it was raining; I remember that we had to check our parishioners' coats on the large and ample side-porch because there wasn't room in the house. It was great fun showing our parishioners the reconditioned rectory because the women, naturally, were dying to see what had been done. In the heart of every woman there is a deep curiosity to see the inside of another woman's home. And when that other woman's home happens to be the rectory of a large city church, the curiosity mounts to a crescendo. I heartily sympathize with this curiosity as I have it myself, and I can understand why the women of any parish would be interested in the way a rectory looks, the way it is run, and the way it is used. This is their right, and in this sense the rector's wife is indeed a public servant. And the rectory, at all times, should be a place in which every member of the parish feels welcome. It should also be a place meriting the approval of every member. The "At Home" included the dedication of each room of the house to God's service, followed by a complete tour.

Calvary Church in Pittsburgh was twice as large in communicant strength as Calvary Church, New York. One of the first things Sam did after accepting this call was to ask the Vestry and staff to check the parish rolls, remove the dead wood, and find out exactly how many people were actual communicants and how many were baptized members. He learned that we had some 1,800 communicants and about 2,500 baptized members. During that first spring, Sam concentrated on his relationship with the Vestry, on reaching out to newcomers, calling on the sick, and counseling and welcoming the many young people who began coming to Calvary in response to his preaching.

By October, Sam was able to write, "Things have opened wonderfully."

In March of our first year in Pittsburgh, Sam had assisted Bishop Pardue (the Rt. Rev. Austin Pardue, Bishop of Pittsburgh) at the funeral of Tom Hilliard, who was in the class of 1917 at Princeton. The next day Sam talked to Tom's daughter Elsie, who invited a group of friends in to meet us at her home the following week. Sam described the amazing results of Elsie's invitation:

"That evening perhaps twenty young marrieds came together. They were all of the most delightful and personable character. We had connections with many members of their families or friends and we had a very gay and enjoyable gathering. 'Would you like to say anything to us?' our hostess asked. I said that I would very much like to do so. And I began by saying, 'I suppose out here in Pittsburgh you have some convictions about free enterprise?' Yes, of course they had. 'Well, have you ever stopped to think where America got her freedom? There is a Greek element in it, but by far the preponderant factor in freedom as we know it is our inherited Christianity.' We played that string for some time. They were graduates of some of our finest universities, yet this thought of the relation between freedom and faith was apparently quite new to them. I reminded them that the same Force that helps us to win freedom also helps us to keep it, by showing us how to use it responsibly and unselfishly.

"All this gave to personal religion and faith a relevance which it had never had for them before. By about 11:00 they were asking 'How do you get this faith you talk about?' I replied, 'The hour is late, but I am good till 2:00 A.M. if you want to go on.' However, they suggested, 'How about meeting again?' We arranged to do so the following week, and on that evening discussed exhaustively how people find faith individually. We met actually five times that spring.

"At the last gathering I said to them: 'I have three things I want your help on. The first is, we need some more men to help with the every-member canvass in the early fall. The second is, we need a lot of good new Church school teachers; lots of you have little children and understand them. (We got six canvassers and seven Church school teachers out of this group.) And here is a third thing: what would you think of gathering together a lot of your friends next autumn and having a course for, say, seven weeks on How to Become a Christian? Let us ask all the young marrieds we know, from any church or from none.' They were enthusiastic and said we must do it."

Sam prepared the seven talks during the summer. When we first met in the fall it was to plan the course. About twenty people came and we spent most of the evening deciding on others to invite. Finally the names of 102 couples were agreed upon. Sam suggested that we not meet in the parish house—he was out to make Christians not Episcopalians—but at the golf club where this group was accustomed to going. Almost one hundred people came to each of the seven weekly meetings. Sam would give them briefly some information and instruction on Christianity and then invite questions. As the weeks went by the questions became less captious and skeptical and more personal and genuine.

Just before our last meeting, several of the men asked Sam to give them the opportunity to sum up and compare what they had learned from previous sessions. So the final meeting was turned over to these men and it was astonishing to hear what they had to say. "Imagine a pagan like me talking to anybody, and especially this crowd that knows me so well, about religion! . . ." Then would follow some point learned, some truth discovered, some experience begun. Others in the group joined in. It was spontaneous, often amusing, natural, and perfectly evident that God as He has revealed Himself in Christ was becoming a reality to them. They were beginning to say their prayers, to say grace at meals, to attend church, and to try to live out their faith in daily work and life.

Then came the question, "What next?" Sam and I were leaving for a month's mission in Texas and the group would be on its own. Most of the young women had been attending my Tuesday talks on how to make prayer effective, so they decided to form their own prayer group and continue meeting each week. This has continued through the years, and good results have come from their steady intercessory prayer and Bible study. The men decided to study the Bible. Once a week they met for luncheon at the Harvard-Yale-Princeton Club. One of the group would report on a book of the New Testament and general discussion would follow.

After our return from Texas we held a reunion for this group about once a month. Usually there was a guest speaker. On one occasion, after listening to the moving words of a newly ordained minister, the young wife of Sam's junior assistant announced that she had never made a real commitment of her life to Christ. She had been a Methodist, and although she had given up drinking and smoking she still felt that she had not really changed. Sam suggested that she make her commitment right then and there. And she did, praying simply and naturally with her friends.

This set off a chain reaction. One of the men had become convinced that he should give his life to Christ but lacked the self-confidence to declare himself. He turned to Sam and asked directly, "Can't you just act *as if* you had done this, instead of doing it?" Sam replied, "If you behaved as if you were married to your wife, when you weren't, you'd be living in sin. You are married or you are not married. You are committed or not committed. Why not do it now?" At the end of this evening it was suggested that we hold a special Communion Service that would be an outward commitment in the body of the Church of our personal commitments in the group.

The following Sunday, gathered for Holy Communion, we said in unison: "And here we offer and present unto Thee, O Lord, ourselves, our souls and bodies, to be a reasonable, holy and living sacrifice unto Thee." This marked a new step of faith for each one of us. We were grateful for a church that provided in its Eucharistic liturgy a formal expression of personal commitment. Many do not know the full power of the Eucharist until they come to it in a spirit that has begun to live in informal fellowship.

Soon afterward the newborn infant of one of these young couples was taken desperately ill. Sam went to the hospital in the middle of the night and made the sign of the Cross on the fevered little forehead as he baptized him. These newborn Christians came together at a special Holy Communion Service united as one person around the parents and for the first time in their lives formed an all-night prayer chain for the baby's recovery. Much to everyone's joy, the baby got well.

It wasn't long before news of what had happened to our young couples spread among their friends and acquaintances. Something had been loosed among these people that went beyond anything Sam had so far experienced in his ministry. Concerning this group, Bishop Pardue commented: "The young married crowd at Calvary ought not to be an unusual phenomenon, in present-day Christianity, but it is. The well-educated, intelligent, and sophisticated young people of today have generally not been led to experience religion in such a way as to make it natural, palatable and personal. Here is an exception. This group are as healthy, normal, intelligent, and full of humor as you will find anywhere in America, and yet they are willing to discuss religion as it relates to their own experience without pious narrowness or spiritual superiority. God grant that hosts of such groups may spring up throughout the land."

In March, 1953, Sam wrote: "The work has gone superbly, yet not too fast. The younger married crowd is the joy of my life. They have grown spiritually by leaps and bounds. Last week when I was to speak at the Church of the Ascension and had laryngitis I got Putnam McDowell of this group to speak for me. He had given the same address at Calvary the night before and he made a profound impression.

"The congregations are growing; had nine hundred on Palm Sunday. They say the largest Palm Sunday congregation in ten years. More important there seems to be an upsurge of spiritual interest everywhere. The young marrieds now want to reach the yet-younger marrieds and carry it to the whole of the city. They are on fire. We can't get over the friendliness and welcome which still continues, or the genuine concern for religion which the old Scotch Presbyterians seem to have made a part of this very climate."

Not long after coming to Pittsburgh, Sam gave a talk before Calvary's Men's Club. He told them that he was not so much interested in building up a great institution as in creating through it a spiritual force that could move in on Pittsburgh and set about to make its human relations Christian.

After the dinner, a man of about thirty-five came up to Sam and introduced himself as Dave Griffith, a worker in the Homestead Plant of the United States Steel Company and the member of a CIO union. He was gentle, hesitant of speech, and had been deeply affected by what Sam had said. He had been thinking along similar lines himself. Sam had no idea at the time what qualities of leadership were latent in this quiet fellow.

A steel strike was in progress and Dave was deeply concerned with trying to settle it. He had some very clear ideas about what should be done. So he brought his problem and his ideas to Sam. At that time, Sam said to him, "Dave, I don't pretend to know anything about industry as such. And I haven't any blueprint as to how this should be done—only a strong conviction that God is the one answer in industry, and we must get people on both sides of the fence in touch with Him. My suggestion is that you reach as many individuals as you can in the mill, make friends with them, open up on God and human relations, and see what you find."

Dave set about doing just that. But one night he couldn't sleep. He had been trying to get the general superintendent, the heads of the company, and the union to agree on letting him go ahead with plans for a weekly gathering in his department where the men could pray and speak frankly about human relations. He had not made much progress. He was certain that this was the right way to begin but he suddenly became aware that his trouble lay in having been trying to accomplish his objective all by himself. Dave got out of bed, knelt, and asked God to make use of him in any way He saw fit.

Things began to happen immediately. At a union meeting Dave got the floor and persuaded his fellow members to appoint a man to serve on a committee of union men, salaried employees, and management. His idea was to have a weekly meeting in his part of the mill, with a short address, prayer, and some discussion. The committee was appointed and the project got under way, and twenty, thirty, sometimes forty men would turn out.

But the real source of the group's strength seemed to be the members' confidence in Dave, and the tremendous amount of time that he devoted to individuals and their problems. One of the men whom he approached to join the group was a Negro. The man was not responding and looked distraught, so Dave asked him what was bothering him. The man remained silent. Finally, he blurted out, abstractedly, "I am in trouble. I've got a wife in the hospital that needs a transfusion and I haven't anybody to give it to her." "What hospital?" inquired Dave. "Let's go along down." Dave gave her the transfusion himself.

The process of quiet cultivation and making friends, dropping a seed here and a word there, went on continually. Four months after Dave had begun this work, Sam asked him how many individuals he thought he had talked with in this way. Modestly Dave shied away from the question, "Oh, I don't know—I guess two or three hundred." Sam said, "Two or three hundred individuals in four months? I'd hate to canvass the clergy of Pittsburgh and see how many of them have talked with two or three hundred people about God and human relations in the past four months!"

Dave wanted Sam to meet some of his friends. Sam suggested it would be a good thing if he brought along some of Calvary's younger married men, and mixed them together. They gathered on a Thursday night in a church basement near the plant. There were about fifteen CIO boys and about five "sons of privilege" from the other group. A really dynamic Christian experience is the only thing that keeps a meeting like that from being split by educational and social differences. Dissension because of diversity of background never arose at all.

On the way home a university graduate said to Sam, "Before I was converted, I should have had little in common with those men: I would have found it hard to talk with them about anything that really mattered. But now it is fascinating to me to be with them and to grow with them in this experience of Christ." Thus the first small seeds of the Pittsburgh Experiment (see Chapter 25) were planted.

During Lent it occurred to Sam that we should have lay speakers at our Wednesday evening services. Sam chose five: a metallurgical engineer, a leading industrialist, an outstanding woman, one of the younger married men, and Dave, who was pleased and not frightened by the prospect.

After the service, one of our older women who, like all the others, had been deeply moved by what Dave had said, remarked to Sam, "I think you may have been brought to Pittsburgh just to set that man on fire." Sam agreed that this might be reason enough.

Sam's success in enlisting the "golf club" crowd led him to the conviction that he should gather a small "inquirers" group of young marrieds, whom I have already described as coming in larger and larger numbers to hear Sam preach. Many young businessmen were among them. They met, twenty-five or thirty of them, with Sam one evening a week for six weeks in 1953 and studied and discussed a simple book Sam had written, distilled from his discussions with the "golf club" crowd, entitled *How to Become a Christian*. This was an intriguing title to young marrieds and many became Christians as a result of the discussions, or revived a flagging zeal that had somehow grown cool. Dave and Caroline Leighton were among them. David was a World War II veteran and a rising young Fisher Body executive. He is now Archdeacon of the Diocese of Maryland.

Sam's first year's experiment with "How to Become a Christian" groups encouraged him to continue, and consequently twice a year thereafter he used this book as a textbook with a series of young marrieds. The groups were never larger than about twenty-five persons. After opening with prayer each member of the circle would read aloud a paragraph and then pass it to the next person, unless it raised questions in the mind of the group. Then there would be discussion. Sam acted as moderator and spoke very little. He never worried if a contentious member carried the subject temporarily into left field. He encouraged the members to answer one another. The discussions never followed a strict time schedule and the meetings invariably closed with spontaneous prayer. It was astonishing how quickly these seeking young people found words with which to address God.

If any member of the group felt led to share any insight or experience of the week before, this was always encouraged. Of course, the meetings became ecumenical and it is heartwarming to think how many of these couples found their Christian vocation through them.

The courses never lasted more than six weeks, and at the end Sam found ways to involve the members of the group in continuing prayer groups, church programs, or groups concerned with the application of one's personal faith to the workday job.

Years of Fulfillment   ▓ 16

FROM TIME TO TIME, AS HE HAD DONE IN
New York and as he did in Pittsburgh, Sam would invite one of his
laymen to speak from the pulpit on special occasions. In the late fall
of 1953, however, he undertook an extensive program of lay witness
that was called "Why Faith?" On four consecutive evenings an outstanding layman was invited to speak from Calvary on his particular
spiritual experience. The speakers were Gertrude Behanna, whom he
had known in New York;* Lee H. Bristol, Jr., then with Bristol-
Myers and now the president of the Westminster Choir School; Dr.
Overton Stephens, a physician from Toronto, Canada; and Ralston
C. Young, the famous Red Cap 42. It was Sam's contention that laymen may understand better than ministers the problems of laymen.
"It is the 'day of laymen,'" he said, "and these laymen have something for us all."

January, 1955, marked the one hundredth anniversary of Calvary
Episcopal Church. The Centennial Service was held on January 23.
All the living former rectors were asked to attend and a number of
them came.

In 1957, the Vestry, reporting on the first five years of Sam's
ministry in Pittsburgh, noted the following highlights: The Church
school enrollment quickly went up to 287 pupils with forty-five
teachers. Boy Scout troops, which had gone out of existence, were
reactivated and a new cub-pack was organized. There was a steady
stream of candidates for Holy Orders sponsored by the Vestry and
rector, and various seminaries were the beneficiaries of theolog-
ical-education gifts. A large procession of young men received
diaconate training at Calvary, and later became rectors of other
churches in the Pittsburgh Diocese. Altogether eight men were
ordained under Calvary sponsorship during these five years.

The endowment fund had grown from $200,000 to almost $750,-
000 during these five years and a new pension and insurance plan

* Under the pseudonym Elizabeth Burns, she told her story in *The Late Liz*
(New York: Appleton-Century-Crofts, 1957).

was made available to staff members, consistent with the latest business practices.

The Vestry guaranteed $2,080 for the extension of Sam's radio programs which, through his entire rectorship at Calvary, were broadcast over Station KDKA at 10:30 every Sunday evening. Funds were made available to start a bookstore in the parish house, with the concurrence of the bishop.

Sam's sermons, during this five-year period, were underwritten initially by the Vestry of Calvary Church and sent out under the title of "This Week's Word." Eventually eight thousand copies a week were mailed to interested persons who requested them.

Numbers of "Retreats" were held for various groups during this time, including the Vestry, the auxiliary Vestry, and representatives from other denominations.

Sam developed through these gatherings a new philosophy for retreats and conferences, which has been perfected still further by the Pittsburgh Experiment (see Chapter 25) and Faith at Work (see Chapter 22). He said of them: "We need an altogether different kind of conference or retreat. To be talked at continually for two days gives little opportunity to absorb or to ask questions. Merely to be silent for the same time, even under direction, may not give the opportunity for exchange which combines growth in experience with growth in fellowship. A conference needs a minimum of structure, and a maximum of liberty under the Spirit. Let a leader speak in an experimental way, or get others to do it, so that the level is the level of experience, not merely of ideas; then call for a period of quiet and waiting on God; then let people express what has been coming to them. When this ravels out into more talk, begin again. We must have spiritually resourceful people on hand, and give new people plenty of chance to break in and ask questions. When the Spirit is present, and the human moderator keeps things moving in one general direction, so that there is not mere chaos of expression, great things happen.

"This is especially true about clergy conferences. The learned addresses of scholars need to be greatly supplemented, if not supplanted, by simple expressions of need and of discovery on the part of the men themselves. Again, experience is the order of the day—not ideas, not the carrying out of a tight, prearranged schedule—but events, with the Holy Spirit given free rein to carry matters in His own direction. I have seen Him more often kept out altogether by stiff

use-struct faith

conformity to schedule than by a few unexpected and informal excursions into the unarranged! We held such a conference not very long ago: the only speakers were lay people, and the listeners were clergy! The tables were turned clear around. Two groups of young laymen, one talking about the effects of faith at the downtown level, the other about life in the parish, a talk on prayer and prayer groups by my wife, and the tape recording of the brilliant witness by Gertrude Behanna were the things that set the pace and level. Then the parsons were free to talk, ask questions, and contribute experience. The time of prayer at the end of the two days, in which everyone took part without being urged to do so, was a memorable experience of power for us all."

At the beginning of Sam's rectorship an auxiliary Vestry of thirty-two men was established, divided into two groups. The groups alternated in teaching in the Church school and in ushering. This Vestry was later increased to sixty men, and the organization of the ushering at Calvary Church is as fine as I have seen anywhere.

A weekly Healing Service of Holy Communion, with intercessions for the sick, which included the laying-on of hands, was started on Wednesday mornings, and to this a number of people in the prayer groups gave faithful support. These Healing Services had been a part of our parish life in New York and Sam believed in both the fact and the efficacy of the ministry of healing.

The Vestry, in a practical note, described the financial situation of the church during Sam's five-year rectorship. They pointed out that in 1952, for instance, the annual receipts of the church amounted to $106,000 and in 1956 they amounted to $180,000, an increase of more than 70 per cent. During this period the income from invested and endowment funds grew from $5,400 in 1952 to $30,400 in 1956, an increase of 500 per cent.

The Church school made significant progress during this era, not only in numbers of children but in emphasis. We moved from a content-centered type of curriculum to one that seeks to relate the gospel to the needs and experiences of children. Weekly teacher-training sessions and classes were provided for eighth-grade pupils, high school students, and adults. Teachers and observers were appointed for each class and a series of family-life weekends was organized.

At the end of the report Sam added his own words: "These five years, 1952-1957, during which I have served as your Rector, have been the happiest and most rewarding years of all my ministry. Words can hardly carry my gratitude to God and to the Vestry and the Staff and the People of Calvary Parish."

Following the Hungarian revolt in the fall of 1956, we worked with all the other churches of the area to help as many refugees as possible through the valiant minister of Pittsburgh's Hungarian American Church. Due to the horrible impact of the Hungarian revolt, Sam again reminded his people of the great danger of Communism. On the back of one of his Sunday church-service leaflets he quoted a French Communist, who was writing for a Communist Party newspaper. It was good for our people to ponder this under the circumstances. The leaflet bore the heading, "Will You Accept This Challenge from a Communist?" and then quoted:

"The gospel is a much more powerful weapon for the renewal of society than is our Marxist philosophy. All the same it is we who will finally beat you. We are only a handful and you Christians are numbered by the millions. But if you remember the story of Gideon and his three hundred companions you will understand why I am right. We communists do not play with words. We are realists and, seeing that we are determined to achieve our object, we know how to obtain the means. Of our salaries and wages we keep only what is strictly necessary and we give up the rest for propaganda purposes. To this propaganda we also consecrate all our free time and part of our holidays.

"You, however, give only a little time and hardly any money for the spreading of the gospel of Christ. How can any of you believe in the supreme power of the gospel if you do not practice it? If you do not spread it? And if you sacrifice neither time nor money for it? Believe me, it is we who will win, for we believe in the communist message and we are ready to sacrifice everything, even our life, in order that social justice may triumph. But you people are afraid to soil your hands."

Distribution of this leaflet was followed by one of our Men's Clubs meetings at which the speaker was Dr. John Turkevich, consultant to the Atomic Energy Commission. Dr. Turkevich spoke on "The Soviet Challenge." All through Sam's ministry, from World War II on, he continually returned to the theme of alertness to the Communist danger, and I was his ardent aide. Having my father on the Foreign Relations Committee of the United States Senate, I knew the threat that the spread of international Communism posed to the free world.

In 1956 we began making large clothing collections for Church World Service; the women of Calvary Church met weekly; twenty prayer groups, a number of service groups, bazaar sewing groups, study groups, and couples met monthly for food and fellowship; a wonderful golden age group met weekly. The parish was literally honey-combed with small groups bent on the Lord's business one way or another.

Sam and I believed that the people of the church should have every opportunity to participate in any activity in which they were interested. The women of Calvary Church have always made an effective contribution to the ongoing work of the parish as well as to other undertakings in the city of Pittsburgh, including hospital auxiliary boards, the League of Women Voters, Planned Parenthood, and good causes of all kinds—and a majority of these women belonged to prayer groups.

Sam and I often wished that young clergy fresh out of seminary were not so deeply indoctrinated with the fear of organized women. Granted some women in church organizations might be termed "battle-axes" or self-appointed priestesses, but these are a very small minority. St. Catherine of Siena is credited with saying, "God does not ask a perfect work but only infinite desire." The women of Calvary were not perfect—who is?—but they longed to serve, and to give and to pray, and they did just that with all their might and main. Sam and I have had the privilege of knowing so many women of this type that we never felt the least bit threatened by a massive phalanx of females.

A family service was held at 9:30 A.M. and the parents of children who went to their classes after the 9:30 service met together with the rector for a time of serious discussion about the meaning of our faith. There were never less than seventy or eighty young marrieds at this meeting, and we had a lively time.

The high point of our Church school year was the annual Christmas pageant. I was delighted with the initial opportunity to supervise its production. We enlisted the aid of Mrs. Bailey Gordon, the assistant fashion consultant at Kaufmann's, one of Pittsburgh's great department stores, to redesign the costumes, and a very able young woman, Miss Phyllis Shoemaker (no relation), a member of the parish who was connected with the Carnegie Tech Drama School, to direct the pageant. So many members of the congregation wanted to participate in the pageant that we had the problem of trying to avoid hurt feelings. We decided that the small children who had the highest attendance records could be baby angels, and that the Holy Family would be the one with the youngest baby at the time of the pageant.

In February, 1957, Sam was invited by the Episcopal Radio and TV Foundation to give a series of talks on the National Episcopal Hour. Sam considered this a tremendous opportunity because thousands of people besides Episcopalians listened to this weekly program. Some fifty thousand letters were subsequently received from listeners to Sam's broadcasts. Four years later, Sam was asked to moderate the Episcopal Hour's first television program, "Track 13," which showed the actual meeting of Red Cap 42's prayer group on Track 13 in Grand Central Station, New York, and became the first of a series of television specials on personal evangelism.

Sam continued in the fall of this year with his couples' groups, which led into his confirmation classes. During Lent the following year, he inaugurated a mission in order to prepare his people further for confirmation. He spoke five times on such subjects as "What Is the Christian Religion?" "How to Begin Spiritually," "How to Keep Going Spiritually," "How to Win Others to Jesus Christ," and "How to Work for God through the Job." He entitled this series "Renewal of Faith," and invited the entire parish to attend.

This same year Sam was asked to speak on the "Art of Living" program of the National Council of Churches, which replaced Norman Vincent Peale on NBC from June through September. Again in 1962 Sam was invited to broadcast for twelve weeks on "the Art of Living" and in 1962-1963 after his retirement and return to Baltimore he broadcast every Sunday night for one-half hour. In fact his final broadcast was made by the Bishop of Maryland from a recording which Sam had made three weeks before his death.

I have already mentioned that Sam used the back of the Sunday leaflet for special messages, such as the quote on Communism (see p. 137). On another Sunday he had a tragedy to report. One of our Vestrymen committed suicide under tragic circumstances the previous week and on the back page of the leaflet Sam wrote this message, which he read from the pulpit: "Surely this is no occasion for any of us to point a finger. Here is a sign of a failure on the part of us all. I feel we failed him in his church. He was of a very sensitive and reticent nature. At times I tried to get through to him spiritually. In his own indirect way, maybe he was asking for help. Why did I not sense his awful loneliness and deep despair? Why does the Church fail to reach through to one of its loyal adherents with a faith sufficient for the dark hour? Are we saying and doing what we should? Are too many of our people merely observing faith, but not really participating in it?

"There may be some others who feel a similar responsibility and sense of failure.

"We believe that the action he took was not God's desire. We know also that many of us do things all the time that are not God's desire, either. I have implicit faith that God, and He alone, knows the whole thought that was in this man's heart, and will go on helping and ministering to him in the other world; for His 'property is always to have mercy.' 'Shall not the Judge of all the earth do right?' (Genesis 18:25). We have commended our brother to God's mercy, and he is in the 'hands of a faithful Creator.'

"But surely we are not meant to let such a terrible event go by as if we had no responsibility concerning it, and as if God were not speaking poignantly to us through it, and asking us whether we have sufficiently let Him into our hearts, so that, if a dark hour comes, we will turn to Him for help, and not fall into the final despair."

In September, 1957, the Rev. Donald Gross came to assist us while studying for a doctor's degree in psychology at the University of Pittsburgh. He was not able to remain with us for more than a year or two because he found that he could not study as he needed to and serve at the same time in a parish ministry. He has since completed his studies, received his Ph.D. and is now back at Calvary Church, which has become a center for one of the first Pastoral Institutes in the church in the United States. Calvary's present rector has had the vision and the courage to initiate it and has received well-deserved support for its launching. This is very much in line with one of Sam's great dreams, which was that young clergy should be trained in personal counseling in depth.

In this same autumn, Mrs. Thomas Hartley, one of our earliest Pittsburgh friends, died. She was a woman in the grand tradition of an old-fashioned lady bountiful. Sam said of her, in tribute, "She was devotedly interested in every phase of our life at Calvary, and in the wider work of the Church beyond its borders. She was the most responsible and thoughtful and cheerful steward of her wealth. She never wished any official position: she never wanted to be thanked and she was endlessly giving of her self, her time and her money." In her will she left $350,000 to the endowment fund of Calvary Church.

In March, 1958, we held a Conference for Christian Vocation, the second or third such conference since coming to Pittsburgh, and it was attended by one hundred college men from nine states and Canada. It is exciting, I think, to realize that this recruiting went on with the same degree of intensity and power with which it had in New York and was the result of Sam's endless visitations to the colleges during all his years at both Calvary Churches.

Again Sam was asked to speak on the "Art of Living" program, from July 8 through September 30, 1958. For the thirteen-week period, 434,000 copies of his talks were requested. Thus his radio ministry spread over the nation as his weekly radio ministry continued over KDKA in Pittsburgh.

Time of Parting   ❋ 17

IN 1960 ALL OF SAM'S BELIEF IN THE PLACE and power of the Holy Spirit in the life of the Church came to a climax.

Sam's association with Dr. Henry Pitney Van Dusen, his friend from Princeton days who went on to become president of Union Theological Seminary, has already been mentioned. They were close colleagues in the early years of Sam's college work in New York as well as at Princeton. Then many years intervened as Sam exercised his priesthood from the springboard of a parish church, and Dr. Van Dusen exercised his in and through great ecclesiastical organizations.

In 1958 Dr. Van Dusen wrote a book entitled, *Spirit, Son and Father*, sending a complimentary copy to Sam. Sam, of course, had been preoccupied with the life and action of the Holy Spirit throughout his entire ministry. However, the book by Dr. Van Dusen focused something for Sam.

As a result of his enthusiasm for this book, and because he felt that there needed to be a further, simpler interpretation of the life and action of the Holy Spirit in the lives of average laymen and women, he wrote a book that he considered in a sense a sequel to Dr. Van Dusen's, entitled *With the Holy Spirit and with Fire*. It has become one of the two or three most widely read of Sam's books. In it Sam speaks of the Holy Spirit and its centrality in the life of the Church and the Christian. He writes: "Pentecost is often spoken of as the 'Birthday of the Church.' This has always seemed to me both true and false—false because our Lord had certainly called out His disciples and formed them into an organic unity and fellowship long before Pentecost; and true because the full meaning of their mission, and especially the power that had been given to them to carry it out, seems to have first really been given to them at Pentecost. Ever since then it has been more or less impossible to speak about the Church without speaking about the Holy Spirit, or to speak about the Holy Spirit without speaking about the Church. We do not find the Holy Spirit only where the Church is: rather we find the Church only where the Holy Spirit is, as Irenaeus said centuries ago.

"The Christian religion, as first experienced in the early Church, was of a nature not easily described. It did not consist principally of theological convictions, though these are there. It did not consist in seeking to live a life of righteousness, though its adherents undoubtedly did so. The nature of that early experience was more like stepping into a stream of power, and being borne along in it. Miraculous things happened to and through them, but they were not the doers of them. They had an amazing unity, in spite of sharp disagreements at times. It must have been exciting in the extreme to be in their midst: one never knew when somebody would start speaking in tongues, or another would begin to tell of his new-found faith in Christ. There seem to have been always two kinds of gathering: the formal kind, where a liturgy based on the events at the time of the original Lord's Supper guided them to perform the service much the same way each time; and the informal kind, which was not so much like our Morning Prayer as like an experience meeting, with a good deal of spontaneous participation by the people. To the first, only the initiated were invited. To the second, enquirers as well as believers were welcome. The power that came to them from the Holy Spirit in both kinds of meetings seemed to continue with them when they separated.

"Our instant need, in this day, is to draw more people, and more groups of people, into that stream of power which is the life of the Holy Spirit in the Church and in the world. This means the Church must begin to do again what once it did, and that is to seek the conversion of individuals to Christ that through Him they may come to know the Holy Spirit. And it means that the Church must learn to do something which it has only intermittently known in the past, and that is how to conduct the kind of small gatherings in which people can be exposed to those dynamic truths of the Gospel which lead into an experience of Christ and of the Holy Spirit.

"Whether to a group, or to an individual, I think the experience of the Holy Spirit is made known as a strongly felt presence. We may feel the presence of the Creator-Father in some part of creation or all of it. We may feel the presence of the Redeemer-Son in a more personal way still. But I think there is often a *nearness* about the presence of the Holy Spirit, as if He were taking the initiative with us Himself. At rare times this will be so luminous, so charged with a sense of the supernatural, that it will almost frighten us; we shall know beyond all questioning that this is no subjective imagining, but a living presence. It is as if He had business with us. He had not just come, He had come for something.

"There is almost always associated with the experience of the Holy Spirit the element of power. Henry Drummond said that 'in the New Testament alone the Spirit is referred to nearly three hundred times. And the one word with which He is constantly associated is Power.' This is not like the physical power of a dynamo—it is power of a different sort. Something comes into our own energies and capacities and expands them. We are laid hold of by Something greater than ourselves. We can face things, create things, accomplish things, that in our own strength would have been impossible. Artists sometimes feel this in a verse or phrase of music or some direction that comes to them, and say that it was 'given' to them. The Holy Spirit seems to mix and mingle His power with our own, so that what happens is both a heightening of our own powers, and a gift to us from outside.

"Today we have hundreds of men with trained minds who can tell us all about the Holy Spirit as the Third Person of the Trinity: but do they know Him as an experience? Millions read by incandescent lights who know nothing either of the properties of light or of how to make an incandescent bulb: light to them is what they see by. This was true of the Holy Spirit at the first. Not theory but experience—not explanation but living power."

Easter was early in 1961, and Sam's Easter message was poignant. I have often wondered whether he had some previsions of the Great Adventure that was coming to him so much sooner than any of us had expected. In his Easter message that year, he said: "Eternal Life—this is the great and unique promise of Christ to man. Eternal Life does not begin with death, it begins with faith. 'This is eternal life that they should know Thee, the only true God, and Jesus Christ whom thou hast sent.' It is and can be the gift only of One Who has Himself overcome death, of One Who was dead and is alive again. The Resurrection is the over-all greatest and most important historic fact spoken of in the New Testament. If Jesus had been divine, but could not overcome death—if He had been our Savior, crucified for the sins of man, but could not overcome death, He would not have been our victorious and all-conquering Lord. Those discouraged and disillusioned followers of His knew on Good Friday that He was gone: and three days later they knew that He was with them again—

changed so that they hardly recognized Him at times, but the same Jesus Whom they did recognize in the end. Never was such a cloud of despair and tragedy rolled back for any man. In the joy and certainty of the Resurrection they went out to conquer the world's heart for Him. That movement which He began has never ended and will never end till all the kingdoms of the world have 'become the kingdoms of our Lord and of His Christ.'

"With the world in its present condition, we seem to live much more under the despair of Good Friday than under the assurance of Easter. How much, then, do we need to hear and believe the Easter message, and to receive the Holy Communion which is His feast and at which He is present as our Host! Though in the Holy Communion we always remember His death, it is the Sacrament of the Living Lord."

I left shortly after Easter for a six-week trip to Korea to see our children who had gone there to work for the Presbyterian Church in February of 1960, as I have described (see p. 75). We had not seen them since and we were both eager to see them. Sam had planned to go with me, hoping to engage in a very strenuous series of evangelistic meetings in both Japan and Korea during our trip. His doctor dissuaded him when he discovered his intention, saying that he thought Sam not only should not go to Korea but should consider retiring from the active rectorship of a local parish. Sam had not been at all well that winter and it was all he could do to meet his commitments, so when the doctor gave us his considered opinion, we both sat down and prayed about whether he should truly consider retiring from the ministry. Accordingly, after having met with the Vestry, he wrote his people in March, 1961, and told them that he felt the time had come to part.

In some ways Sam's retirement was sudden, because we had not supposed that his continued ill health would lead to this decision. He remained at Calvary until January 1, 1962, which completed his ten years there. But after the March announcement, we moved into a time of transition. The high point of this whole year's work was the great expansion of the Pittsburgh Experiment, the launching of the Anglican Fellowship of Prayer, and Sam's tremendous interest in and emphasis on the work of the Holy Spirit in the life of the Church. It was the subject of a series of sermons that year and the theme of all the small-group meetings.

And so our wonderfully exciting and fruitful ten years at Calvary came to an end. As I have studied the way in which Sam exercised his rectorship here, I have again been struck by the emphasis on both the gathered Church and the scattered Church. Sam often used to say to me that no rector should initiate more than one or two great new emphases and experiments. A parish can't stand it. So accordingly, Sam never experimented with the liturgical service. He also encouraged continuation of the traditional activities of a lively parish.

Sam had a wonderful series of senior wardens in Mr. Lucius Robinson, Mr. Greier Coolidge, Mr. William Howard, and none better than Mr. John Smith, who was his senior warden during his last years at Calvary. A canny American from the Tennessee mountains, a retired president of a Pittsburgh bank who had been on the Vestry on several occasions and taken outstanding responsibility in many areas of Pittsburgh life, he knew instinctively how much the business community could take in the way of pressure and how much it would not take, and he was always a wise and witty counselor.

I shall never forget the final Christmas pageant. It was held on a Sunday morning for the first time, because that year of 1961 Christmas Eve fell on Sunday. All the members of the pageant outdid themselves, knowing how much we loved it, and it was even more beautiful than usual. One innovation of this particular pageant was the introduction of a donkey from the children's zoo on which the Virgin was to ride down the aisle. The donkey's keeper was so excited over the honor to his charge that he combed and brushed and powdered the beast profusely before delivering him to us. As donkeys will, this one got halfway down the aisle and stopped dead. Joseph could neither pull him nor push him, and the Virgin stood helplessly along side. In desperation Joseph gave him a resounding swat on the flank, and the church was filled with such a cloud of powder that all the children sitting nearby began sneezing lustily. Finally the donkey was urged down the aisle, the Holy Family found their places, a dozen or so baby angels marched down beside the angels and archangels, and the pageant went on to its moving and beautiful conclusion.

The day after Christmas I left Pittsburgh for Burnside, so that it might be reasonably settled when Sam arrived, and I was not at Calvary Church when Sam preached his last sermon there. One hears often of the tearful partings of congregations with their rectors, but I don't believe there was ever a more tear-filled parting than this one.

Sam was not an emotional man by nature, but this leave-taking was too much even for him, and he told me when he arrived at Burnside that he was glad I had not been there because he doubted very much whether I would have survived it. I had found it heart-rending even to attend the farewell reception, at which the ladies of the parish presented me with a gold bracelet with a medallion on it, and my prayer group with a small gold Bible in which was inscribed, "May the Lord watch between me and thee when we are separated one from another." Somehow those time-worn and familiar words symbolized what we all felt for one another—what we will always feel for one another both in this life and in the life to come.

And so the curtain fell on the joyous and wonderful adventure of thirty-six years in the ministry of two Calvary Churches, and it began to go down on Sam's ministry in this world.

Helen Kromer, in the musical revue *For Heaven's Sake*, has caught the thrust of Sam's whole ministry in her chorus, "One Man Awake":

One man awake
Can waken another;
The second can waken
His next-door brother.
The three awake
Can rouse a town
By turning the whole
Place upside down.
The many awake
Can make such a fuss,
That it finally wakens
The rest of us.

One man up,
With dawn in his eyes,
Multiplies!

IV
A CAMPUS MINISTRY
OUT OF
A LOCAL PARISH

COLLEGE WORK

REV. DR. ERNEST GORDON
Dean of the Princeton University Chapel

Time and time again I am asked if the undergraduates of today are more interested in religion than those of forty years ago. Invariably I reply by saying, "I don't know. I have to leave that to God. What I do know is that you cannot measure faith in terms of progression from one generation to another, but only in terms of the spiritual progress in the life of each individual within his own generation."

Jesus called His disciples one by one. When He called them, He called them by name, and gave to them His own nickname or love name. His work with men was face to face work. It was by encounters which demanded responses. This was what Sam Shoemaker had learned supremely well from His beloved Master. He had learned as a disciple what it means to follow Jesus Christ and having learned as a disciple he became an apostle who reached out to others to draw them into that same experience of the risen Christ.

During the few times he visited Princeton at my invitation he always met a number of lads in this face to face way. In this encounter something happened: a flagging spirit was strengthened, a trembling decision was made resolutely, and the course of a man's life was decided.

On Campus—From
Calvary, New York ░ 18

SAM NEVER LOST HIS EARLY INTEREST IN
school and college work and recruiting young men for the ministry, the first faint inkling of which began to develop during his undergraduate days at Princeton and his exposure to the spiritual greats of that day, Dr. Robert E. Speer, Dr. John R. Mott, Dr. Sherwood Eddy, and others. As we have seen, this interest was fanned into flame in China and developed further when he returned to become Executive Secretary of the Philadelphian Society in Princeton in 1919-1920 and in 1922-1923. During this time at Princeton, he began visitations to other schools and colleges which he continued throughout his life.

After accepting the call to Calvary Church, New York, in 1925, there was very little opportunity to visit the colleges. In the 1930s he was forging links between his parish and the worldwide Oxford Group movement; and he was busy establishing his work at Calvary Church. True, he continued to counsel many young men, but they were largely those who had been attracted by his preaching or by the Thursday night meetings at the church, or who had come in contact with Sam at the large assemblies of the Oxford Group in the United States and Canada and England.

During World War II most of our young men were in the service. Nevertheless, a continual stream of young men and young women from far and wide kept coming and going at Calvary House in New York during those war years. Fellowship with them left many vivid memories.

Shortly after the close of World War II, young men who had seen service overseas began finding their way to Sam and Calvary in larger and larger numbers. One of these was Bardwell Smith (the son of Gertrude Behanna), who wrote the Foreword to this book. It was he who returned from China to find his mother lying unconscious on her bathroom floor as a result of an overdose of barbituates.

Bard began accompanying his mother often to Calvary Church, where Sam got acquainted with him. He had returned to Yale with a

veteran's grant and was one of those in the postwar years who, with
Bob McLean, Mac Symington, and many others, helped to establish
daily Christian cell groups in the chapels and colleges of Yale University.

Many of these men went into the ministry, others into business
and industry. They all carried into their chosen vocations the vision
and commitment described so vividly in the following evaluation by
Bard of Sam's ministry at Yale during this era. "In my own instance,
Sam came at a very formulative period. I talked with him several
times and it was through these conversations that I became aware of
the genesis of such ideals as the basic dignity of mankind, the worth-
whileness of life, the triumph of love over hate and greed and self-
centeredness, etc. With this intellectual assent, I gradually felt a
power greater than myself urge me on to make a personal decision, a
commitment to follow Christ."

In May, 1950, Calvary Church gave us the wonderful twenty-fifth
anniversary reception that I described in Chapter 12. As Sam's work
in the colleges had proved so significant during this postwar era, Bob
McLean, a friend of Bardwell Smith and Kelly Clark (who is currently dean of the cathedral in Kuala Lumpur in the Diocese of
Singapore), was asked at this time to tell the story of Sam's ministry
at Yale. He said: "I will try in these few minutes to give you an idea
of what college has been like during the last four years. It has been
disturbing in that most of us have felt the same forces, tensions, and
anxieties that pervade the lives of people all over the world today. And
yet it was the very realization of these forces and tensions that made
many of us search for a *vocation of service,* and for a philosophy of life
that we could apply to it. It has been at this point that Sam has
helped us.

"Not many of us got through college without taking at least one
course in religion or ethics, and yet all we had to show for it was a
knowledge of a few religious movements, or a bare insight into the
Christian ethic. At this point we were prone to take one of two
positions—either we felt that Christianity was good, if it was true;
or even more pessimistic, we agreed with Professor Stace of Princeton that the God of our time was dead!

"We were not long with Sam before we realized that it was not
God that was dead but ourselves! Noteworthy in friendship with him
has been the fact that many have been immediately drawn to ask of
him the basic question of life and to share with him the deepest

experiences of their own lives. I think the highest praise that can be attributed to Sam is that it was not long after I had met him before I had come to a new understanding of the person of Jesus Christ, and this has been true of many of my friends. . . .

"Sam helped us to see the nature of Christ's mission and the nature of our destiny, and it was not long before we were ready to adopt those spiritually athletic disciplines of prayer and sharing in cell groups that are necessary to the freeing of the human consciousness from the tyrannies of this world in order to enjoy a new life in Christ.

"And yet I do not want to give you an overly optimistic picture of what has happened at Yale. To say that there has been a university-wide religious revival would be to tell a falsehood. However, I think it is significant that forty to fifty men, bound together in the common discipline of prayer and fellowship, are beginning to grow spiritually and to see all of their lives within a Christian context. And many who have been searching for a philosophy of life to apply to their vocation of service have found in Christianity the ultimate answer.

"Sam in his ministry to us has shown us that the living Christ is always ready to lead us on our way back to our ever-patient and all-loving Father. The decision remains with us as to whether we are willing to adopt those disciplines that will bring us out of our ego-centricity into a God-conscious and God-centered life."

Sam wrote in his diary of 1950-1951: "One of my deepest interests all through my ministry has been putting the claims of the Christian ministry before the kind of college men who would do a good job of it. Whenever and wherever this could be done, in small groups or large, I did it. I suppose at least two thousand of them have attended one or other of these college conferences. And in the winter of 1950-1951 this was all stepped up. I spoke to about twenty-seven college groups, including Lehigh, Williams Amherst, Yale, Harvard, Haverford, and Columbia. This often included preaching at Sunday Chapel and then speaking informally in the evenings and seeing a lot of people personally. Many influences touch the life of a man who goes into the ministry, and for any one person to claim 'credit' for it is, I think, insufferable conceit, so I have never sought to keep anything like a record of how many men were so influenced. But many of them still speak to me or write to me about the influence that one of these conferences or a personal talk about the will of God had upon them."

In 1950 Sam was particularly active with seminarians. He said: "I
went down and talked to them this fall—*about 500 of them*—at
Rock Island. If we could just leave aside the questions where we
disagree and concentrate on conversion, prayer, witness, and fellowship we might begin to see things happen. Some of the fellows at the
Theological School at Cambridge, Massachusetts, asked me to come
along and talk to the Canterbury Club, and I got there on Sunday
afternoon and went to old Trinity. We met in an upstairs room, and
it was absolutely packed with students—250 to 300 there from all
universities, M.I.T., Cambridge, E.T.S.—everything that exists
around that part of town.

"I was aware of two fellows, plus the wife of another one, who
were looking after that group and watching me pretty closely. Afterward they came over and said: 'We want to talk to you sometime,' so
I suggested that we get together tomorrow. We had one of those
marvelous times that God gives you, and they went a few steps ahead
and we became a team. We decided it would be right for them to
bring a couple of their friends in for a separate meeting. A distant
cousin of mine from Kentucky was there—he was keen for real
spiritual things—but I asked him whether he had really let go and he
said he hadn't. Usually we have some prayer about these things and
he was having a tough time coming through on saying a prayer of his
own. It was his real decision but much deeper than I had any idea of
at the moment. Two other fellows came in and we started to talk; the
third came in. We talked enough and I said I thought the time had
come to keep quiet a bit, pray aloud if you feel like doing it. They
prayed in short sentences. One fellow said 'That is it, Lord.' That is
the real meaning of Amen. Bob [Sam's cousin] had never prayed
aloud in his life, and he prayed naturally. It was, upon my soul,
about as near an experience of Pentecost in its quality as anything I
have ever experienced in my life. It was confirmed by the signs that
followed. These letters say more than I can say myself. 'Words can
never express the experience you brought into my life, into the lives
of everyone here in E.T.S. in Boston. I want you to know how
appreciative we all are and how much your interest meant and helped
me to hold on to this new power that God has given in my ministry
through you, and I thought it might be like the Lord to start in this
place. Sam, although we may not be an initial spark, at least there
are four of us who have been set truly afire and will have this fire to
take with us as we go out into the church. When I first read your

book on the ministry I felt a strange impulse to see you. How marvelous is the memory of our conversation with you and God—the three of us in the sacristy of the church!'

"Another letter: 'We have two additions to our own cell now. G's room is being used to organize a group composed of five Anglo-Catholics. There have been three other students. It is working up degree by degree. Those who come to scoff remain to pray. G.B., and I are determined to go through with our plans for a preaching mission. Life has a much greater and richer meaning for all of us these days.'

"From G, who was a lawyer before he went into the ministry: 'I have been putting off writing to you on the theory that something disappointing would happen. But things just seem to get better and better and I had better get this off while I still have a chance to give a half-way account of it all. Our group at Trinity has grown to about twenty and we are dividing up for want of space.' "

On February 29, 1952, Sam wrote an important letter to the young men in the colleges. In it he said, "As one of my university friends, I want you to know about a very important step in my life. In December I was called to Calvary Church, in Pittsburgh, and after some time of consideration and prayer, it seemed to me right to accept the call. I take up my work there on March 30.

"One of the considerations which made me hesitate was that I thought it might interfere with the work I have been doing in various colleges. When I put this before the Vestry in Pittsburgh, they not only said I must keep on with the college work, but they put an item in the budget to help toward the cost of flying to ensure my keeping on with it.

"Before I go to Pittsburgh, I am to be in Princeton, March 2-6; in Lehigh, March 9-12; and in Boston and Harvard, March 16-21. Next year I shall be making dates to visit various places where I have been before, and others that are new.

"There is something stirring on the university campuses today that is mighty close to revival. If God wants to fan it into revival, let's tell Him it's all right with us—He can count on us."

Calvary Clergy School ▨

AND NOW ANOTHER FLASHBACK IN ORDER TO DE-
scribe another of Sam's growing preoccupations. Sam was concerned
not only with undergraduates but with seminarians and fellow clergy
who needed to find a more meaningful ministry. With this in mind,
he and two others, the Rev. Canon Quintin Warner of London,
Ontario, and the Rev. Ernest Churchill, who became associate rector
of Calvary Church in 1945, sat down one day and prayed together.
The result was the idea of starting a Calvary Clergy School. They believed that Calvary House was an ideal place in which to hold such a
school, situated as it was, and as they said in their first prospectus,
next door to the Church Missions House of the Episcopal Church
and around the corner from a number of other large church headquarters. The school was inaugurated by Sam, Canon Warner, who
had been for twenty-eight years rector of Cronyn Memorial Church
in London, Ontario, and the Rev. Ernest Churchill, who before coming to Calvary had been for thirteen years rector of Grace Church
at Nyack, New York.

These three wrote and sent out a prospectus, from which I quote:
"Good leaders and clergy who are more effective in working with
individuals have always been needed in the Church. The realization
that there never was a time when the need was greater than at
present has helped Calvary Episcopal Church in New York City to
accept the challenge and grasp the opportunity that confronts the
Christian Church today."

On September 16, 1945, Sam wrote, "The Calvary Clergy School
opened last night. There were seven men here. Quintin Warner is
here as Warden and Ernest Churchill and his family have arrived
from Nyack where Clax Monro succeeded him as Rector of Grace
Church."

The primary purpose of the school was to provide *supervised* internship for pastoral training. "Such training," said the prospectus,
"is essential for the high order of leadership needed by the Church to
meet the new challenge of today. . . .

"By living, working, praying, studying the Bible, and worshiping together in a closely knit fellowship, the members of the school learn through actual experience what the evangelistic responsibility of the Church is and how it can be met.

"The members will receive ten months' training in a supervised internship. They will work in both general and mental hospitals, do parish calling, personal counseling, preaching, conduct various types of meetings, work in the Church School, and other parish organizations. In addition to this, they will be in close relationship with great religious leaders, attend many outstanding meetings and services, and have the repeated opportunities that only a city like New York offers. All their work will be supervised and regular reports will be required.

"The school is also prepared to help the following individuals by having them as members of the school from one week to some longer period of time: (a) Those who need to reorient their lives. (b) Those who are spiritually dry and want refreshment. (c) Those who want to do some special consecrated work. (d) Those who are lonely and need fellowship.

"Regular weekly seminars have been held on Thursday afternoons, with eminent clergy speaking.

"These seminars will be continued each week, not only for the regular members of the Clergy School, but for the benefit of a larger group of the clergy in the Metropolitan area, as well as for any others who are free to come.

"Conferences are held three times each year; namely, in the fall, the winter, and the spring. They begin on a Monday afternoon and continue through a Wednesday evening.

"Members of the Clergy School, with trained leadership, take part in small groups which speak at churches and other places, upon invitation. Such speaking is not only training in group fellowship and participation, but has been an effective means of revitalizing the church work done in various churches and localities.

"There is often a need in the life of young ministers for something to bridge the gap between the academic training of the seminaries, and the actualities of the working ministry in the world. Something is called for that corresponds to the 'internship' of the doctors.

"In some churches there is provision for a period of training, as in the Diaconate of the Episcopal Church. But what often happens is that (a) a young man is put to work under a busy parish minister who may have little time or skill for training an assistant; or (b) he goes to work in a small church by himself, where he has little if any fellowship with an older clergyman, or oversight from him.

"It is felt that there are several fields in which young clergy need generally to go deeper if they are to achieve a more spiritually effective ministry:

"(1) Personal devotional life. Learning the various ways in which the life of prayer becomes a reality, and prosecuting those ways which seem most helpful at the time, with the assistance and cooperation of others who are making a similar experiment.

"(2) Reading in some of the spiritual classics, and the lives and writings and spiritual movements of men in the past who have contributed most to the enrichment of the life of the Church.

"(3) Knowledge of how to work with individuals, helping them to a strong and saving faith. Young ministers need to learn to meet the different problems that arise in the lives of their people. There will be great emphasis on the study of individual counseling, and at weekly meetings of the group there will be discussions of the most effective methods.

"(4) Fellowship. The church should be a melting pot for great varieties of people, with no prejudices or barriers. Clergy should be trained to draw people into fellowship with each other.

"(5) Cooperative effort. The tendency of clergy to become 'lone wolves' must be offset. The Clergy School represents a community in which the men will work and receive training as a unit in fellowship and team-work.

"Special opportunities will be provided for the men in training at the Clergy School to meet personally outstanding leaders of various Communions and occupations, both in the informal seminars at Calvary House and at their own churches, hospitals, clinics, or places of business.

"Among the leaders who already have consented to meet with the men of the Clergy School are:

"The Rev. Henry Sloane Coffin; John Foster Dulles; Mr. Frank Goodman, Executive Secretary, Department of National Religious Radio, Federal Council of Churches of Christ in America; the Rev. Frank C. Laubach, educator, of the Congregational Church; Rufus M. Jones; the Rt. Rev. Henry St. George Tucker, Presiding Bishop of the Protestant Episcopal Church; the Rev. Henry Pitney Van Dusen; Mr. Ellis Van Riper, power maintenance worker, New York City transit system, Section Chairman, Transport Workers Union Local 100, C.I.O.; and Dr. Edwin G. Zabriskie."

I remember vividly the number of clergy that came from all over the country and from every denomination for the very large Clergy Conferences that took place three times a year. I remember even more vividly the conferences held for college men who might be considering the ministry and whom Sam recruited as a result of the enormous amount of activity in which he engaged in the Ivy League colleges, in particular, during those years. We rarely had less than a hundred young men at our Thanksgiving and pre-Easter conferences from Princeton, Yale, Harvard, Williams, Amherst, and other colleges. It was a lively and wonderful time.

Dr. John Oliver Nelson, director of the Commission on the Ministry of the Federal Council of Churches, who has himself taken part in nearly all these conferences, says, "Of all the movements of inner dedication leading men into the Christian ministry, none that I know of has been and can be so effective as the program which has gone forward at Calvary Church."

Several young clergy, the products of these conferences, have written me of Sam's influence on their lives—and so the ripples spread and spread. Here are two such letters, which came to me after Sam's death: The first is from Hal Edwards, Jr., associate minister of the First Methodist Church, Santa Ana, California.

"Dr. Sam, in his own right, has been to me and to thousands of young fellows an 'Unfinished Symphony.' There are many things that I wish Sam could have told me—but the miles and distance have kept us apart physically. His letters have been refreshing streams into my life. His prayers have been felt. His books have penetrated to the life-level in my own experiences. He has always been quick to say that he was not at all perfect, and that all of us shall be, in a sense, very real problems to ourselves as long as we live. He has made it easy for me to grow in the Holy Spirit's guidance.

"So, Mrs. Shoemaker, I want to thank you for sharing your husband with this nation of ours. I am sure that the influence of this man will live on through many many years to come in the lives of those of us who have found Fresh Life in Christ Jesus through his ministry. I am interested in knowing if he ever finished his autobiography. If the book never gets written, I am sure that it will be written in history, in the lives of fellows such as myself."

And the second letter is from the Rev. Jonathan L. King, Church of St. John the Divine, Mount Vernon, New York.

"I know, and rejoice in the fact, that I am one among *many* who can truly say that 'Sam' was the most wonderful person I have ever been privileged to know. He had a way of getting right down to the heart of things, to the things that really count in life. He had a gift for opening heaven and earth to you in such a way that you could never again be the conventional Christian you were before. In him you saw the light that is Christ; in his presence you felt the warmth and radiance of God's love; and in his friendliness you experienced a joy that made life seem supremely worth living.

"Of course, the best memorial that 'Sam' could have is the love of God which burns in the hearts of the thousands whose lives he touched and of the scores of men, who like myself, are in the ministry because of him."

On Campus—From
Calvary, Pittsburgh ▓ 20

ONE OF THE REASONS FOR SAM'S RELUCTANCE TO break his ties with Calvary Church, New York, was, as he intimated, the extraordinary generosity of the Vestry in permitting him to spend a great deal of time in college work. They felt that his ministry with college students was a meaningful one and that everything should be done to encourage him to continue with it.

Sam said of it at the time, "The student work has been growing like everything. I have had lunches for businessmen where two young fellows would speak about what they had got going spiritually and how they had received the call to ministry through our work in the colleges."

He described in some detail the renewal of his college work at Princeton. "The work at Princeton began in March, 1951; how long a hiatus since 1924 with the Philadelphian Society. We had a meeting of twenty-five undergraduates at the Smiths' house [my parents' home in Princeton] at the instigation of Guy Holliday and other undergrads who had been in some of my Burnside summer evening cell groups. Kelly Clark came along and told what had happened at Yale.

"In May, 1951, we had another group of sixty-five at the Smiths. Bill Cohea, Ren Jackson, Neill Hamilton, and Bruce Larson of the seminary have formed a really effective team which carries on. A quiet but very significant undergraduate awakening is taking place. It is fascinating to see it grow and spread. There are 150 in cell groups at Princeton alone."

It was during these years that Sam was actively involved, at the invitation of Dr. John Mackay, then president of Princeton Theological Seminary, in equipping seminarians for a vital ministry. Among them were Bruce Larson, currently Executive Director of Faith at Work (one of the "living movements" described in Chapter 22); Bill Cohea, of the Chicago Business Industrial Project and first Executive Director of the Pittsburgh Experiment (see Chapter 25); Neil Hamilton, who is at present in San Anselmo, California; and Renwick

Jackson, Professor in the Theological Seminary at Rutgers in New Brunswick, New Jersey.

Bill Cohea, Ren Jackson, and Neill Hamilton were mobilized by Sam for evangelism in the colleges. They called themselves "the University Mission." They were sponsored by an Ecumenical Committee of prominent laymen and clergy and were supported by the Presbyterian Board of Education. Their impact on both men's and women's colleges was powerful and hundreds were brought to Christian commitment. In fact, their appeal was so challenging that the Presbyterian Board began to get cold feet—an interesting illustration of the clash that occurs over and over again between a vital organic movement of the Holy Spirit and the slower-moving impact of the organized church.

Sam said of the Mission, 'I have watched them at work many times, and consider them to have as great a talent for reaching students spiritually as any men I have ever met. They touched hundreds and hundreds in the twenty-five or so colleges which they visited. Many of these young people say openly that this was the first thing that ever really awakened them to Christ, and some of these were connected with churches. I have watched their approach—the almost perfect point of contact; the humorous, deep presentation of the gospel in the vernacular (which is the way Christ Himself spoke); the flow of countless stories of individual boys and girls, like the hearers, for whom the experience of Christ had become a reality; the flow of personal interviews taking every waking hour they had, the most exhausting and rewarding kind of self-giving imaginable; and great conversions getting under way—conversions that had to be left to the local religious authorities to conserve and nurture. This was done in complete loyalty to the Church's historic faith. It was done in the fullest possible cooperation with the existing forces of their own and other churches on the campuses. It was done in a spirit of entire teachableness, admitting mistakes when they were made, and open to new truth and procedures, which, of course, did not extend to heeding the counsels of those who themselves do nothing about direct evangelistic work.

"A lawyer, a layman, who knows their work at first hand and has seen it in operation says of them, 'I have seen it work. The results are unbelievable, effects incalculable. I have seen heterogeneous, diverse temperaments, intellects, personalities, held together in big bull sessions, important bull sessions, where the subject under discussion is the most important subject in the world. I have seen these boys lead groups in prayer, seen those groups transformed into devout and prayerful units. I have seen dissension, argument, intellectual sophistry, intellectual pride and arrogance swept away by the Holy Spirit. I have seen and felt that Spirit flood in through a college group with tidal intensity, and the personality of each one in the room suffused with virtually indescribable experience. The creative approach of this group is nothing short of a crusade, a new weapon to bring to a highly educated group the realization of the great and tender miracle of the Love of God in Jesus Christ.'

"There is nothing 'separatist' about all this: it was discovered that every fellow in the cell-groups is attending the church of his choice, many of them returning to the church precisely because of what has happened to them in the cell. This is true of one of my Calvary boys at Princeton, who had slipped away from the church entirely. Of course, they are in constant touch with the religious authorities on the campuses, and with Dr. John Mackay, the president of Princeton Seminary."

Yet the committee of the Presbyterian Church charged with responsibility for these things withdrew all support after only a year's trial. And these were the grounds:

"1. Apprehension concerning possible involvement in an independent evangelistic movement apart from the Church."

(How often has an official church body begun an effective movement toward awakening? When has it not been necessary for a vital movement to scratch gravel by itself till it has proved its worth, when the Church "makes virtue of the faith it had denied"? Committees do not beget spiritual movements, any more than they beget babies. Inspired men beget them. Are these inspired men part of the Church, or are only the committees part of the Church?)

"2. The visits produced rather sharp reactions pro and con."

(Can you imagine anyone reading the Acts of the Apostles, or studying the history of spiritual awakenings, who would be surprised at "sharp reactions pro and con"? Has the living presentation of the gospel ever produced anything else? The same gospel which convinces also convicts. Here is rather a badge of authenticity than a proof of unsoundness! "Criticism of evangelism," as Dr. John Mackay said in this direct connection, "is in the grand tradition.")

The blunt comment of one who knew this situation intimately was, "the gap between the impact of evangelists, and the often complete

spiritual powerlessness of the incumbent on the spot to bring about
such results, is so wide that in order to save his face the incumbent
must deny their power."

The issue was not pressed successfully. Another "movement of the
Spirit" on a university campus was discontinued by "the structure."
What a tragedy!

Setbacks did not discourage Sam. In September, 1953, he wrote in
his diary, "The day after Sambo was born [his grandson who was
named for him] I preached at West Point. Had two services of
cadets in the chapel. At the 11:00 service, General William F. Dean
was present, home after his long imprisonment in Korea. I gave them
'Faith and Freedom' as the basis of a nation's life. Going out, General Dean shook me by the hand and said, 'That's the finest thing I've
heard since I came home.'"

It was during this year, too, that Sam resumed his visits to Yale
University at the invitation of Chaplain Sidney Lovett of Dwight
Hall, and again succeeded in recruiting a number of tremendously
vital young undergraduates. One of them, Franklin Vilas, who is now
rector of St. John's Episcopal Church, Beverly Farms, Massachusetts, tells in a letter to me of his own confrontation with Sam while
he was a freshman at Yale in 1953 and describes Sam's method of
work: "I read recently the issue of *Faith at Work* [published after
Sam's death] which contained the tributes to Sam, and they recalled
once more to mind the debt which I owe to him—not because of
anything particular which he did, but because he was himself, and
being himself was open to the power of the Holy Spirit.

"Over the last five years in which I have been in the ministry, and
previously at seminary, I have run into countless people who have
been reached by the Holy Spirit through Sam. It is my growing
conviction that he was a one-man revival, and that he fulfilled the
title of one of his own books *Revive Thy Church—Beginning with
Me.*

"In reflecting back on my experience at Yale, I would say that
Sam's influence was felt when I was there in three different ways.

"The first was through the groups which were founded at Yale
through his leadership. My own experience was one of being taken to
a group in one of the residential colleges by Ted Riegel, a friend who
had known of Sam and the group movement earlier. The group was a
typical 'cell,' which had as its seminary adviser Bob Raines of the
Divinity School. It was composed of undergraduates, among whom
numbered Bill Schneider, the present Chaplain to Episcopal Students

at Harvard, Don Colenback, now an Episcopal clergyman, Doug King, now a Presbyterian missionary, and several others.

"The key factor was 'Koinonia'—the fellowship of the Spirit. I believe that these groups, which spread about the campus, were tremendously important in creating the atmosphere within which Sam did one of his most important works. I can remember meeting with Sam and perhaps twenty others for a prayer meeting right in the lounge of Calhoun College. It was a moving experience for me. So, firstly, there were the groups which were begun through Sam's influence, and which continued as the Spirit worked through the undergraduates.

"Secondly, there were the personal consultations which Sam held with various and sundry undergraduates. Sam had a facility for being around at a crisis time, a 'kairos,' in people's lives. Perhaps he drew to him those in trouble. At any rate, he also had the gift of presenting the challenge of Christian Commitment in a personal way which was challenging and not sentimental. He was able, apparently, to be led by the Spirit in these situations, and I am sure that much of his real work was done in this way—personally, quietly, without much publicity.

"You will know that there was some criticism among the clergy in various places about Sam's approach to individuals. If I were to be fair, I would say that precisely because Sam attracted the unsettled and emotionally overwrought, as well as the spiritually confused, his direct methods may sometimes have been damaging to specific individuals. But I don't feel that this in any way detracted from the great importance and value of his approach. For the several whom I know who were put off by this approach, I know a dozen more like myself for whom it was exactly the right thing.

"Thirdly, there was Sam's public approach—his preaching, conferences on the ministry, etc. I can still remember a sermon he preached at Yale the first time I heard him in 1953, in which he challenged the students to Christian commitment, and then said, in effect, 'Shame on you, sons of privilege, who have the finest education money can buy, and who have as your only goal in life to lounge selfishly in your suburban homes while the world goes to ruin, and while thousands starve for Christian service.' This kind of preaching had its effect (I can't remember whole phrases from too many sermons) and that particular sermon shocked many into some kind of re-evaluation.

"I would say, then, that in those three ways—the groups, the personal counseling, and the public ministry—Sam had a great effect on the lives of many college students.

"I would not say that Sam's influence was the only influence upon me in those years at Yale. The college chaplaincy and my own religious quest had much to do with my future course. But *Sam was crucial,* as were those great individuals whom he had touched—Bob Whitaker and Bob Raines of the Yale Divinity School, Ralston Young and the others whom I met in New York.

"In short, I think that Sam's evaluation of himself as a doorkeeper was a good one, and the words of one of my friends spoken right after Sam's death were ones which rang true, 'A great old warrior goes to his reward.' "

In an article entitled "College Work Today" in *The Church Review* of the Church Society for College Work for April, 1954, Sam shared the distilled essence of his wisdom in regard to college work. He wrote, "I believe that two things are substantially true. One is that the undergraduate of today has a greater realization than the one of a few college generations ago of the fact that religion has and must have an intellectual backbone. When he comes to consider the subject at all, he expects to use his mind, and wants you to use yours. He may not agree with your theological position, he may not even understand it; but he will not blame you for having it. He has much more respect for Christianity as intellectually a real 'world-view' than he used to have.

"The other is that he realizes that religion to survive at all cannot remain in an amorphous and disorganized condition. There must be a Christian organization, to carry the faith to oncoming generations, to continue the Christian movement, to try to say those things that are specially relevant for one's own time out of the rich treasure of faith and history, and to provide seeking people with brothers to seek with them and to worship and work with them.

"These things seem to me to put the present generation of college workers far ahead of where we used to be years ago. The cry then was for nothing but ethics, and these held in the thin air of sheer individualism. There is much more to build on now. I suspect that the respect for theology is in no small measure due to the departments of religion that have been created in so many places, as well as to a world situation which calls for something much more potent than individualistic ethics. I suppose that the realization of the need for some kind of body to channel the faith and spirit of Christianity is due in part to the failure of certain kinds of liberalism and secularism to give any meaning to life, and the need for some continuing force that speaks up for the faith as an adequate interpretation of existence.

"Many a student knows there are needs that his studies and learning cannot satisfy. When it comes to values and meanings, religion comes into the center of the stage.

"Then there are certain needs that seem to belong specially to our time. I graduated into a world at war, but it never occurred to us that we would not defeat the Germans and go on as before. Who today expects anything to 'go on as before,' and who wants it to?

"As I talk with students one by one, two problems come out in about three out of five cases: the problem of *loneliness*, and the problem of *lostness*.

"Of course, if these two needs are typical, there never was such a time for religion to come into the picture. *The Church* is the real answer to loneliness. *Redemption* (but this needs a more vernacular word when you talk to them about it) is the answer to lostness.

"There is a great gap, I think, between the objective presentation of the facts of religion (in courses of religion), or the claims of religion (in university missions, and steady work through chaplains or Christian Associations) and the actual discovery of faith by individual students.

"We face the ever-present problems of 'communication.' It is acute with your eager, not too well-informed minds. No matter how well a professor of religion may teach, or how well a student pastor may preach or talk, he never knows whether what he is saying 'gets over,' as the parson in the local church does not know it, without some kind of closer grips with individuals.

"I would plead for two things in this connection.

"One is for more men and women close to the undergraduates who speak in the vernacular. I think Jesus did that.

"My second appeal is for more time to be given to individuals in the kind of interviews that start at least a working spiritual experiment, if they do not clinch a decision. We desperately need clergy everywhere, but especially on campuses, who know how to act in this field. We need research in it, not based on books, but on talks, hundreds of them, thousands of them. We need bright young men who can hold their own intellectually, but that by itself will not do. They need understanding and caring as much as intellect. They must learn that there is no substitute for knowing the human heart at first-hand, and for approaching people in the spirit of prayer, humility, and self-giving.

"For years I have been especially interested in getting more men and better ones into the ministry. Clergy and bishops sometimes ask the best method for this. Never the indiscriminate net, I should say—but *the rod and line!*

"We need more young men in the ministry who will dedicate their younger years, and maybe their older ones, to working on the campuses of our land. They will need to be converted men who know how to make the great Christian experience of new birth and new life real to others. In a world as potentially dangerous as ours, there is no use sending students out into it fortified only with some religious arguments or even beliefs. They need to get deep into the living experience of faith. President [Nathan] Pusey of Harvard says, 'It is leadership in religious knowledge, and more, in religious experience of which we now have a most gaping need.' I think some of our seminaries may be training men to give people more in 'religious knowledge' than in 'religious experience.' It is not good enough. But we are in a new day when the president of Harvard is saying things like that!"

The Very Rev. John Coburn, dean of the Episcopal Theological School, in Cambridge, Massachusetts, summed up in a few succinct sentences Sam's impact on American college undergraduates during the years of his ministry among them: "The news of Sam's death, while not unexpected, came as a very sharp dropping of a curtain on a memorable and in many ways unique life. There are not many like Sam given the church, and only one in a generation. Of his influence and impact upon the lives of hundreds—thousands—of young men, there can be no question. More than almost all the rest of the clergy combined, he laid it right on the line for men to make a decision about the ministry, and in my experience he never made a mistake."

V
THE LAITY IN ACTION

Living Movements, poems, and babies do not come from committees.

SAMUEL MOOR SHOEMAKER

Unless there is at least one living movement within the structure of the Church in every generation, the institution will tend to crystallize and die for lack of Spiritual Power.

HENRY PITNEY VAN DUSEN

Living Movements
and the Small Group   ▨   21

ONE OF SAM'S CARDINAL EMPHASES WAS THAT every parish should have within it one or more small groups that meet for the deepening of the spiritual life. He was developing this idea when he talked of the need for another kind of spiritual gathering than the formal service or the parish organization. He felt that many were finding this need best satisfied in what is often called a spiritual "cell," which is a small, informal company that meets for prayer or fellowship or study or work or all four together.

As Sam pursued the idea of small groups he began to discover more and more areas for small groups. The genius of these little groups is that a few people are drawn together by common need and faith. God then gives the spark of fire. People quietly unite in such a fellowship and so a Christian "cell" is formed. And in that cell, hopefully, the individualism and selfishness, the self-consciousness and fear, the defeat and despair of many a man and woman are turned into unselfish service, freedom of expression, hope, victory, and faith through Christ.

Such a meeting may begin with an informal prayer. It may proceed with a brief but relevant exposition of a passage of the Bible. It may be right for one man to tell enough of his own story, or the story of his situation, to give a flavor and set a pace, which is like leaven that begins permeating the others.

Sam felt that as a newborn child needs warmth, food, love, and attention, so a newborn Christian needs someone who will stick by him for a time and bring him into a living fellowship. As children suffer from gas and colic, a reborn person has his ups and downs in the early stages of spiritual growth. A chance to meet with several others regularly will see him over the first stages. This person will also be brought into the full fellowship of the church. Of course, this would mean some systematic instruction, the study of the right kind of books, and being introduced to the power and the value of formal worship.

Individuals and small companies are the secret of the awakening of our parishes. It takes meeting after meeting to get things ground into the bones of those who are converted—Christian ideas, Christian caring, Christian fellowship, and Christian worship.

Sam wrote his own quadrilateral of evangelism—conversion, fellowship, prayer, and witness. One side in this quadrilateral of evangelism is fellowship. Jesus did not drop the seeds of the gospel into a dozen individual hearts. He drew a dozen men about Him and kept them with Him till they grasped who He was and what He wanted to do in the world. When you come to Him, you don't just come to Him, you come also to His followers, His Church, His Body.

Sam summarized the principles behind the functioning of the small Christian group as follows:*

"1. Nothing happens while we merely think about starting a cell, so pray for God's direction and try something. Everyone makes mistakes, but he who wants to be used will find both like-minded people and a practicable plan.

"2. Keep the group *small*. If you must enlarge, then form a 'heartbeat' out of those three or four who are most spiritually in earnest and meet with them for prayer and planning at a different time from the larger meeting.

"3. Accent *friendliness*—it is a sign of love. It is emotional release which leads people to say what they think and 'this will be created largely by the leader's hospitality to them and their ideas.'

"4. Keep the room, whether in home, church, or office, coolly ventilated and eliminate glaring lights and unnecessary noise. Avoid using a table.

"5. Welcome *silences*—they can lead to conviction and conversion when used patiently, without fear or embarrassment.

"6. A silence closed with the Lord's Prayer helps a cell to gain unity and strength and leads individuals to rediscover their voices.

"7. *Draw out* those who are moving forward spiritually, or have just made a decision of some kind, and let the meeting take flavor from them. If debates arise, suggest that those who are in disagreement talk through the points at issue privately at another time. . . .

"8. Use the Bible when you find a story which relates to the life of the cell or the outreach of that life in the community and world.

"9. Keep the separate meetings *short* and stop on time. . . .

* Samuel M. Shoemaker, *Revive Thy Church—Beginning with Me* (New York: Harper & Row, 1948), pp. 95-97.

"10. *Follow up* all meetings by talks with one or more friends individually. Get the habit of praying aloud with one other person. In your own devotions, ask God to show you what to do next for 'A' or what further step to suggest to 'B.' Think of those who come as you think of your children, and ask vision for them."

In his book *By the Power of God*, Sam clearly stated the importance of the "living movement" to the Church and the Church to the "living movement" when he said:

"Sometimes the Church is humble and far-sighted enough either to accept the new spirit when it appears, or to incorporate it later, as part of the Church's life and work. There exists a tension here. It appears that nearly every movement of the Holy Spirit is more vital near its beginning, while it is misunderstood and not accepted; and tends to lose edge and power as it is 'taken over' by the Church. Corrective as to doctrine, ministering the 'means of grace' must come from the Church to the new movement. New life must come into the Church from the movement. Such movements need to allow for what is given through the Church and the Church in its organized capacity needs to allow for what is given directly by the Spirit. We may expect some misunderstanding, and some difficulty. We have a right to expect of the organized Church that it have some spiritual insight, and recognize what is clearly from God, and admit that this, too, is an organic part of the life of the Church.

"The old, organized Church needs the new invasions of the Spirit for freshness and reality, for a return to first loves and first principles, for renewal and awakening and a rediscovery of the spiritual power that is often lost by sheer custom and routine. . . . And the fresh and spontaneous movements of the Spirit need the old Church for balance, for historic perspective, for an understanding of the faith, and for provision of the regular 'means of grace.' It *is difficult to keep* these two elements in balance, but it can and should be done."*

---

* Samuel M. Shoemaker, *By the Power of God* (New York: Harper & Row, 1954), p. 144.

Faith at Work   ▨ 22

WHEN SAM BECAME RECTOR OF CALVARY
Episcopal Church in New York City, along with the training of
a staff, he felt it necessary to develop a midweek meeting to which
the laity could come to witness and to learn. In January, 1926, he
began the Thursday evening meetings, which continued for many
years and which trained thousands of laymen to give witness in the
workaday world from which they came and to which they returned.
Over the years, the attendance at these meetings numbered into the
many tens of thousands, and their influence extended into the far
corners of the world. For here was found the sharing of spiritual
experience by ordinary individuals, confronted with the common
problems and situations of life. They talked about these things naturally; the emphasis was on the will being given to God, and on
what He could do to guide and use a life so given to Him. There was
laughter and fellowship and challenge, costly decision and gay adventure; these people had found an answer. They learned how to share
simply, intelligently, and convincingly what they had found, and
many a life discovered a new direction and learned what it meant to
be in touch with the living God, through those meetings.

There is a great deal being said and written nowadays about the
ministry of the laity. A lay woman, Amelia S. Reynolds, in her book
*New Lives for Old,** describes one of these early Thursday night
meetings:

"The group itself meets in the Hall of Calvary House, which has
been made beautiful by hangings, tapestries, and religious paintings.
Before Calvary House was built, if unbeautiful surroundings could
have discouraged it, it would have faded away. When we grew too
big for the rectory, we moved into the old gymnasium, where Mr.
Shoemaker, sitting under a basketball net, had anywhere from one
hundred to one hundred and fifty people on camp chairs as close to
him as they could get, for the men who built the gymnasium were not
interested in acoustics.

* Westwood, N.J.: Fleming H. Revell, 1929.

"Mr. Shoemaker is apt to begin the meeting with a prayer for the presence of the Holy Spirit in the place. . . . Then cheerfully, informally, he begins. One night it may be with an analysis of the interview between Christ and the Woman at the Well; how He drew her out, brought conviction of sin, and how she went out to tell a whole city about Him. Or it may be the story of someone who had surrendered the night before. Then, with his eyes twinkling, he asks: 'I wonder if Bill hasn't something for us tonight. It came during the staff meeting this morning that he might lead off.'

" 'That's all right with me, Sam,' calls a boy of twenty-five from the back of the room.

" 'Guess you better come up here,' says S.M.S., Jr. 'Crowd's too big to hear you tonight where you are.'

"Bill, a big and handsome and attractive youngster drops into a chair by the leader. 'I've been having a great time,' he says. 'When I remember that kind of a cuss I was four years ago, how I was so unhappy in college (although I seemed to have everything), that I got drunk just to escape myself—and think of now!' Then he tells the story of a boy whom he brought to faith in Christ the week before, the son of a missionary, by the way.

"The meetings of this group are better drama than any that goes on on Broadway, but the group meeting is not held merely to interest people. The purpose is to give a chance to make real to outsiders a God-inspired life through stories of such lives, and to take members of the fellowship further in their experience of Christ by witnessing as to what has happened up to date.

"The other night I saw here a bishop of our Church soon to return to China, a former Mohammedan now turned Christian, who is studying at a seminary; a secretary of a Y.W.C.A. from the Middle West; a wealthy businessman from New Jersey; a charming girl with her husband from Tennessee; a curate from a neighbouring parish."

During the last five years of our participation in Moral Rearmament the Thursday night meetings were discontinued, which in retrospect we knew was a mistake. So after our split with Moral Rearmament, we reactivated the meetings under another name, "Faith at Work." These new Thursday evening meetings came to have the same tremendous impact and power that had been shown originally when Sam started them in the late 1920s.

It is hard to disentangle the outreach of Calvary Church parish from the tremendous ecumenical outreach this living movement represented. We were never unaware of the important fact that Calvary was an inner-city parish and that the ministry of the laity was an integral part of the development and outreach of such a parish.

Actually the reactivated Thursday night meetings of the 1940s started in the boiler room of Calvary Church parish house. A Jewish painter named Bill Levine was hired to do some repainting in the interior of Calvary House and, naturally, the janitor, Herbie Lantau, who was the sexton as well, made friends with him.

One day Bill Levine found his way down to the boiler room, fell into conversation with Herbie, and Herbie was able to persuade him so convincingly of the advantages of what it meant to become a Christian that Bill reached out for it. So Herbie astutely suggested that they begin meeting frequently in the boiler room for the sharing of experience, Bible study, and prayer.

Herbie, as a member of the Calvary Church staff, had had drummed into his ears, "Be a witness where you are." So he chose as his place of witness the boiler room. This became Herbie's chapel, and for a couple of years this is where he and his friends met. It was at this time that someone made contact with Ralston C. Young, Red Cap 42 at Grand Central Station, and he found his way to Calvary House and joined the boiler-room group. He felt so at home in that boiler room and found such new faith himself through his fellowship with these other men that he decided to start a group of his own on Track 13 in Grand Central Station. He has often said since that Grand Central Station was his cathedral just as the boiler room was Herbie's.

One Christmas after the beginning of the group in the boiler room, we recruited some of our boiler-room personnel for the Calvary Christmas pageant. It was a truly moving pageant that year because the Wise Men were Bill Levine the converted Jewish painter, Herbie Lantau the janitor, and a very handsome young Negro who had also joined the group. A Christmas pageant takes on vivid life when the actors are themselves people who have met the Christ child face to face and bowed before Him in obedience and in love.

The boiler-room group gradually became larger and moved up to the second floor of Calvary House where it met every Monday afternoon, attracting all sorts of people from messenger boys to business executives.

The men's group at Calvary had picked up a lot of men who felt lonely and without fellowship when Moral Rearmament departed, and a large conservation job needed to be done, so the boiler-room group joined this one. But hundreds more joined and became part of this group who never had any touch whatever with Moral Rearmament. Irving Harris, who assumed the editorship of the *Calvary Evangel*, counseled with countless people throughout these years and became the principal architect of the Monday afternoon men's group as well as the Thursday evening group.

The men's group at Calvary, like all healthy organisms, has proliferated into any number of offshoots: I have already mentioned Ralston C. Young, Red Cap 42, and the group on Track 13. Then there was the group Ed Cabaniss started in the Joseph Dixon Crucible Company in Jersey City, of which he was vice-president and then president.

The principles that governed Alcoholics Anonymous (see Chapter 24), which at this time met on Tuesday nights in the Great Hall of Calvary House, and the principles that governed Faith at Work, which met on Thursday nights, paralleled. Sam often said that this basic approach was "fundamental for anyone with problems," and then he added with humorous insight, "for everyone has a problem, is a problem, or lives with a problem."

Sam insisted that the small-group action, of which he became a greater and greater advocate in his ministry, always started with personal counseling and continued in "group therapy." We called it fellowship. Social workers began using this method with narcotic addicts, neurotics, prisoners, and in many other specialized fields.

In our own informal way it is possible that we helped to beat out in creative experimentation the principles and procedures which have now permeated so many special fields of work. Dr. Cotton, a leading New Jersey alienist from 1890 through 1910, made a prophetic statement when he said, "If you find a principle and procedure that will operate with the most difficult cases you have a principle that will operate with the most normal."

In 1943 a significant weekend conference was held at Calvary House. Between four and five hundred were there. Speakers included Dr. Henry Pitney Van Dusen; Lt. Comdr. C. Leslie Glenn; Ellis Van Riper, labor leader; H. Alexander Smith, U.S. Senator; Carl Vrooman, Assistant Secretary of Agriculture under President Wilson;

Olive M. Jones, former president of the National Education Association; Alys Smith; and David Lawrence, editor-in-chief of *U.S. News and World Report.*

We laid down an over-all plan, which looks something like this when you set it in outline:

1. *Goal:* The Kingdom of God on earth. A world-order based on the life and teachings of Jesus Christ.

2. *Unit-objectives:* Christian Homes; God-guided Education; Honest Business; Unselfish Use of Possessions; Right Race Relations; God-led Statesmanship; Christ's Kind of Peace.

3. *Means and Methods:* Conversion of Individuals to Christ; Listening to God; Loyalty to the Church and the Bible; Fellowship, Prayer and Training Groups; Literature; Impact on Situations; Co-operation between Christian Groups and People.

We didn't quite achieve our objectives on that weekend, but we did set a good many wheels in motion.

Sam wrote in his diary three years later, "It was in February, 1946, that my article about Ralston Young, Red Cap 42, appeared in the *Readers' Digest.* I had come to know Fulton Oursler and he said to me one day, 'Sam, I know there are some stories in connection with your work that ought to appear in the *Digest.* I gave him quite a lot of material, and he was not long in coming back at me with the idea that by far the best and most dramatic of them was Ralston's. As the story of a man letting God use him in a somewhat commonplace calling, I hardly know its equal; and it was gratifying when, on the *Digest's* thirtieth anniversary they published the hundred most asked for articles throughout those years, this had been one of them. Ralston and Sadie have gone to innumerable places to speak, and the story of them has gone wider still. They are among my dearest friends, and I rejoice in the wonderful way in which they have been used. Some silly people have wanted him to go into the ministry, others to create a chapel in Grand Central: thank God he remains a layman, and his only 'chapel' has been the empty car on Track 13 where on Monday, Wednesday, and Friday noons he conducts his meetings. His and hers together has been a most signal ministry." Ralston was one of the leaders of our Thursday night meetings.

One evening "Gert" Behanna turned up, brought by Tom and

Blanche Page. She gave her magnificent and moving witness, which she has repeated before thousands of groups since, with the same telling effect, for she is surely an instance of the "great redemption."

Another night, a middle-aged housewife, Dorothy Bennett, who lived in a tenement under the Third Avenue elevated told how she and an East Side social worker, who also attended our meetings, became deeply concerned about the way in which they observed teenage kids hanging around the innumerable bars which lined Third Avenue in the 1940s between 23rd Street and the Bowery. They did not know what to do about the situation themselves, but they had an uneasy feeling that teenage kids watching drunks reeling in and out of bars were not experiencing the best possible influence. They agreed to meet to pray about this matter. Every day at noon they sacrificed fifteen to twenty minutes of their lunch hour and met in the Calvary Church chapel to pray.

The evening that Dorothy Bennett spoke, the Rev. Shelton Hale Bishop, rector of St. Philip's Church, Harlem, and a regular attendant at our Thursday night group, was present. It was June and he was tired. He was planning to go off on a much needed summer vacation, although that week a child of eleven had stabbed another child to death with an ice pick in the very block on which St. Philip's Church stood, and he was gravely troubled. When he heard the witness of the housewife in regard to her prayer intention, he began to think uneasily about the fact that while St. Philip's Church stood on one of the most overpopulated blocks in the whole United States, it was doing nothing about the people who lived on this block except those who belonged to St. Philip's. Among the inhabitants of this block, of course, there were thousands of children who spent most of their lives on the streets.

He returned home, spent a sleepless night, and the next morning he had received his direction from the Holy Spirit. It was to make available the facilities of his parish house during the week to do a work of salvage for the children of that block. He announced it from his pulpit the following Sunday and asked for volunteers to help. Immediately, trained social workers and others volunteered their services for the summer. Many of the members of our Thursday night group, both white and Negro, joined the volunteers and he was able to start a work in his parish house that took the children of that neighborhood off the blistering streets and gave them all kinds of opportunity for creative and constructive fun throughout the long summer months. I remember his telling the story of one group of young gang members who wandered in and began to make trouble. He got hold of these boys and said to them, "Boys, we're glad to have you come here, but we will not welcome you unless you tie in with our program." The leader rather truculently said, "What is it?" He began to tell them what they could do. They not only tied in with his program throughout that summer, but they became the most responsible and creative group of young leaders in the whole project.

Father Bishop described very movingly the two or three rows of children who began coming and sitting in the front rows of the church on Sundays. They had no other church affiliation and it had been gently suggested by many leaders of the group that they might be interested in attending the church. Many of these kids, as they became older, were baptized and confirmed and became good, solid members of his younger congregation. But his purpose was not to build up his congregation; his purpose was to serve his community, and he found the inspiration for this service at a Faith at Work meeting in Calvary Church on a Thursday evening in early June many years ago because a lay woman shared her prayer concern.

We shall never know the total effect of the boiler room group, then the Monday men's group, and finally, the Thursday midweek group. Mr. John H. Ryder, a former president of the New York Advertising Club and founder of the Job Finding Forum, was a member of the Monday group. He has said:

"It was at Calvary Church where Sam was rector that I first came in contact with the tremendous power of laymen witnessing. It was there that I first learned that laymen were really the Church. That's why I accepted the chairmanship of Laymen's Sunday—withal reluctantly, because when Lex Capron, Wally Speers, and some others suggested it, I thought it was a good thing but that somebody else ought to do it.

"My organization had about four thousand clients—these clients were scattered all over the United States and Canada. Each of them received a mat telling of Laymen's Sunday. A great many of these clients reprinted the mat that I am sure didn't know a thing about the event, but it did cause inquiry, and I became a member of the Board of Managers of the United Church Men who were and are now well equipped to handle the day. Don Calame, the executive director of the United Church Men, told me that in 1964 they estimated about four hundred thousand men in pulpits publicly doing something for

Christ, standing up as men who are trying to work for Him. Four hundred thousand men is a lot of men and as far as I am concerned, it could never have happened unless it had been for Sam and his church.

"As you know, many years ago I was asked by members of the New York Advertising Club to teach men how to find a job. I reluctantly accepted after pressure because I had no knowledge of how to find a job, not having been out of work since I had been in my teens. But Sam and the fellowship at Calvary encouraged me and God's gracious Spirit saw me through and so the Job Finding Forum became a reality.

"I think in the old days I would probably have been willing to chip in one or two hundred dollars to help a distressed brother, but I am sure I would never have given the time, effort, and prayerful thought to the subject of job finding had it not been for what I had found through Sam and our other spiritual pals.

"The Forum was saved from possible disaster many years ago when we had a fire in the Advertising Club and Sam welcomed us down to the Great Hall at Calvary and there the Job Finding Forum functioned for some time until the damage at the Advertising Club had been repaired and we could return to our quarters."

A living movement needs a magazine which tells its story, and so *Faith at Work* evolved, growing out of the *Evangel*, the small parish monthly, which Sam inherited from former rectors. Many parishes have their own magazines. But some years ago the *Evangel* began emphasizing the great central verities of Christianity, particularly Christian experience. The magazine is now read all across the nation in every state and in more than one hundred countries of the world. It is read in Tokyo, in Berlin, in Edinburgh, and Capetown; in fact, almost wherever men say, "Show me—I am from Missouri," or ask, "Can faith really make any difference?"

In describing its purpose Sam said: "*Faith at Work* is not a popular 'how to get ahead' manual. It is not concerned with offering faith as the key to wealth, popularity, and success. It makes no attempt to prove that through faith life can be made easy; rather, it tries to make clear that through faith at work life can be made great. *Faith at Work* is a meeting in print." Every month it carried a sermon or an article by Sam.

In 1956 the *Faith at Work* magazine moved from Calvary House to 40th Street first, and then to Madison Avenue, New York, where the combination magazine and movement still has its headquarters and continues to exercise an amazing influence in hundreds of places, both by the printed word and by teams of people going out all over the country and abroad to witness.

Faith at Work reports that there are now fourteen regional inter-denominational church-sponsored conferences held every year throughout the United States. More than 400 laymen, 250 teenagers, 150 clergy, and 200 women attended the New York conference in midwinter of 1966. Numbers of small paperback books describing this amazing lay ministry are sold throughout the world annually.

The clearest and most profound testimonies of the outreach of this work poured in, in letters from men and women from all over the country, when Sam died. These people had found something "special" through Sam, the *Faith at Work* magazine, and the meetings of Faith at Work.

One young housewife wrote: "I have never forgotten my year at Calvary House.

"I have wanted to write ever since the death of Dr. Sam. I had so wanted him to know that my Bill, for whom I wrote to you both for help many years ago when we were in Ohio, has come so very far in his search for his Faith and his Lord.

"He finally made a decision. . . . Since then his Spiritual Growth has been wonderful—at this point he feels he is being called to the Priesthood, but not in the ordinary sense of a Parish Priest. Rather, he feels he should stay in the teaching, business world, with assisting on Sundays, etc. He is deeply concerned about Christianity in the Business World."

A Roman Catholic friend, who had been one of our Faith at Work people, wrote me: "I 'hear' the Church Expectant rejoicing over your Sam's death even as the Church Militant mourns over the loss of one of our greatest 'crusaders for the Lord.'" And an Episcopal lay woman from Alabama wrote: "Through meeting Sam and serving Christ through Faith at Work we have found our greatest sense of satisfaction and fulfillment so far. Sid and I are more grateful than I can find words to express for Sam's very real and vital part of our spiritual life. And what a *glory* to know that we are only two of the thousands who can say the same thing! So we, Sid and I, send you our dear love and prayers, and join you in rejoicing and thanking God that such a servant as Sam Shoemaker lived among us and is *Living Still* with Him."

Churchmen who have not understood the vast outreach of Sam's work with individuals and small groups have sometimes sneeringly accused him of being "pietistic." But are the kind of men and women I have told of in these pages "pietistic"? Are they not the "leaven in the lump," the light of the world, the candles on the candlestand to which our Lord so often referred? As Gale D. Webbe has written, "Grace having found and created a channel in man pours with power and ever more power into the whole world of men."

Grass-roots Ecumenicity   ❇ 23

ONE DAY THE THOUGHT CAME TO SAM THAT IT might be beneficial for some of the informal spiritual groups to bring together their leadership, not to federate or to make any pronouncements but to exchange experiences and, as E. Stanley Jones once said, "to 'cross-fertilize' each other." Sam and Dr. Jones did not work in exactly the same way, but in many ways they were after the same thing. So Sam wrote Stanley Jones and Glenn Clark, as representing the Ashrams and the Camps Farthest Out, suggesting a day or two around the first of January each year for dialogue and prayer. Both thought it an inspired idea. Then they enlisted Frank Laubach, who is known around the world for his literacy work; Melvin Evans, of Human Development in Action (Chicago); Congressman Walter Judd; Abraham Vereide of International Christian Leadership; and Norman Vincent Peale. Sam also wanted Rufus Jones—and the canny old Quaker came with his suitcase packed, ready to stay if it were worthwhile but, Sam thought, a little skeptical. He liked it, stayed, and came back each year. Later John Peters of World Neighbors joined the group.

This group, which met in Washington, D.C., continued to meet for several years. As individuals need to meet with other individuals, and take an honest look at their own shortcomings, and receive strength from fellowship with one another, so do groups based on Christian discipleship need to do the same thing. We must be willing to learn from one another, to appreciate one another, but to avoid the temptation to boss one another. This is an important expression of the ecumenicity for which we all pray.

The importance of these gatherings did not lie so much in the actual meetings themselves, but in the exceedingly fruitful results of the cross-fertilization, which Sam hoped would be their result. It is not necessary to describe the great movements of the laity which have continued to thrive with the help and prayers of these men for one another in their undertakings. For instance, I have in my hand the most recent news report on the activities of International Christian Leadership, which has indeed gone places and done things since those early days in the 1940s when Dr. Abraham Vereide met with this cross-fertilization fellowship group, and which resulted in the annual Presidential Prayer Breakfast in Washington, as well as annual governors' and mayors' prayer breakfasts around the country.

In attendance at the 1966 Presidential Prayer Breakfast were more than seventy presidents of national and international labor unions, more than one hundred leaders in the field of industry and business, the chancellors and the presidents of a number of universities and colleges, and prominent men from the courts, from communications, and from every other phase of economic life. Senator Frank Carlson of Kansas, who presided at the meeting, said: "The growth of the prayer breakfast movement during these past thirteen years has been remarkable. As a result of this Breakfast, practically every governor in the United States holds an annual Governor's Prayer Breakfast in his own State capital with the leaders of that State. And literally hundreds of smaller regular groups are meeting to foster faith and freedom in this land and around the world.

"New prayer groups which meet weekly are being organized among businessmen, civic officials, secretaries, clerks, housewives, college and university students.

"Now there is a growing appreciation for the values gained when leaders meet in the spirit of prayer, recognizing that our ultimate hope and trust is in our God."

World Neighbors, another movement fostered by this fellowship, is now established in more than three thousand villages in underdeveloped areas of the world and has helped to date more than 3,150,-000 people.

This work preceded by many years the Peace Corps, and I don't doubt that it had some influence on the ultimate formation of the Peace Corps. It is part of the people-to-people program of which former President of the United States, Dwight D. Eisenhower, is General Chairman.

One of the results of the fellowship these men experienced together was the holding of interdenominational conferences for laymen at Calvary House during the 1940s, which became an annual event during Sam's rectorship.

In a newspaper clipping of May, 1951, such a conference is described under the heading: "300 from U.S. and Canada at 3-Day Conference."

The article says: "The conference, an annual event at Calvary Church, drew delegates from all parts of the United States and Canada, 'to develop an effective Christian leadership among laymen,' according to the Rev. Dr. Samuel M. Shoemaker, rector of the church.

"Dr. Shoemaker and the Rev. Canon Quintin Warner, of London, Ontario, opened the conference Friday night with a discussion on 'Our World and Our Opportunity.'

"In his sermon, 'Christian Leadership Today,' at the morning service, Dr. Shoemaker said, 'The success of the Christian enterprise is the heart of the world's future welfare. There is no sign of hope anywhere else.'

"'The onrush of Communism makes people realize that one needs a philosophy, and not just a gun, to meet Communism. For Communism is a deadly belief, and only a true belief can conquer a false one.' he said."

So at the same time Sam was carrying on with his parish duties and commitments and was busy recruiting young men for the ministry and for Christian vocation in the colleges, possibly his most significant contribution had to do with the way in which he was presenting laymen and women of all types of backgrounds with the challenge of Christian commitment and Christian action in the government, business, home, and international world.

What a pity that the great church power structures are not more eagerly listening to and hearing the lay people who are engaging in far-flung and significant action in the lay movements of our day. We seem so concerned on the official level with thinking through and implementing our own message that we scarcely have the time or will take the trouble to hear of the way in which this message has already been heard and is being implemented in group after group of the kind that I have described.

I often asked Sam why he didn't take more trouble to explain to the people in the ecclesiastical power structure what he was doing and to try and get them to hear him. He would shrug his shoulders and answer me almost with despair, "My job is to reach as many people as I can for Christ before I die, and they will be my testimony. I haven't the time or the strength to try and explain to the people in the structure what I am doing. I am too busily engaged in doing it."

However, it was always Sam's hope that sometime, somehow, the organic prayer and action fellowships would find a way to work happily with the ecclesiastical organization, and I am sure that he is adding his prayers in heaven to this intention as this also is hopefully part of the great ecumenical grass-roots Christian action of our day.

A Rescue Mission and
Alcoholics Anonymous ❧ 24

CALVARY CHAPEL—THE PLACE WHERE, BRUCE
Bairnsfather said later, "a Carpenter still mends broken men"—
was an old unused East Side chapel when Sam fell heir to it at the
time he became rector of Calvary Episcopal Church, New York City.
It came about in this wise: When Sam accepted the call to Calvary
Church, the original 23rd Street Chapel and Lodging House, brought
into being through the vision of Dr. Francis Lister Hawks and
Bishop Satterlee (the Rt. Rev. Henry Yates Satterlee), was standing
idle. As I mentioned earlier (p. 50) Sam walked restlessly and
musingly past it on several occasions, and then went back to the
rectory and jotted down in his diary, "It has always seemed to me
that a vital church should be reaching, not only the settled working
people with homes and families, but also those without any place in
society, the homeless, friendless, faithless derelicts who have lost
everything. While we work with people of sufficient privilege to find
their way into the rectory and church, what is happening to men in
the Gas House district to the east of us? I looked at the practically
unused chapel at 246 East 23rd Street which we own. There it is,
waiting for a real function, for the right man to open it and minister
to the hundreds of men who stand about idle or drunken or quarrel-
ing or bewildered, in that neighborhood."

While these thoughts were coming to Sam, God's ideal man for
this work was looking longingly at that closed door, praying that it
might open to him so that he might begin rescue work there. His
prayers were answered. He found Sam and they met together. He
was Henry Harrison Hadley, II, the son of the Samuel H. Hadley
spoken of in William James's *Varieties of Religious Experience.* The
son had been converted three days after his father's death in 1906.
Henry Hadley had been in Christian work traveling throughout the
United States, and believed that he should settle into local work. He
and Sam talked and prayed about the possibilities of 23rd Street. It

was going to take a considerable sum to open up this fresh work; Sam had been at Calvary but six months, and the extra expenses of material alterations had already been heavy. On December 11, 1925, he had a memorable meeting with the Vestry. They considered it all carefully. It seemed to them that the spiritual significance of such a work in the Gas House district, and what it might mean both to the men of that neighborhood and to the Calvary Church people, was so great that they must make the venture of faith. Sam contracted to be responsible for securing half the sum needed if the Vestry would be responsible for the other; it would take five thousand dollars a year to maintain it; and they agreed to try the experiment for six months. They took one word of the name from "Calvary Chapel" and one word from the old "Galilee Mission" that had been founded by Dr. Satterlee, and called it "Calvary Mission."

The Mission was opened on February 1, 1926, when a great many of Calvary's parishioners were present. Men began to be changed and, as "Harry" Hadley used to say, to "stick." The Mission was maintained for the surprising figure of ten dollars a day, though fifty-seven men slept in the beds and forty-five received two meals a day.

One of the parishioners, Amelia S. Reynolds, described it vividly:

"Calvary Mission did not stand out prominently on that dilapidated block of East 23rd Street. The lighted cross in front of it hardly showed against what remained of the daylight. The Mission room came on you suddenly. The clean, bare, yellow place, hard benches, a platform one step up, the piano with the girl from another world softly playing hymns, and against the wall, a huge black cross. One by one men drifted in. There was no talk—some of them fingered hymnals. Once, when the girl at the piano played a refrain which they knew, the men half hummed, half sang it. Mr. Hadley, looking healthy, well scrubbed and with the very shiniest shoes, read a chapter in the Bible. I could not tell whether the men listened. He made comments afterward, and I still could not tell whether they listened. They seemed sodden with an exhaustion that was of heart, body and spirit. Then they sang three or four gospel hymns that I did not know. The men sang the sentimental ones with vigor—atrocious musically, but nevertheless catching. Mr. Hadley told the story of his own life and conversion. The men listened.

"Then a man from the benches got to his feet—generations of

Anglo-Saxons back of his gaunt, hook-nose face—little smiling lines around the eyes—a fine face. 'I want to give thanks for seven days without drinking.' He sat down.

"They sang, rather low, a hymn which was called a hymn of invitation. A man in the room burst out crying and came forward to the front row and knelt with his back to the platform. Muffled by his arms, you heard through his sobs: 'Oh, Lord! Oh, Lord!' He was quite drunk. For ninety days, somehow, he had kept straight, and the wife who had put him out of the house ninety days before for the sake of her children had promised to receive him back that night. He had been sleeping in a lodging house where every night drink had been offered him and somehow he had managed to refuse until this night, when he was overwhelmed with happiness at the thought of going home. Happiness sapped his strength. Now the door of the place that he called home was shut against him by his own hand, but nothing that he could do could shut the door of the Mission against him.

"As Mr. Hadley knelt by them each night, they knew a man who had won the fight that they were fighting. As he told them of his wasted youth, they, knowing his present life, saw the everlasting miracle. Nothing remote or fantastic here. Just a man once broken, now whole.

"There was a final prayer period. The men who had not come forward drifted out. The men on the front bench waited for little talks with Mr. Hadley. The girl at the piano said as we walked through 23rd Street, 'It's hard to do right for twenty-four hours. Trying to do it forever is hard.' "*

Bruce Bairnsfather, the creator of the famous "Old Bill" cartoon during World War I, moved into the neighborhood. He was interested in Calvary Mission, and drew for Sam a moving poster, with a Bowery-type character standing against a wall, the Cross showing from round the corner, and the caption, "There's a place near by, where a Carpenter still mends broken men."

Up till 1936 the attendance at the meetings of the Mission totaled 210,403, of which 39,149 came forward to ask for special prayer, 147,896 were given beds, and 228,657 were fed.

One of the many persons to come to Calvary Mission was Bill W. In the recent book *Alcoholics Anonymous Comes of Age*

* Amelia S. Reynolds, *New Lives for Old* (Westwood, N. J.: Fleming H. Revell, 1929), pp. 35-38.

Bill describes his contact with Calvary Mission and subsequently with Sam and the Oxford Group through the Thursday night meetings in Calvary House. In it he says:*

"One day while pretty maudlin I got a great idea. I figured it was time I did some religious investigation on my own hook. Remembering that Ebby, an old drinking friend of mine, had been lodged by members of the Oxford Group at Sam Shoemaker's Calvary Church Mission, I thought I would go and see what they did down there. I left the subway at Fourth Avenue and 23rd Street. It was a good long walk along 23rd Street, so I began stopping in bars. I spent most of the afternoon in the bars and forgot all about the Mission. At nightfall I found myself in excited conversation in a bar with a Finn named Alec. He said he had been a sailmaker and a fisherman in the old country. Somehow that word 'fisherman' clicked. I thought again of the Mission. Over there I would find fishers of men. Oddly enough it seemed like a wonderful idea.

"I sold Alec on coming along, and soon we reeled in the front door of the Mission. Tex Francisco, an ex-alky in charge, was right there to meet us. He not only ran the place; he proposed to run us out of it. This made us quite sore as we thought of our good intentions.

"Just then Ebby turned up, grinning. He said, 'What about a plate of beans?' After the food, Alec and I had slightly clearer heads. Ebby told us there would be a meeting in the Mission pretty soon. Would we like to go? Certainly we would go; that's why we were there. The three of us were soon sitting on one of those hard wooden benches that filled the place. I had never seen a Mission before and I shivered a little as I looked at the derelict audience. There was a smell of sweat and alcohol. I could well imagine how much suffering was represented in this gathering.

"There were some hymns and prayers. Then Tex, the leader, exhorted us. Only Jesus could save, he said. Somehow this statement did not jar me. Certain men got up and made testimonials. Numb as I was I felt interest and excitement rising. Then came the call. Some men were starting forward to the rail. Unaccountably impelled, I started too, dragging Alec with me. Ebby reached for my coattails, but it was too late. I knelt among the shaking penitents. Maybe then and there, for the very first time, I was penitent, too. Something

* *Alcoholics Anonymous Comes of Age*, 1957—AA World Services. 305 East 45th St. New York City.

touched me. I guess it was more than that. I was hit. I felt a wild impulse to talk. Jumping to my feet, I began.

"Afterward I could never remember what I said. I only knew that I was really in earnest and that people seemed to pay attention. Ebby, who at first had been embarrassed to death, told me with relief that I had done all right and had 'given my life to God.'

"Upstairs after the meeting I saw the dormitory where the derelicts slept. I met a few who had made good recoveries. Some were living at the Mission, working outside by day. Eagerly I listened to their stories. I sobered up very fast and the dead weight on me seemed to go on lifting. With a qualm I remembered Lois, my wife. I had not phoned her and she would be worried. I must tell her all about this. It was good to hear her sigh of relief at the other end of the wire."

Bill goes on to tell of his association with the Oxford Group, Calvary Mission, Dr. Silkworth's Towns Hospital, and of his own work. He also writes of his association with Sam and of the beginnings of Alcoholics Anonymous.

The insights Sam gained through his obedience in bringing into being Calvary Mission, as well as his experience in working with the Oxford Group, later inspired Bill to write the famous Twelve Steps of Alcoholics Anonymous.

Bill says of this, "It was from Sam that co-founder Dr. Bob and I in the beginning absorbed most of the principles that were afterwards embodied in the Twelve Steps of Alcoholics Anonymous, steps that express the heart of AA's way of life. Dr. Silkworth gave us the needed knowledge of our illness, but Sam Shoemaker gave us the concrete knowledge of what we could do about it. One showed us the mysteries of the lock that held us in prison; the other passed on the spiritual keys by which we were liberated."

Twenty years later Sam was one of the principal speakers at a great Alcoholics Anonymous Assembly in St. Louis, and Bill describes the occasion: "Dr. Sam looked scarcely a day older than he had almost twenty-one years earlier when I first met him and his dynamic group at Calvary's parish house in New York. As he began to speak, his impact fell upon us there in the Kiel Auditorium just as it had upon Lois and me years before. As always, he called a spade a spade, and his blazing eagerness, earnestness, and crystal clarity drove home his message point by point. With all his vigor and power of speech, Sam nevertheless kept himself right down to our size. Here was a man quite as willing to talk about *his* sins as about anybody else's. He made himself a witness of God's power and love just as any AA might have done."

And all this began in the old Calvary Mission in the Gas House district on East 23rd Street the night that Bill and Alec reeled through its doors.

Sam used to say frequently that if everyone sitting in the pews of our churches had the same sense of gratitude and the same ability to give themselves that the AAs have in reaching and salvaging drunks, we would have a very different America.

Two of the most moving letters I received at the time of Sam's death were from AAs. One was from an attorney in Washington, who wrote: "We have lost in body—but will always keep in spirit— the best and dearest friend and leader we have ever had or ever will have.

"This can't be a letter of condolence, though it is one of heart-felt sympathy. Rather, it is a letter of appreciation for Sam and for God's Grace that sent him amongst us, the agnostics, the spiritually crippled, the sinners, the drunks, those that travail and are heavy laden, to refresh us, to give us courage and peace, and above all, as Sam used to put it, to give us an introduction to God.

"No one in our lifetimes could have touched as deeply and as surely as many lives as Sam touched—nor as lastingly. B and I want you to know how grateful we are and will be to the end of our lives for the grace and strength that Sam gave to us."

And the other was from a very noted actor, who wrote: "His books have been a continuing inspiration to me all these years, and I have always spoken of him as though of a very close friend. Of course, as you must know, his name repeatedly bounces up in AA meetings and among AAs in conversation everywhere. I feel certain in my heart that his spirit, as his Master's, will live on and on in an ever-widening circle among those who seek His way."

The Pittsburgh Experiment ▓ 25

SOON AFTER COMING TO PITTSBURGH, SAM, with his usual creative vision, conceived the idea of "Pittsburgh as famous for God as it is for steel." He was able to sell this vision to his enthusiastic "golf club" crowd. About this same time, *Fortune* magazine, researching the apparent resurgence of religion among businessmen throughout the country, sent Duncan Norton-Taylor to call on Sam and ask him what was happening in Pittsburgh. As a result of their conversation, the article "Businessmen on Their Knees" appeared in *Fortune* in October, 1953, which caused quite a stir throughout the country.

Excerpts from the article, describing the beginnings of what was to become "the Pittsburgh Experiment," follow:

"In Pittsburgh, in one of the great powerhouses of the nation's material strength, one of the most remarkable religious manifestations is taking place. Pittsburgh's dynamism is in some ways inseparable from its old Scotch-Irish Presbyterian background, so perhaps it is not too surprising to find the city nourishing such a movement.
. . .

"The demands that most of the orthodox Protestant churches have made on their followers have been somewhat querulous and limited. Financial contributions and some cooperation in the church's social activities were about all that clergymen have dared expect. Regular church attendance could be hoped for, but not presented as a necessity to salvation. . . .

"In March, 1952, Dr. Shoemaker had accepted the rectorship of Pittsburgh's Calvary Episcopal Church. Among the fish that he went after were members of Pittsburgh's well-endowed, splendidly nurtured, and studiously casual 'Golf Club crowd' (their own phrase). 'The Lord loves snobs as well as other people,' Dr. Shoemaker had told himself, and carried his convictions right into the Pittsburgh Golf Club, and in the end there was a minor revolution along a highly strategic Pittsburgh social front."

In his book *The Experiment of Faith*, written in 1957 when the

Pittsburgh Experiment was well launched, Sam was able, as a result of earlier experiments with religion in office and factory, to outline some of the principles and techniques that evolved, as well as to describe the way in which it worked in and through the lives of men on the job.

"The first thing we need is some new thoughts about the practicalities of daily life in relation to our religion. We often behave as if God were interested in religion, but not in life—in what goes on in church, but not what goes on in a mill or a farm or a broker's office. This point of view overlooks something. It forgets that Christianity began, not when religion got carried farther up into the skies, but precisely when it was brought 'down to earth.' It has often been called the most materialistic of all religions, because it is constantly concerned, not with a God above the skies, but with a God Who came to earth and lived here.

"As Christians, we are not called to leave behind us the body, money, work, amusements, statecraft: we are called upon to redeem *these things by using* them for God. Unless we hear this kind of teaching in churches, we are not hearing an authentic preaching of the religion of the Incarnation—which means the enfleshment of the Son of God. Jesus' coming into the world has forever banished the idea of the incompatibility of material with spiritual things. I say it without hesitation: there is nothing more 'spiritual' or holy about going to church than about going to the office, if you go to both places to serve and obey God. . . .

"But how is this spiritualization of the material to come about? Business is so vast, so impersonal, so hard at times—where shall anything spiritual take hold, or seem other than a sentimental intrusion? If anything is to happen to Christianize business, it must concern, first, the changing of the individuals who are part of the business scene, in some of their basic attitudes and beliefs; and, second, it must manifest to them that there can be a different kind of human relations in business, and that this is the primary situation where God enters the picture of business.

"Our first need, then, is to let our conversion extend to our job. We cannot close this gap between 'God' and 'the world,' but we can lessen it. There is no use in our saying we are even attempting to be 'converted' when we live as if our faith and our job were in two irreconcilable compartments. Much nonsense has been talked during the last seventy-five years about the need for a 'social gospel' as well as a 'personal gospel.' Christ made no such distinction.

"The second thing that can happen is: *God can give us a new motive in business.* To be sure, we must be practical and realistic concerning 'profits,' for unless a business is successful enough to be making money, it cannot meet its payroll, let alone anything due to investors. Making things, selling them, and receiving money for them, is of the essence of business. Do not let us fool ourselves here: schools sell education, hospitals sell health, churches sell faith, and all of them—however noble their motives—are in some sense in business. *They must exist in a practical world where we find ourselves all together and all interdependent.* But the thing we sell may have a very true value to the person who buys it, and it may be a real service to him that we make it available. No man ought to market anything he knows is inferior to what he says it is. We can put honesty above sales.

"A third thing which can happen is that an individual, or group of individuals, can go to work to establish more of what may be called general justice. Justice demands that in a free and democratic society a qualified person should be given a chance to do any work of which he is capable, without regard to religion, color, or anything else that differentiates him from the majority or from a ruling group. . . .

"A fourth possibility is starting a group within the company. A man's influence is not doubled, it is multiplied, when he gets into fellowship with another man, and they pray, and feel their way with God, and act. Start praying for a spiritual teammate. Get into solid fellowship with him. Draw in one or two more as it seems guided. Soon there will be a nucleus with which God can begin doing business in the company.

"Business is meant to be a channel of God's power, the main and chief extension of the church in the world. God may never have any other access to certain people except that one who believes in Him happens to work alongside them.

"I know, and I think everyone knows, that this kind of religion is going to call for a real change, starting in ourselves. Many years ago I was trying to help the son of one of this country's best-known industrialists. The young chap was drinking heavily and his home was threatened. We worked with him for some time. Then one day I had to say to his father, 'Do you know one thing that makes that boy drink? It is your domination of him.' This enraged the father. He invited me out of his hotel room, and I went. An hour later he called me on the phone, 'Can I see you?' 'Certainly,' I answered. He came to the apartment and sat down and said, 'I run an empire all day. It's hard to change your gears when it comes to the family.' 'Yes,' I told him, 'I realize it must be.' Tears came into his eyes and he said, 'Unless God helps me to change I cannot do it.' We knelt down and he sobbed out his prayer of penitence for his willfulness and domination, then he prayed for the son. God wonderfully answered those prayers. But, like many another prayer, that one had to be answered in the *self* first."

The Rev. Donald James, the executive director of the Pittsburgh Experiment, tells his own story of how Sam enlisted him. What he does not tell is that he was led to seek ordination and is now an Episcopal priest, serving with permission of the Bishop of Pittsburgh as director of the interdenominational Pittsburgh Experiment during the week and serving at the bishop's direction in churches of the diocese on Sundays—a new form of industrial ministry if you will, and a highly effective one. But here is his own story:

"At age eighteen I became angry with God and decided if He was a God of love, He had a peculiar way of showing it. My dad had died when I was fourteen, and my mother died three years later. At the death of my mother many adult friends had crowded around trying to be helpful, but I was in no mood for coddling. Like most teenagers, I wanted freedom. This desire to be free of the overprotectiveness of adults, coupled with little or no desire to live, led to my decision to enlist in the Marine Corps in World War II.

"My career as a Marine proved to me that I could function as a man if manhood meant drinking, fighting and sex. But deep down inside I was a frightened person. I had enough religious training as a child to know that something was wrong, but not enough to know what to do about it. To add to my confusion, the war ended before I had been killed. I had not wanted to come back—but I did. Why me? Sixty per cent of my buddies didn't make it!

"Back home after the war I ran into another problem I had created four years earlier that I had not planned to have to face. After my dad died I had lost my incentive to study and my grades in school had dropped to a level that just earned a high school diploma. When I tried to enter college under the G.I. Bill, I found I would have to attend night school to take some of my high school subjects over again if I were to bring my grades up enough to qualify for college. Through much luck and the influence of an uncle, I was able to get a job in the accounting department of a railroad. The next four years were good ones. I made enough money to do almost anything I wanted to do. My school work was passable and I entered the University of Pittsburgh Night School. My social life had become more responsible than it had been in the service.

"My love life between the age of twenty-one and twenty-eight, in retrospect, seemed to follow a pattern. I was either hopelessly in love or strictly animal in my interest.

"Finally, at age twenty-seven, a phone call from a close boyhood friend, asking me if I would join him and another friend of ours on a date was the beginning of the way back for me. A college mate of theirs was coming to town for the week-end, and they needed a date for her. The young woman I met that night turned out to be a fabulous gal. Before the week-end was over I was convinced that this was the one for me.

"As the romance grew, both our families began to voice concern about our marrying. Her family was not happy with my lack of religion and other personal traits. My relatives were not happy with my financial ability to assume the responsibilities of married life.

"It is said that love can conquer anything, but from my own experience, it requires a lot of painful surgery in the conquering.

"I did not help matters by my attitude of resentment toward her family and my frustration in a new job. As our tensions mounted, so did the frequency of my getting drunk. Finally, after four or five months I realized that something had to be done if the marriage was to survive. I loved my wife, but I did not know what to do or to whom to turn for advice. The thought came through that I had to go to church and I had to pray. Joan and I had decided that we wanted to find a church to join so that when children came we would have some place to have them baptized and send them to Sunday school. But, we did not wish to become too involved ourselves. We decided to avoid the denominations we formerly belonged to. When I suggested that we should go to church, Joan agreed, but she was unable to keep her side of the bargain. As we sat in strange churches, she filled up with tears as she thought of the family estrangement, and I was extremely embarrassed and felt guilty. This ended our church hunting for several months, but I was still plagued with the thought that I had to keep my end of the deal and go to church.

"Finally, after six months, I about ran out of churches. I had been to every one I could think of. The next Saturday night I picked up the local papers and the top listing on the church page was 'Calvary Episcopal Church . . . Dr. Samuel Moor Shoemaker, Rector.' When I saw the name I remembered where the big Gothic structure was, and decided to attend. The name 'Shoemaker' meant nothing to me.

"As I walked into Calvary I was immediately impressed and a little frightened by its size. I no sooner sat down when the lady sitting next to me turned and said, 'My name is ———— and I believe you are new here.' I quickly looked down, for I thought I was improperly dressed, or that something was noticeably wrong, because in the six months I had been attending churches, no one had ever said 'hello' to me. Granted, I didn't look good. I usually had bloodshot eyes and smelled like a hangover, but I needed to be welcomed.

"When I regained my composure from the shock of being spoken to, I said, 'Yes ma'am, my name is Don James.' She then asked, 'Mr. James, have you ever been in an Episcopal church before?' to which I replied, 'No.' She went on to say, 'Our service is a little different from what you have probably been accustomed to, and if you would like, I would be very happy to hold my Prayer Book over in front of you and point to the proper place so that the service might have more meaning for you.' I was very grateful for her kindness. The service was beautiful, and Dr. Shoemaker preached his usual moving and practical sermon.

"At the close of the service the woman turned to me and said, 'Mr. James, we have a coffee hour at this time, and I would be very happy if you would come with me. I would like to introduce you to some people your own age.' I quickly thanked her but excused myself on the grounds that my wife was ill, which of course was not true.

"I was sufficiently impressed, however, to return to Calvary the next three Sundays in a row. Each Sunday I was approached by someone who introduced himself and invited me to the coffee hour. The second time I accepted and met many young couples, and I also met Dr. Shoemaker. Little did I know then the effect these people and Dr. Sam were to have on my life.

"After four weeks of my own attendance, my wife decided she wanted to go with me. To make a long story short, after we had gone together for one month, we decided we wanted to join. As I approached Dr. Shoemaker on the porch of the church, it was with great self-satisfaction. I'm sure I had the look of a satisfied puppy. After all, 'I' was now going to church regularly; my drinking was reduced, and not only that, but my wife was now going with me. 'Sir,

Joan and I would like to join Calvary,' I said, in a tone of voice that gave the impression, 'you lucky guy!' Dr. Sam smiled and said, 'Well, Don, that's great. We sure would be happy to have you but I would like to ask you and Joan to wait six months.' This statement stopped me cold. Most churches I knew anything about didn't have any waiting period. I protested mildly, explaining that my wife was expecting and we wanted to join so that the baby could be baptized at Calvary. Dr. Sam explained that even though he probably could make arrangements for us to be confirmed by the bishop quickly, he still preferred that we wait at least six months. 'I want to make sure that this is the last change you two ever make,' he said. As for the baby, he promised to baptize it any time we wanted, whether we were members or not. He was the boss, so I was stuck, and a little confused.

"Several months later, he called me and asked if we would join a group of young marrieds to review a book he had written entitled, *How to Become a Christian.* I quickly accepted, figuring that my wife needed this instruction. As for me, I was doing fine, but I would go for her sake. It took about three weeks for me to realize that my wife had more faith in her little finger than I had in my whole body. By the end of the six weeks' course, I was not quite so cocky, and saw for the first time in my life the implications of professing a belief in Jesus Christ. When the course ended, Dr. Sam suggested that some of us might want to continue meeting weekly on our own, without him, to study the Bible. Four of us couples decided to do this. We began to meet in the Parish Hall to study the Book of Acts.

"Then came a phone call that trapped me into going to a businessmen's luncheon in the downtown Y.M.C.A.! Once inside the small room off the Y.M.C.A. Cafeteria in downtown Pittsburgh, I became confused. I had expected stern-faced characters who would ask me if I was saved and give me a tract on the evils of sin. But it didn't happen. As each man in turn introduced himself to me, I was impressed with their warmth and seeming sincerity in saying they were glad to know me. The men ranged in age from thirty to forty-five.

"After I had been introduced all around, the men resumed their eating. As I began to eat, I tried to pick up the conversation around the table. I was looking for any signs of pious talk, but I heard none. Some were discussing the problems of crabgrass; others were sharing stories of their children; a couple of golfers were replaying last Saturday's game, and still others were talking about their jobs. Several times one or another of the men would try to draw me into their conversations. My apprehension caused me to answer with one word if possible.

"So far, so good, but about the time I had begun to relax, a voice louder than the others, rocked me. 'Fellows, it's my turn to moderate the meeting, so let's get going. Let us pray.' All the men bowed their heads and the moderator said a short prayer asking for God's guidance as we tried to find and do His will.

"Before I could get my hearing off and my mind elsewhere, he continued, 'Let's discuss today where it says in the Bible if someone strikes you on one cheek, you're supposed to turn the other cheek. As far as I'm concerned that's a lot of garbage.' The last phrase popped my eyes, ears, and mind open as nothing else could have. I was flabbergasted. I thought these guys were 'pious idiots' but he had just criticized the Bible and used language not usually associated with pious men. 'I'm a salesman,' he said, 'and if I go around turning the other cheek to my competition, they'll kick my brains out. Sooner or later my boss will get disenchanted with my ability to sell and I'll lose my job. If that happens I won't be able to feed my family, and don't tell me that it's God's will that my kids starve.'

"This man was smart . . . he thought as I did. I couldn't have agreed more if I had made the statement myself. The moderator didn't amplify his statement, he immediately turned to the man on his left and said 'What do you think?' The next man agreed with him and gave equally good reasons for his position. The third man to speak didn't agree, and he gave an equally good reason and story to back up his belief. So it went around the table, each man supporting his position with an actual story in most cases. The discussion became heated at several points, with fists being shaken back and forth. I sat there spellbound. When it came my turn to talk, I passed. This was too hot for me.

"Finally the moderator broke in, 'Fellows, we better say our prayers and get out of here before we all get fired. Anyone who wishes may offer a prayer and we'll close with the Lord's Prayer.' The first man began, 'Dear God, please help John (the moderator) to realize he can turn the other cheek, Amen.' Immediately another man prayed 'Dear God, please be with Al's wife, Mary, and heal her, Amen.' This fact had been made known during the luncheon conversation. The third man said, 'God help me, I have a decision to make this afternoon, and I don't know what your will is, Amen.' Each man around the table offered a short, pithy prayer concerning something that had been discussed either over the lunch or during the meeting. When it came to my turn, I passed. The meeting closed with everyone saying the Lord's Prayer. Again they all greeted me warmly and said that they hoped I would come back the next week.

"As I walked back to my office, I was a very confused young man. What I expected I hadn't found, and what I had found was better than anything I could have expected. Their honesty and sincerity were almost beyond belief, but I returned the two following weeks.

"During the third lunch, I shared with the man across the table the fact that I had a problem with my boss; I hated the sight of him. I felt that he stood for everything that I didn't like. When the moderator began the meeting, my new friend stopped him and suggested he hold his topic until the next week, and that they all hear my story to see if there was anything that they might suggest that would help me. At this point I recounted in detail my tension and frustration with my supervisor. Many of the men knew and understood my problem because they had had a similar one. One of the men, after telling about a previous problem with his own employer, told how he had prayed for his boss each day for thirty days. He said that the results were amazing and described how God had worked. At first I refused on the grounds that our bosses were different and that it wouldn't work with mine. The group applied gentle but firm pressure and each agreed to pray with and for me. Finally I succumbed and then they told me how to pray, honestly admitting my frustration in everyday language. Thirteen days later the boss came to me and asked what was the matter with me. He said that I wasn't fighting him the way I had been. I refused to answer him, but I couldn't wait to tell the group. Whereupon they told me that God had done something for me and that I had taken the credit. They said that sooner or later I would have to tell the boss that I had been praying for him. This, they said, was what is meant by 'witness.' Five days later my boss demanded to know what had caused the change that had come over me. I told him of my prayers, much to his surprise. My surprise came when he asked me why I had been praying for him. I expected to be fired when I gave him my reasons for disliking him, but it didn't happen. Instead we discussed each reason. Once I had heard his side, things really began to change between us. We became extremely close when he began to share his problems with me."

In a booklet written by this same Don James, who went on from these first experimental steps with the Christian life, to become executive director of the Pittsburgh Experiment, we are given a glimpse of its purpose. This purpose evolved out of the creative experience and experiment of the young businessmen and the executive director himself.

The spiritual growth achieved by the executive director in the few years between his exposure to Dr. Sam and the men of the Experiment and the writing of this pamphlet is a striking illustration of what the Holy Spirit can do with a group of men who wake up and come to "obey" Him.

Founded in 1955, the Pittsburgh Experiment consists principally of laymen, who are brought together in small groups in an organic rather than an organizational way. The Rev. William H. Cohea, Jr., a Presbyterian clergyman was the first director of the Pittsburgh Experiment, between 1955 and 1958.

"The Pittsburgh Experiment is designed to encourage people to bring Christianity into their normal daily dealings with each other. Primary emphasis is placed on the conduct of business relationships.

"Our times call for inspired lives and inspired relationships both at home and in business.

"The small groups of businessmen provide an opportunity for discussion and growth that is not possible in most churches. This does not imply that church attendance is not necessary. It only means that in addition to the sacraments and common worship afforded in the church, we all need a small-group situation. In smaller groups men feel free to discuss their doubts and concerns in the application of the truths they hear in church.

"Regardless of prior association with a local church, or the lack of it, it has been our experience that after one full year of attendance in the small group, the men are twice as active in their local parishes. At the end of two years 80 per cent are tithing on gross income, not because they have been brain-washed on the subject, but because they are daily reading Scriptures and saying their prayers and feel that they can do no less.

"As a result I have seen men get involved in every kind of situation in the community and become instruments of redemption and reconciliation. Through the rebirth of individuals we are seeing rebirth of whole areas in our community.

"The prayers and efforts of fifteen to twenty employed Christian businessmen in Pittsburgh alone have resulted in approximately four hundred men finding employment over a three-year period. Most of the men found their own jobs as their experiments in prayer brought about increased confidence and a renewed faith in God's love and concern. Others found work through leads provided by those men who were employed."

One of the leaders of this group of businessmen which became known as Employment Anonymous tells his typical story: "As we met at lunch with unemployed men, we found that they often had something more than just an employment problem. They had lost initiative, aggressiveness, and confidence in themselves, and certainly had lost faith in their God. We encouraged them to try prayer, and some of them embarked on a thirty-day prayer experiment. We suggested that they pray each day for thirty days that God would give them the will to work. This seemed to change many of the men and they found a new confidence, a new faith, and went out with a new attitude.

"At later meetings they reported that when they went for interviews they seemed to be better received, and undoubtedly made a better impression. A number of 'success stories' tended to reinvigorate the men who were still looking for work. Those who first found employment would come back to the meeting the next week, tell of their experiences, and testify to the power of prayer and the change it had made in their lives.

"One man said that he had left the first meeting and began to pray regularly that he would find a job. Sometime later, when preparing for his daily period of prayer, he stopped a moment and said to himself, 'Mel, you've just been praying for work. Perhaps it's time to pray that the Lord will strengthen your faith.' The next day the phone rang, and a man who had interviewed him some weeks before asked if he was still looking for employment. And the following day he went to work.

"Hearing a story like that gave new courage and faith to men who had thought their problem insoluble. One man who had been unemployed for eight months started on a thirty-day prayer experiment to ask for the Lord's help for his situation, and twenty days later went to work in a position better than he had even hoped for. He was so convinced that prayer was the answer that he started an unemployed neighbor on a similar prayer program, and prayed with him for help in his situation. The neighbor went to work just twenty-nine days later.

"The amazing thing about all of these cases was that the job each man found fitted his qualifications perfectly. The coincidences which occurred could only have been the work of the Lord in answer to prayer. None of the men who have tried to help in this work are trained in employment or personnel work, and we have no magic formula. We tried to open any doors we could and contacted people around the city to let them know of these men in need of work. The results which occurred, however, were far beyond our limited means, and came for the most part from changes in the men themselves."

Another of the many forms of expression taken by the Pittsburgh Experiment concerns America's huge housing developments, which tend to be mighty impersonal. Individuality and initiative can be destroyed in these sterile, look-alike communities, unless we share God's love and give their residents something to live for.

The Rev. John Garvin served, under the Methodist Church, nearly one thousand families in such a federal housing development. Their needs included marital counseling, spiritual counseling, jobs, food, clothing, and legal aid. Obviously one man could not do all this. A church was providing funds for some of these needs, but if the job was to be done, it would require many, many dedicated men and women who would give of themselves, their time and talents.

As the word got around, through couples' groups in Pittsburgh, some of the couples prayerfully decided that the three hours spent each week in Bible study and discussion could be better spent helping these people. When they offered their services, the Rev. Mr. Garvin was ready. He had lined up several groups of couples living in the development who were willing to meet with people from outside to discuss some of the problems they faced.

One couple who met with people in the development tells this story: "Where does one start with a divorced mother of three babies, two unemployed alcoholics, and a married couple with unbelievable domestic problems headed for the divorce courts? Since we had no training in social work, we went each Sunday night to meet with these unlovely children of God with a smile on our faces, love in our hearts, and a prayer on our lips. We spent the first month in getting acquainted, establishing trust in each other and, most important of all, coming to love one another.

"Then we were guided to ask, 'What do you want out of life?' June (wife of the miserable marriage) replied, 'I want what you have.' This gave us the opening we had been waiting for. We told them that anything admirable they might have seen in us was due to Christ in us and not anything that we had achieved by our own efforts. We gave each of them a Phillips translation of the New Testament. We read, discussed, and prayed. Then, and only then, did the miracles begin to happen.

"June and Bill, reading their Bible one night, came to the realization that God did forgive them for their sordid past. To the average layman, this may be common knowledge, but to June and Bill it was a miracle. What a sense of relief to know that no longer must they live in the shadow of guilt.

"Elaine, the divorcée, each morning prayed to God for strength and guidance to meet her daily problems. She found that as each day passed she had the strength to meet them. To Elaine, this was a miracle.

"John, an alcoholic, just a few weeks dry when he became part of the group, found that merely getting rid of the habit was not enough. He needed something to fill the vacuum. And this was God.

"All these people are members of a church, but they did not attend. From their own admissions the organized church was not relevant in their lives. Now they are back in their respective churches but still rely on the love and warmth of the group. Admittedly, this is a limited experience, but we know it to be absolutely true because we were a part of it, and we thank God for it."

Radio Station KDKA found through an audience listener survey that approximately ninety thousand people regularly listened to the program "Faith at Work" in a fifteen-county area in and around Pittsburgh. We knew from the correspondence we received weekly that the program was also heard as far west as Kansas, as far north as two hundred miles beyond Toronto, as far south as South Carolina, and in the areas between. From these facts we realized the responsibility and opportunity we had in sharing this ministry with upwards of 100,000 persons each week.

In 1964 there were three occasions to be seen and heard on TV. The director of the Pittsburgh Experiment was interviewed over educational station WQED-TV on the "Key to the City" program. This is a program conceived to inform the Pittsburgh public of interesting personalities and projects in the city. Also on WQED-TV, one of the laymen of the Experiment moderated a panel designed as a public information service to better inform the public of the problem of alcoholism and how the program of Alcoholics Anonymous serves the community.

The Pittsburgh Experiment was used as the subject of a series of programs entitled "Assignment Pittsburgh," which is moderated by John Roberts and seen over KDKA-TV. This half-hour program concerned itself with the group of men of the Experiment interested in the unemployment problem. A kinescope of the program was made into a film.

The Pittsburgh Experiment holds annually a conference of five hundred businessmen and their wives, a conference for about four hundred teenagers, and a conference for an equally large number of college-age youngsters.

In recognition of his services to the city of Pittsburgh, the Junior Chamber of Commerce gave to the Rev. Donald James, director of the Pittsburgh Experiment, the award of Pittsburgh Man of the Year in Religion in 1965, just as in 1955 they had awarded it to my husband, the man who motivated Mr. James into the work.

Fourteen prayer, study, action, business, and news luncheon groups have been established in downtown Pittsburgh, which meet weekly.

The places of employment of the members of the current Board of Directors of the Pittsburgh Experiment are interesting in themselves: Jones & Laughlin Steel Corp.; Gooding Rubber Co.; Coal Traffic Bureau; Pittsburgh Bridge Co.; Arthurs, Lestrange & Co., Brokers; Pringle & Breslin; City Solicitor of Pittsburgh; Cunningham Schwartz Co.; Crucible Steel Co.; U. S. Steel Co.; Westinghouse Electric Corp.; and Pittsburgh Press.

The places where the discussion-prayer groups take place throughout the week are also interesting; all are in Pittsburgh unless otherwise designated:

Monday	7:10 A.M.	Duquesne Club, Sixth Ave.
Monday	12:30 P.M.	ALCOA, Alcoa Building
Tuesday	12:00 NOON	Employment Anonymous office, Downtown YMCA
Wednesday	12:00 NOON	Oliver Building Restaurant, Smithfield St.
Wednesday	12:00 NOON	Jones & Laughlin Steel Corp., Pittsburgh Works
Thursday	12:00 NOON	Jones & Laughlin Steel, Aliquippa, Pa.
Thursday	11:45 A.M.	Jones & Laughlin Steel, Gateway Center
Thursday	12:15 P.M.	United States Steel Corp., Downtown
Thursday	12:00 NOON	Williams & Co., Calvary Methodist Church

Thursday   12:00 NOON Beaver group, Beaver Restaurant, Beaver, Pa.

Friday   12:00 NOON Gulf Oil Research Center, Harmarville, Pa.

Friday   12:00 NOON Trinity Cathedral, Downtown

The daily prayer of the members of the Pittsburgh Experiment illustrates the seriousness of their purpose:

I take God the Father to be my Lord,
I take God the Son to be my Saviour,
I take God the Holy Spirit to be my sanctifier,
I take the word of God to be the rule of my life,
I take the people of God to be my people,
I now commit myself, mind, body and spirit to my Lord and Saviour, Jesus Christ, and I do this freely, fully and forever,
In the name of the Father, and of the Son and of the Holy Spirit. Amen.

VI
THE BATTLE WON

This Is the Victory   ❧   26

SAM WROTE BEFORE HIS DEATH, "THERE ARE,
in every situation, two factors: there is what happens, and there is
how we take what happens. How we take what happens goes back to
what kind of person we are, and what kind of belief we have about
life as a whole. If the whole scheme of life is not a scheme at all but
a chaos, if there is no thread of purpose running through it all but
only confusion, then our misfortunes are just part of the general
mess. But if God is, and if life is His creation, with meaning in the
middle of it, then we may hope to discover a pattern which will both
give coherence to it all and help to interpret any one event in the
unfoldment."

We can hardly believe in the love of God as He revealed it, and
then believe that at death all of life is dashed to pieces and nothing-
ness. As our faith becomes for us the passionate center of our lives,
and we gladly accept the Christian belief about immortality, death
becomes a further experience in life.

I agree with G. K. Chesterton when he said, "I had it in the
beginning and I am more and more coming back to it in the end, my
original and almost mystical conviction of the miracle of existence
and the essential excitement of all experience."

Sam felt, as our Lord knew in Gethsemane, that his experience of
going through the gate of suffering before death was in the books for
him. Sam did not feel that he would be healed in this world, and he
reiterated to me on a number of occasions a conviction that he
carried all through his life from the time of his early ministry: that
God would allow him the full privilege of suffering as so many other
men and women suffered; because he felt that he had been so blessed
with gifts, with opportunity, with spiritual power, and with success
that somehow for a completely full life he needed also the experience
of bodily suffering.

During the last two years of his life this experience came to him in
abundance. As time wore on Sam spent more and more time alone,
gathering his forces for the great final confrontation.

It is a joyous thing that just two weeks before his death he was able to hold a meeting in the living room at Burnside for his friends in Green Spring Valley who had never had the privilege of hearing his most famous convert, Gertrude Behanna. On that evening, although very weak, he was able to introduce her to some seventy-five of his friends and relatives with his old mirth and charm, so that people said after the meeting, "Why Sam looks much better than he has in months." The day after, he went to the hospital, never to return. And when I drove him down the beloved driveway from our home, he did not look back.

When Sam was very young, he wrote a poem entitled "A Prayer in Bed." It reads:

> Dear Lord, one day
> I shall lie thus and pray
> Stretched out upon my bed,
> Within few days or hours
> Of being dead.
> And I shall seek
> Then for the words to speak,
> And scarce shall find them,
> Being very weak.
> There shall be hardly strength
> To say the words if they be found, at length.
>
> Take, then, my now clear prayer
> Make it apply when shadowy words shall flee;
> When the body, busy and dying,
> May eclipse the soul.
> I pray Thee now, while pray I can,
> Then look, in mercy look,
> Upon my weakness—look and heed
> When there can be no prayer
> Except my need!

As I sat in the corner of his hospital room, hour after hour, sharing with him the experience as well as I could of going through the gate of death, I was led to say aloud to him so that he might hear it, the great words from the Sanctus, "Holy, Holy, Holy, Lord God of Hosts: Heaven and earth are full of Thy glory, Glory be to Thee, O Lord most high"; and the words of the Gloria at the end of our marvelous Communion Service, "We praise Thee, we bless Thee, we glorify Thee, we give thanks to Thee for Thy great glory, O Lord God, Heavenly King, God the Father Almighty." Then I would re-

peat the Twenty-third Psalm or some of the words from the seven-
teenth chapter of the Gospel of St. John, or verses from the eighth
chapter of Romans.

Sam had once made the comment, "The priest is as much a priest
on a sickbed as before the altar." He did not forget this in the agony
of dying, for every time I repeated to him the great words, his face
would light up with a look of quiet recognition. His sister and I
commented on a most extraordinary thing that took place just three
days before his death. Suddenly, in spite of the fact that he was only
semiconscious, all the lines and marks of desperate illness were
erased and for a few hours his face was young and beautiful and
radiant.

She and I have not understood why this should be except possibly
that deep in his subconscious His Lord was renewing his real self—
the essence of him as a priest before He should take him finally into
the Great Life.

In a letter that I wrote to our daughter Sally, in Korea, who was
not with us when her father died, I described to her the last hours
and his funeral and burial in the old churchyard of St. Thomas'
Church, Garrison Forest, Maryland, where he had gone as a boy,
where his grandfather and grandmother and parents and so many of
his family lie under the old oaks.

I wrote, "Nickie and I were with Daddy when he died, thank God.
He died at 10:30 P.M. We had the beautiful usual evening prayer
from the Prayer Book with him, for those absent from us, for trust-
fulness, for those we love, and he wasn't, of course, rational, but
somehow he got it.

"Please don't grieve over the difficulties of Daddy's last illness,
because the pain stopped completely three days before he died, and
while he was irrational there was no more pain and this I ascribe to
prayer; the prayers of all of you out in Korea and everybody else
everywhere.

"The second half of the last day he was with us he was increasingly quiet. When his body stopped breathing we felt in a strange way
that his spirit had already left.

"Daddy was brought back here and placed on his bed, just as Pops
was and Ma was, if you will remember, and we arranged our flowers
all around him. He had asked that he be buried in his purple cassock
with Uncle Lulu's [his great uncle who had been rector of Emmanuel Church, Baltimore] surplice and his Easter stole and the

Prayer Book right by him. It gave me the warmest sense of comfort and joy to slip in and out and have prayers for him, although I felt that while his tired old overcoat of a body was there, he was on his journey and was so busy that he couldn't concern himself for awhile even with us at Burnside. This rejoiced my spirit.

"We brought his body downstairs on Sunday morning, just as we did with his father and his mother and with James. I went to the early Communion Service with Carrie and Page and Chal and Kitty and all the nephews and nieces and Sister. It was wonderful. Then we returned to the house and his body was placed in a closed casket before the long mirror in the parlor. Sister and I had chosen a most exquisite pall of green with a cross of small white mums on the top. Imbedded in the heart of the cross, a band of red carnations.

"Everybody came from far and wide for the funeral; old Calvary friends from Calvary, New York, Alys and Jack Smith all the way from California, Tobe and Ellie [Samuel Shoemaker Johnston, rector of St. Andrew's Church, Kansas City, Missouri, his nephew], Sherry and Margaret Day, Ralston and Sadie Young, most of the staff from Calvary, Pittsburgh, with the rector and many others. Mother and Daddy stayed with me, your in-laws joined us on Monday, so did Bill Wilson of AA and dear Williard Monroe [one of our most faithful Negro Baptist minister friends from New York].

"The church was jammed. Beloved Don Wilkins came all the way down from Pittsburgh and played the organ, and the vested clergy who attended the funeral came in procession behind Jack Scott, the assistant minister at St. Thomas who acted as crucifer, singing 'Jesus Christ Is Risen Today.' It was glorious. At the end of the service we all walked out to the churchyard singing 'For All the Saints' at the tops of our lungs; Nickie with her head up and the tears streaming down her face."

One of the beautiful letters which I received after the funeral was from Bishop Lawrence, (the Rt. Rev. Frederic C. Lawrence, Suffragan Bishop of Massachusetts), in which he said:

"Coming home on the plane Katharine and I were wondering what our lives would have been without Sam. How many others whose lives have been changed must be saying the same thing. Bill Schneider, with whom I had an appointment today (our new Episcopal chaplain at Harvard) told me how much he owed to Sam. How wonderful to think that Sam was still reaching young men today just as he reached men in 1922 and after.

"I think of my first talk with Sam at Silver Bay, my summer with him at Grace Church and my first decision, my ordination, our wedding and yours, my consecration. The service today had a marvelous lift. I am sure that the service in Pittsburgh will too but I am glad that this was in Baltimore where all those came who cared the most."

Ken Taber, one of the young deacons of the Diocese of Maryland, who had met with Sam on the Burnside terrace the summer before his death, wrote, "I felt the necessity of a word to you. As you know I am a most recent friend of Sam's, but in our brief friendship he penetrated my heart. I do not fully appreciate the profundity of his spirit nor that which he gave me but I feel the attraction of a dim light shining in the midst of a dark cavern. In some sense he was and is a 'father' to me and I felt a great loss in his death. But I also felt a great glory. It was a feeling I have never experienced at any funeral, one of confidence and joy. The true meaning of death came to me in his death. He was a man who walked with Jesus while he lived and he is a man who is resurrected with Him in his death. There is little question that in his passing I have experienced a conversion along life's way and thank God for all this. For me now death is not a 'passing away' but a 'being immersed in' the very Person in whom 'we live and walk and have our being.'"

Sally wrote: "My darling Mother, how wonderful to hear your own voice last night on the telephone, and how wonderful to know that our beloved Daddy is gone to be with his Lord. Think what a joyous time he must be having. Court was reading last night after you called that marvelous passage from Revelation 7 about the great multitude from all nations and kindreds and peoples arrayed in white standing before the throne praising God forever and ever. What a glorious promise! As terribly as we are going to miss him at this point I can only feel gratitude that God has taken him home, and gratitude that He will continue to look after us even as He has taken care of Daddy. Meanwhile, my Darling, we are with you in spirit every second of the day knowing that God is there. Give our Nicklet a hug and tell her that our prayers are with her too. At choir this week we're singing, 'I heard the voice of Jesus say, Come unto Me and rest, Lay down, thou weary one, Lay down thy head upon My breast. I came to Jesus as I was, Weary and worn and sad, I found in Him a resting place, and He has made me glad.' Korea is nearer Heaven than America. All my love, LaLa."

The week after Sam's funeral was a week of pain and triumph. It was natural that Calvary Church, Pittsburgh, would wish to hold a memorial service in Sam's honor and that the bishop would wish it to be a memorial Eucharist; so on Thursday, November 7, 1963, at 3:30 o'clock this memorial service took place. I knew that I could trust the marvelous liturgical sense of the new rector of Calvary Church and the loving concern of himself and the bishops to think through every detail connected with the service, but I must admit that my heart sank when I saw the kind of day that Nature provided for us. The great occasions of our life in Pittsburgh seemed to be marked by rain—our arrival, our first Easter, our 'at home,' and now this. Rain, rain, rain, but it didn't dampen the ardor of the people of Pittsburgh one bit as they poured into the church to pay their last tribute to Sam. I had no idea what would happen or whether there would be many there to express their love. Nickie and I sat in one of the front pews surrounded by all the members of the prayer groups, whom I had requested to sit around me.

I had not been told what form the procession would take, and when the Easter hymn, the same one we had sung at St. Thomas' in Baltimore, opened, I was amazed at the procession that swept down the aisle singing it. There must have been almost one hundred people in this procession, which included the full Calvary choir, the Auxiliary Vestry of Calvary Church, the past and present members of the Vestry of Calvary Church, the wardens of Calvary Church, the Ecumenical clergy in their vestments and the Diocesan clergy in their vestments, the clergy who were postulants and candidates through Sam as well as those associated with him on the staff of Calvary Church. Then came the visiting bishops, the Epistoler who was the executive director of the Pittsburgh Experiment, the Gospeler who was the Rev. John Baiz, the bishop's chaplain, and the bishop as well as the members of the board of the Pittsburgh Experiment. Nickie and I had never imagined such a glorious procession, and the rafters rang to the great words of the Easter hymn which was followed by "The Strife Is O'er," as the procession concluded.

The Eucharist was celebrated by the bishop with the assistance of those clergy who had been particularly close to Sam in his ministry at Calvary, and it brought tears to my eyes to see and to worship with the glorious company of God's faithful people who came forward to make their Communion at the three altars of the church in honor of their friend and rector who had entered into the larger life. I think I knew every single member of the almost one thousand people who came that day to do him honor, and I shall never in my life forget the sound of the responses and the glory of the hymns rising from a thousand throats. I am sure Sam was quite overwhelmed with surprise and gratitude at such a tribute. The bishop—and this is unusual in connection with a burial service in the Episcopal Church—said some beautiful things about Sam before the celebration of the Eucharist:

"On the eve of All Saints' Day, 1963, 'Sam' Shoemaker passed to Paradise. "The *Living Church,* one of our national Episcopal magazines, said that Dr. Shoemaker was unquestionably one of the greatest evangelists this Church has ever produced. I am sure that most all of us would agree with this evaluation.

"I have known Dr. Shoemaker for nearly forty years, and while he was in Pittsburgh we became intimate friends. Various things about him left an indelible impression upon my consciousness.

"First, he was ceaseless in his desire to bring people to a deep personal experience of Christ.

"Second, he wrote twenty-eight books and innumerable sermons, as well as pamphlets. He always expressed himself with rhythmic phrasing that carried a punch and a challenge to anyone who would read his message.

"Third, I admired him for his great courage, for there was no man he feared to challenge on behalf of his Lord and Savior.

"Fourth, he had an undying conviction that every man should be converted to Christ. Such conviction cannot help but win people, and his impact was worldwide.

"Fifth, he had an almost incorrigible sense of humor. I have never laughed more heartily with anyone than with this great man.

"Sixth, he had a unique personality which had a built-in kind of electricity which fairly crackled with vigor, energy, and magnetism.

"Seventh, he was a man of great faith in the power of prayer, and he was able to communicate this faith, through others, to the ends of the earth.

"Eighth, he was one of the founders of Alcoholics Anonymous. He knew men in their depths of despair and he has helped an almost unlimited number of men and women who have had alcoholic problems.

"Sam was one of the greatest Christian personalities I have ever known, probably the most unique and the most effective. As his bishop and personal pastor, I shall never cease to thank God for his innumerable gifts to the needs of the souls of men. 'May he grow daily in the Land of Light and Joy.' "

In the *Church News* of December, 1963, a reporter wrote of the memorial service for Sam in Calvary Church, Pittsburgh: "I didn't know the man too well; or rather I should say, he didn't know me too well.

"But like hundreds of others of all races, denominations, social categories, I attended a memorial requiem in his honor at Calvary Church, Pittsburgh.

"Literally thousands of people in Pittsburgh, New York, Baltimore, and other places paid tribute to the memory of Dr. Samuel Moor Shoemaker at separate, yet spiritually linked, services. There was no mawkish sentiment; no sentimental eulogies. Just expressions of thanksgiving to Almighty God for having given the world such a man."

The mayor of the city of Pittsburgh, Joseph M. Barr, added his tribute to others at the memorial service: "Pittsburghers were gratified but not surprised when Dr. Shoemaker in 1955 was named one of the ten greatest preachers in the United States by a national magazine. The message which Dr. Sam brought to Pittsburgh during his decade in Pittsburgh was never a bland or a quiet one. He attacked all of the backward failings of humanity with fierceness, wit and relevancy. But Dr. Sam was never pessimistic. He saw and made others see a shining future for Pittsburgh as a city under God."

In New York, at Sam's first Calvary Church, the rector had invited Dr. James Kennedy of the Church of the Ascension and the Rt. Rev. John Bentley, who had been a parishioner of ours during our last years at Calvary, New York, to take part in a memorial service, and a great many of Sam's clergy friends from other churches in the city were present, including Arthur Lee Kinsolving from St. James Church and Norman and Ruth Peale from the Marble Collegiate Church.

"Tuie" Kinsolving wrote: "Sam was probably the first person in my life experience who translated the Christian way into more practical and intelligible challenges and commitments. He was a man of such proportions that in himself he was a movement in the Church and in the lives of men. I can hardly believe that his earthly life is completed.

"To you, dear girl, there are no words that can express my sense of the meaning of your partnership."

Jim Kennedy, the following Sunday, had printed on the front of the leaflet of the Church of the Ascension a most beautiful tribute: "Thanksgiving and faith go hand in hand. Understanding of this comes often in a single moment, as I experienced recently, after a memorial service for the Rev. Dr. Samuel M. Shoemaker, one-time rector of Calvary Church, New York. When I spoke to his wife, Helen, four words came naturally and quickly to my lips, 'Thank God for Sam.' The reason for that expression of thanksgiving for the life of a man goes back to a conversation with Sam some twenty-five years ago which changed the direction of my life and gave me a strong new understanding of faith in a God who gave men a new center of obedience in Jesus Christ. It was through Sam Shoemaker that God gave me a revealing perspective of my life in relationship to His life and renewed my faith and sense of direction under His guidance. 'Thank God for Sam.' "

And in the memorial copy of the *Faith at Work* magazine, Dr. Norman Vincent Peale said the following: "Of course, I loved Sam devotedly as did we all, and I count my long friendship with him as one of the greatest blessings God has granted me. I have known many men in the ministry who have been quite outstanding in their effectiveness. Some have excelled in preaching, some in the pastoral office, others in administrative affairs, a few in mass evangelism. Many of these were truly great and good men. But no man has excelled Sam Shoemaker in sheer spiritual depth and persuasive power."

Letters poured in from all over the country and all over the world. They were not the usual condolence letters. Their significance lies in the reiteration over and over again of what Sam had meant person-ally to the writer, of the way he had brought each writer into a particularly significant experience of Christ and His Church. They came from bishops, from clergy, from old and young, rich and poor.

One such letter was written by Dr. Theodore D. Stevenson, a member of the Commission of the United Presbyterian Church. He wrote: "I want you to know how grateful I am for Sam. Perhaps more than anyone I have ever known, he influenced my life by his witness and superb ability to interpret God's word and will to me."

Canon Green (Bryan Green) said of him: "He has done more than any other living minister to help forward the work of evangelism within the Protestant Episcopal Church of America."

Dr. E. Stanley Jones, the great Methodist evangelist, wrote: "I've thought of you often and all my thoughts turn to gratitude and prayer. Gratitude for Sam and for you. I need not tell you what I thought of him—that is beyond expression. He was God's anointed. And I can never think of him except with praise to our Heavenly Father. And you, Sister Helen, knowing what kind of a Christian you are I know you will not bear this, but use it. You will take it up into the purpose of your life and make something out of it—something by which you can help others."

And Billy Graham said: "Words cannot express adequately the sense of personal loss I have felt at the home-going of our beloved Sam. What a blessing it has been for me to talk and especially to pray with this giant among men. I doubt that any man in our generation has made a greater impact for God on the Christian world than did Sam Shoemaker."

He truly let through the light, and it is fitting in thinking of Sam to remember the words of Henry Ward Beecher: "When the sun goes below the horizon he is not set; the heavens glow for a full hour after his departure. And when a great and good man sets, the sky of the world is luminous long after he is out of sight. Such a man cannot die out of this world. When he goes he leaves behind him much of himself."

RADIO MINISTRY
The Rev. Canon Samuel Moor Shoemaker, d.d., s.t.d.

Year	Program	Station	Auspices
1945	Your Life Today (weekly)	WJZ, N. Y. C.	Federal Council of Churches
1946-1952	Gems for Thought (brief daily programs)	WJZ, N. Y. C.	Federal Council of Churches
1947-1951	Faith in Our Time (Sunday)	WOR, N. Y. C.	Federal Council of Churches
1948	Radio Chapel (Sunday)	WOR, N. Y. C.	Federal Council of Churches
1949-1951	Radio Chapel (Sunday)	WOR, N. Y. C.	Federal Council of Churches
1952-1961	Faith That Works (Sunday)	KDKA, Pittsburgh	
1954	Faith in Our Time (Sunday)	WOR, N. Y. C.	National Council of the Churches of Christ
1957	Episcopal Hour	(10 weeks, for the Episcopal Radio and TV Foundation. Tapes sent to radio stations in 44 states of the United States, and to Korea, Philippines, Puerto Rico, and the Virgin Islands.)	
1957-1958	Art of Living (12 weeks)		National Council of the Churches of Christ
1958	Episcopal Hour	(10 weeks, approximately same as above.)	
1960	Episcopal Hour	(10 weeks, approximately same as above. Letter from Mrs. Caroline Rakestraw of the Episcopal Radio and TV Foundation, July 26, 1960: "We have as of this date sent out approximately 50,000 copies of the 1960 Episcopal Hour.")	
1962	Art of Living (13 weeks)		National Council of the Churches of Christ
1962-1963	Faith That Works (Sunday)	WBAL, Baltimore	

BOOKS WRITTEN BY DR. SAMUEL MOOR SHOEMAKER

Realizing Religion. Association Press, 1921.
A Young Man's View of the Ministry. Association Press, 1923.
Children of the Second Birth. Fleming H. Revell, 1927.
Religion That Works. Fleming H. Revell, 1928.
Twice-born Ministers. Fleming H. Revell, 1929.
If I Be Lifted Up. Fleming H. Revell, 1931.
The Conversion of the Church. Fleming H. Revell, 1932.
Christ's Words from the Cross. Fleming H. Revell, 1933.
The Gospel according to You. Fleming H. Revell, 1934.
Calvary Church Yesterday and Today. Fleming H. Revell, 1936.
National Awakening. Harper & Row, 1936.
The Church Can Save the World. Fleming H. Revell, 1938.
God's Control. Fleming H. Revell, 1939.
Confident Faith. Fleming H. Revell, 1939.
Christ and This Crisis. Fleming H. Revell, 1943.
How You Can Help Other People. E. P. Dutton, 1946.
Living Your Life Today. Fleming H. Revell, 1947.
How You Can Find Happiness. E. P. Dutton, 1947 (Religious Book Club selection).
Revive Thy Church—Beginning with Me. Harper & Row, 1948 (Presiding Bishop's Book for Lent).
Freedom and Faith. Fleming H. Revell, 1949.
They're on the Way. E. P. Dutton, 1951.
The Church Alive. Drift Press, 1952.
How to Become a Christian. Harper & Row, 1953.
By the Power of God. Harper & Row, 1954 (Religious Book Club selection).
The Experiment of Faith. Harper & Row, 1957.
With the Holy Spirit and with Fire. Harper & Row, 1960.
Beginning Your Ministry. Harper & Row, 1963.
Faith at Work, a symposium edited by Samuel Moor Shoemaker. Hawthorn Books, 1958.